Designing Business

Designing Business

Multiple Media,
Multiple Disciplines

Clement Mok

Adobe Press

San Jose, California

Published by Adobe Press, Adobe Systems Incorporated

Library of Congress Catalog No.: 96-75902

ISBN: 1-56830-282-7

10 9 8 7 6 5 4 3 2 First Printing: May 1996

Printed in the United States of America by Shepard Poorman
Communications Corporation, Indianapolis, Indiana.

Published simultaneously in Canada.

Adobe Press books are published and distributed by Macmillan
Computer Publishing USA. For individual, educational, corporate,
or retail sales accounts, call 1-800-428-5331, or 317-581-3500. For
information address Macmillan Computer Publishing USA, 201
West 103rd Street, Indianapolis, IN 46290.

For my colleagues at Studio Archetype

Contents

Foreword

You should recognize Clement Mok's name. He is one of the new generation of digital visionaries and practitioners. *Designing Business* makes that all the more apparent, and Clement is to be commended and congratulated. His viewpoints and design sensibilities are providing a foundation for the new world of the Internet.

Yet the word "Internet" does not begin to describe this new world's potential. That is one of Clement's points – our language and cultural metaphors have not caught up with the information age. A new media type is emerging: businesses are undergoing a transition from paper and broadcast formats to a hybrid of dynamic media that harnesses the power of computers and software. For the first time in history, a business can economically communicate with all of its employees, business partners, and customers at the same time.

Communication is essential to business, and design is about creating that communication. Most people consider business and design to be at opposite ends of a continuum between commerce and art. Clement exposes us to the line of that continuum, and then adds a z axis to the x, y plane. This new dimension of communicating is called computing.

Adobe Systems has been at the forefront of several technological shifts in computing, all of them benefiting our customers and propelling them forward. The latest shift changes how the business world thinks, how it markets itself, how it sells, and, most important, how it provides value.

Business must change its thinking when it deals with the computing medium. Creating a Web site is only a first, modest step. This new medium is incredibly competitive. It lets corporations and two-person startup companies vie for the same customer, and it removes small corporate size as a barrier to entry. That is where Clement's book is so vital. Businesses that use the computing medium to provide valuable information and visual richness and to establish valuable relationships will be the winners. Until every executive, designer, marketing, sales, or product manager understands how to create that value, competitive advantage will be easy to spot.

Adobe develops software solutions to help a business and its design teams develop that value.

It's a fascinating time to be involved in the technology. It's also a fascinating time to be designing a business. The ability to communicate directly with individuals, by "singlecasting" rather than through broadcasting, is revolutionizing our society. The old world is not going to disappear – after all, you are reading this on paper. What's important is that the new world is opening onto a fascinating and rewarding new age.

Charles M. Geschke
President
Adobe Systems Inc.

Acknowledgments ———————————————

The most difficult project I have ever worked on was writing this book; the easiest and most pleasurable was listing the many people who contributed to it. I've used many pages of this book to present their ideas and creative efforts, but I have only two pages to thank all of them. This absurd juxtaposition in no way reflects the reality of my indebtedness.

I must begin with four individuals who held up signposts for me: Richard Wurman, who cleared the way for me to be a designer not only of things, but of understanding; Milton Glaser, who inspired me above all others; Steve Jobs, who allowed someone who flunked high school math to work with computer engineers; and finally, the late Skip Sagar, a friend, a mentor, and a coach in helping me design my life and my businesses.

Any number of people are both friends and colleagues, among them Charles Altschul, David Berlow, Roger Black, David Brown, Chuck Byrne, John Casado, John Clippinger, Moira Cullen, Michael Cronan, Michael Donovan, Bill Drenttel, Hugh Dubberly, Randy Fields, Stephen Frykholm, Caroline Goff, David Goodman, Nancye Green, Rick Grefé, Pat Hansen, Jessica Helfand, Carolyn Hightower, Tom Hughes, Peter Lawrence, Stuart Malin, Doug May, Chee Pearlman, Bob Powers, Chris Pullman, Tom Reilly, Barry Reder, Margaret Richardson, Jennifer Saffo, Paul Saffo, Louis Sagar, Karen Himba, Rick Smolan, Paul Souza, Linda Stone, and Peter Vedro. All have contributed to this book by the forcefulness of their achievements.

Brad Husick and Lillian Svec not only participated in many of the projects mentioned in this book but were instrumental in putting forward many of the ideas described in it. Lillian and Wendy Richmond were early readers who took the time to ask hard questions.

I want especially to thank my colleagues at Studio Archetype – Mark Crumpacker, Amanda North, Peter Rack, Eric Wilson, and Lillian Svec – for contributing to this work and for ideas and inspiration; my administrative assistant, Stephanie Shoemaker, for managing my life with such dedication and order that I was able to write this book and still keep up with my other work obligations; and all the current and past employees whose heart and soul are the essence of the company's success. I also want to thank Samir Arora and Dave Kleinberg of

NetObjects, that entrepreneurial part of my life, for granting me time away from a startup company – I promise not to do it again for a while.

Ann Burgraff and Brad Husick were instrumental in launching the CMCD business, a move that took me beyond the design world and led to many of the business and design ideas in this book. Equally important are Doris Mitsch and Claire Barry, who pushed me into new arenas of technology and media by the absolute virtue of their skills, focus, and talents.

In one way or another, all our clients' projects, as well as our relationships with the clients themselves, have added to this book. Herman Miller and Revo were especially willing to go along with our ideas without knowing where they might lead; Carl Halverson, Tom Mandt, and Ron Buck at IVI Publishing, Stuart Spiegel at QVC, Tom Hughes, Bill Heston, and Natalie Angellilo at PhotoDisc, Lovester Law at Bill Graham Presents, Jim Peterson at 3Com, and Barak Berkowitz and Steve Cavalierli at Logitech.

E.M. Ginger, my editor, not only led me through the ordeal of sorting, coalescing, and structuring my ramblings into succinct prose, she passed on to me some of her enormous knowledge of books and a new respect for print, the quintessential medium. This book couldn't have been published without her.

I want to thank Josh Michels, my design assistant, for allowing me to change my mind all the time throughout this long process; David Bullen for contributing typography befitting a book on design; Karen Roehl-Sivak for following up on the nitty-gritty of rights, clearances, schedules, and budgets; Michael Conti for handling production so skillfully that I never thought twice about it; and Cathy de Heer and Linda Yeo for their exacting eleventh-hour editorial work.

Patrick Ames, my publisher, encouraged me to write this book when all I had was a handful of diagrams and sketches, with not a word in sight. Amazingly, he not only facilitated its development but helped shape the structure and premise.

I make endearing reference to my parents and family, not just for their forgiveness when I didn't call, but for somehow understanding how important all this is to me.

And finally, thanks to Indi and Murphy for their unqualified devotion.

I thank you all. This is really your book.

Introduction: Embracing Chaos

The very subject of this book makes it a work in progress. We – all of us – are living through a media revolution as computing technology changes everything around us. It's chaotic, it's complicated, and many people find it uncomfortable. No one truly understands where computing is taking us; experts and trustworthy guides don't exist, and no one can find their way alone.

Historically, it has taken decades for the dust to settle when a revolution in communication technology takes place, such as the invention of movable type or radio broadcasting. Even considering today's collapse of product and technology time lines, the pace of the change we've been seeing for the past few years is far from slowing down. For weeks I grappled with how to write about this moving target, what to cover, and in what detail. In the end, I decided to focus on the cross-section of design and business that I'm familiar with. Both design and business apply a combination of art and logic, and the more I examined the links between design and business, the clearer their partnership with the computing medium became. In trying to frame the opportunities the computing medium sets forth in terms of relevant fields and disciplines, I realized that it all comes back to design.

Working with new technologies doesn't mean we have to reinvent the wheel – design's purpose has always been to define and solve problems. What new technology alters is the environment in which problems reside. For one, technology generates what I call the "multiplicity" phenomenon: the growth in the number of communication media, from newspapers, magazines, and television to online services, Web sites, Internet radio, hybrids of computers and televisions, personal network agents, and all the other forms that digital communication technology takes. Furthermore, technology is advancing now at an exponential rate.

To businesses, the consequence of those two factors – the multiplicity of communication options that computing technology is generating, combined

> **Complex problems require complex solutions.** Skip Sagar

with the speed at which the technology is evolving – is chaos. The need of businesses to communicate about products or services hasn't changed, but business and design approaches do need to change in response to the technological environment.

This book is not about shifting paradigms, re-engineering, or "being digital." It's not about learning to use a computer. This book is about using design to find order and opportunity in the chaos the computing medium is generating; using design in this way leads directly to making a business viable.

Technological innovation is important, but it tends to dazzle people with what's possible instead of lighting the way toward products that people can understand and use. Making things understandable and usable isn't particularly glamorous, but it's good business. For every successful Silicon Valley company, numerous others met quick deaths because they ignored that principle. Businesses recently have begun to recognize the importance of usability in their products, but now there's a catch: products have to be developed at a breakneck pace.

Developing a usable product or service takes time, planning, and attention to detail. Because market conditions change so fast, though, it's easy to over-analyze them. That makes it hard for businesses to stay profitable and designers to come up with creative ideas.

The coverage of design disciplines in this book is directed at solving the problems the chaos – as we know it now – is generating in the business world. Business people armed with an understanding of those disciplines can take advantage of the opportunities the computing medium offers. They can define new creative dimensions and new ways to run businesses.

This book should be understandable to most people with a design background or even exposure to a company's creative department. Formal design training isn't necessary to follow the examples and principles it sets forth. In fact, some designers may have more trouble with certain business propositions than business people may have in understanding design issues.

This book follows a progression from problem to solution to implementation to case studies, showing how the links between business and design are becoming more evident with each step digital technology advances. Chapter 1, Designing Business, shows why the computing world deserves all the hype it gets yet is dangerous to businesses. Chapter 2, Multiple Media, Multiple Disciplines, examines the "multiplicity" phenomenon and the speed of the development of digital media; explains how design disciplines shape communication media; and shows how understanding the relationships among design disciplines and communication media leads to adapting business principles to the wacky digital world we live in. Chapters 3, 4, and 5 examine three relevant design disciplines – identity design, information design, and interactivity design – and how they help businesses cope with the behavioral problems of the computing medium. Chapter 6 is a series of case studies that explore the places where design and business meet.

This book discusses a number of ideas that are best conveyed in interactive format, and so it's accompanied by a CD-ROM containing examples of projects that demonstrate those concepts.

In the past, people have outlived and outwitted monumental media transformations, and we'll survive this chaos too. There are no quick answers, though, because the future is wrapped in the design process, only to be unveiled by teams of people from multiple disciplines, all asking: What is valuable? What is usable? What is better?

FOLSOM

FULL BAR · ART · LUNCH · INTERNET · DINNER · · · · · · FULL BAR · ART · LUNCH · INTERNET · DINNER · MUSIC ·

American Food Around

OPEN

SF Weekly

16

Designing Business

de·sign (dǐ-zīn ′) v. **-signed,** **-sign·ing, -signs.** –tr. **1.a.** To conceive or fashion in the mind; invent. **b.** To formulate a plan for; devise. **2.** To plan out in systematic, usu. graphic form. **3.** To create or contrive for a particular purpose or effect. **4.** To have as a goal or purpose; intend. **5.** To create or execute in an artistic or highly skilled manner. –intr. **1.** To make or execute plans. **2.** To have a goal or purpose in mind. **3.** To create designs. –n. **1.a.** A drawing or sketch. **b.** A graphic representation, esp. a detailed plan for construction or manufacture. **2.** The purposeful or inventive arrangement of parts or details. **3.** The art or practice of designing or making designs. **4.** Something designed, esp. a decorative or an artistic work. **5.** An ornamental pattern. **6.** A basic scheme or pattern that affects and controls function or development. **7.** A plan; a project. See Syns at plan. **8.a.** A reasoned purpose; an intent. **b.** Deliberate intention. **9.** A secretive plot or scheme. Often used in the plural. [ME designen <Lat. designare, to designate. See DESIGNATE.]

busi·ness (bǐz ′ nǐs) n. **1.a.** The occupation, work, or trade in which a person is engaged. **b.** A specific occupation or pursuit. **2.** Commercial, industrial, or professional dealings. **3.** A commercial enterprise or establishment. **4.** Volume or amount of commercial trade. **5.** Commercial dealings; patronage. **6.a.** One's rightful or proper concern or interest. b. Something involving one personally. **7.** Serious work or endeavor: down to business. **8.** An affair or matter. **9.** An incidental action performed on the stage to fill a pause between lines or to provide detail. **10.** Informal. Verbal abuse; scolding. **11.** Obsolete. The condition of being busy. [ME businesse <bisi, busy. See BUSY.]

Surrounded by the fantastic forms that technology takes, it's easy to think we've landed on another planet, but the down-to-earth reality is that business will have to live with the constant arrival of new technologies for some time to come. Further complicating that reality is the fact that introducing an innovation into the marketplace doesn't guarantee its success. On the contrary, it's the ability of humans to adjust to change that controls whether new technology is accepted. The Internet's twenty-year "overnight success" shows that technology evolves much more quickly than humans adapt to it. People adopt ideas when social, personal, and financial trends intersect – a confluence that may seem random but that usually happens "by design." Design, in its broadest sense, is the enabler of the digital era – it's a process that creates order out of chaos, that renders technology usable to business. Design means being good, not just looking good.

Everything Is Designed

Everything around us is designed. One of the most pervasive examples of good design is highway signage. In small-town Kansas or metropolitan Los Angeles, highway signage is reliable, consistent, and understandable. People everywhere can use it easily because someone thought about which typefaces could be read from a distance during the day and at night, which colors provide the most readable backgrounds, and where each sign should be positioned so that a driver in a fast-moving car can quickly comprehend it. Highway signage is a designed system.

We may not be able to see or feel computing technology, but just like highway signage, it affects us in very real ways. After a software engineer writes a software application, someone designs a graphical user interface for it. Most people think the design is in the interface (the look and behavior of what's on a computer screen), but what can't be seen – the internal structure of the software – is designed too. It's the design of that internal structure that allows the software to facilitate people's activities (as word-processing software does) or make possible the spread of new ideas (as Web browsers do).

Because digital media make it harder to discern what is designed, designers and consumers of digital media are both finding it more difficult to identify what's relevant to their concerns. A book's design (the way its elements appear on the pages) and functionality (the relationship between two levels of headings, for instance) are easy to see. Compare that to the functionality of a software application, which lies in its processing capability. A user's access to an application is through the application's graphical user interface; the shapes and navigational tools the user manipulates on screen are the only visible manifestation of the application's structure. The application and the interface, therefore, are interdependent – one cannot be changed without affecting the other. Furthermore, in software design there are rarely only two design factors, and the dynamics between them vary from case to case.

The biggest challenge designers face in working with the computing medium is not mastering the various technologies that are its constant companions, but introducing meaning and life into the products and services on the human side of the screen.

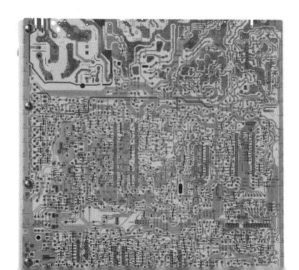

Ever wonder who designs the signage for our highway systems? It's amazing how consistently highway signage is implemented and how carefully it is designed. Is it based on a graphics standards guide? What typefaces are used? Who is responsible for the legibility of the typography – since, in this context, bad typography and bad graphics can kill. The other items on this page are also the result of careful design.

Technology Is Not Neutral

"Guns don't kill people, people do" is a controversial statement, and the idea that a computer isn't more than a tool in a designer's hands is equally debatable. Technology, whatever form it takes, has a bias, and we expend considerable energy countering that bias. Our changing habits and values reflect the way we're adopting digital technologies and

Go Corporation introduced pen-based computing in the United States in 1990; other pen-centric computing businesses sprang up soon afterward. Computing technology is ahead of its time – so far ahead, in fact, that it may have been superseded before the public had a chance to accept it. Old habits die hard.

abandoning old methods of doing things, as well as the speed at which we're doing so. The tradeoffs aren't all immediately apparent, and it's impossible to gauge the full consequences of the proliferation of digital media.

Displacement

As people adopt digital technology to accomplish everyday tasks, they abandon older technologies, and along with them habits, technical skills, methodologies, conventional points of view, historical perspectives, values – any or all of the above. When new technology is adopted, it displaces something, but there's not a one-to-one relationship between the old and the new. It's only by understanding what we're giving up by using new technology that we can influence the way technology fills the void.

Before written language, people communicated ideas largely through storytelling. Once people were able to record ideas with writing, they abandoned the oral tradition. A world of rich literary traditions took its place, but because few people could read and write until many centuries later – when movable type was invented and books became widespread – the ability to understand writing resulted in the centralized power on which civilizations were built.

Instead of giving us more time, the efficiency of digital technology is making time a luxury. Who has the time to sit back and reflect on what they've accomplished or created? Business schedules used to include a day or more for mailing deliverables to clients. The fax machine robbed us of interesting ways to say "It's not finished" in the 1980s, and now electronic file transfer has left us speechless.

Another irony of digital technology is that in spite of the amazing powers of communication it gives us, there are now more events for disseminating information than ever before. Even though the Internet and online services are supposed to supply us with all the information we could ever need, people flock to new media conferences. Likewise, e-mail replaces much of the communication that used to take place in staff meetings, but not all of it. Apparently, information isn't enough – people need the warm, fuzzy feeling they get from being in the same room together, too.

It's commonly believed that technology automates everything, making tedious processes a thing of the past. However, software such as spelling checkers don't truly take the place of dictionaries and proofreaders. It's easy to be fooled into thinking that technology solves problems more neatly than it really does.

Multiplicity and Speed

In addition to the displacement that comes with any new communication technology, digital technology is imposing two other phenomena: it's opening a multiplicity of communication options to both businesses and consumers, and it's making those options available very quickly.

In the 1960s, a traveler bought tickets by calling individual airlines directly. In the 1970s, travel agents began mediating the traveler's relationship with each airline, but the relationship was still a singular one. Now, digital technology has expanded the number of channels airline customers can use to make transactions: they can view flight schedules, make reservations, and purchase tickets through Web sites or any of several online services. In the eyes of consumers, this kind of multiplicity of channels is quickly changing from a novelty into an essential service.

The speed at which technological innovation is hitting the business world and work environments is now impossible to ignore. It has become a considerable factor in product development cycles, icon design, stock offerings, and everything else that relates to doing business.

We believe that we live in the "age of information," that there has been an information "explosion," an information "revolution." While in a certain narrow sense this is the case, in many ways just the opposite is true. We also live at a moment of deep ignorance, when vital knowledge that humans have always possessed about who we are and where we live seems beyond our reach. An Unenlightenment. An age of missing information.

Bill McKibben,
The Age of Missing Information

"Binhexing"
 "Imaging"

"FTPing"   "Prototyping"

"FEDEX it"   "Acrobat it"

"Profiling"

"Repurposing"

"Authoring"

"DeBabelizing" "Link it"

"Modem it"

Harness Technology

The task of designers and businesses is to find a way to bridge the old with the here and now; their biggest challenge is to create a context for the many choices the computing medium presents to consumers. How can car dealers and manufacturers, for instance, go about providing consumers with the option of purchasing over the Internet as well as from showrooms or by phone? It wasn't long ago that businesses created products for the general public and imposed a standard of taste that changed yearly. When there were only a few television channels, everyone watched the same sitcoms because they didn't have a choice. Now technology allows companies to use demographics and psychographics to get their messages across in specific, targeted ways, while at the same time,

The avalanche of digital technology often puts us in the uncomfortable position of not knowing how to describe what we are doing, so we make up new words from technical terms to describe the tasks we perform every day at work. Language is thought of as a living thing because it's the result of the way we live. New additions to our language help people say what they mean – although they can take awkward forms, as in the use of the word "author" as a verb, or whimsical ones, like the word "spam" in all its grammatical permutations.

Sometimes people find themselves in the uncomfortable – and embarrassing –

situation of not being able to find a word to describe what they see or do – what a new phone service does, say, or how a new technology can be used. With computing technology becoming so pervasive so quickly, the right-word void affects everyone, but it's experts explaining the technology who seem to suffer from it most – at technology conferences, they can be heard using the word "thing" more than anyone else.

the unpredictability of technology makes it more difficult for companies to plan ways to implement strategies such as multiple distribution channels.

These dual challenges and opportunities are changing the dynamic between businesses and design studios. Businesses used to hire design studios to fulfill their graphic needs. In the context of the technological leaps we're making now, designers must be more than contractors; businesses and designers must collaborate. Each professional on a project team has a separate body of knowledge to contribute to the process of designing a product or service, but because no one member of a team can have a definitive understanding of digital technology, they must share their expertise and experience.

Designers are in a position to promulgate new values and to define and quantify the effects of those values, and over the next ten years, their optimum role will be to design "understanding." The age we're living in now is an incredible time because of the extent to which designers, business people, engineers, and technologists can redefine their roles. It's not often that anyone can influence his or her profession; most of the time we fill prescribed roles. Designers who involve themselves in clarifying company vision and technological innovation have more freedom and thus deliver better products and services to businesses.

Technology is forcing businesses to reinvent themselves. Corporations must recognize information product planning and information architecture as valuable processes and make them part of corporate structure. Businesses that understand the importance of implementing access to information know that good design is good business.

Sometimes, designers abandon messages completely in favor of style. But in Selected Notes to ZeitGuys, *a CD-ROM catalog of 126 illustrations, writer Mark Bartlett and designer Bob Aufildish put the latest graphic design gimmick into the service of the content. Originally conceived for print, the title presents a series of screens, each a composition of illustrations. Each composition appears out of focus until the user moves the mouse pointer over a part of it: then that part of the composition pops up, in focus. Together, the compositions tell a story, but only at the user's prompting. The title turns the mouse and cursor into a metaphor for the mental process of distilling sense from a text made oblique – blurry – by layers of meaning.*

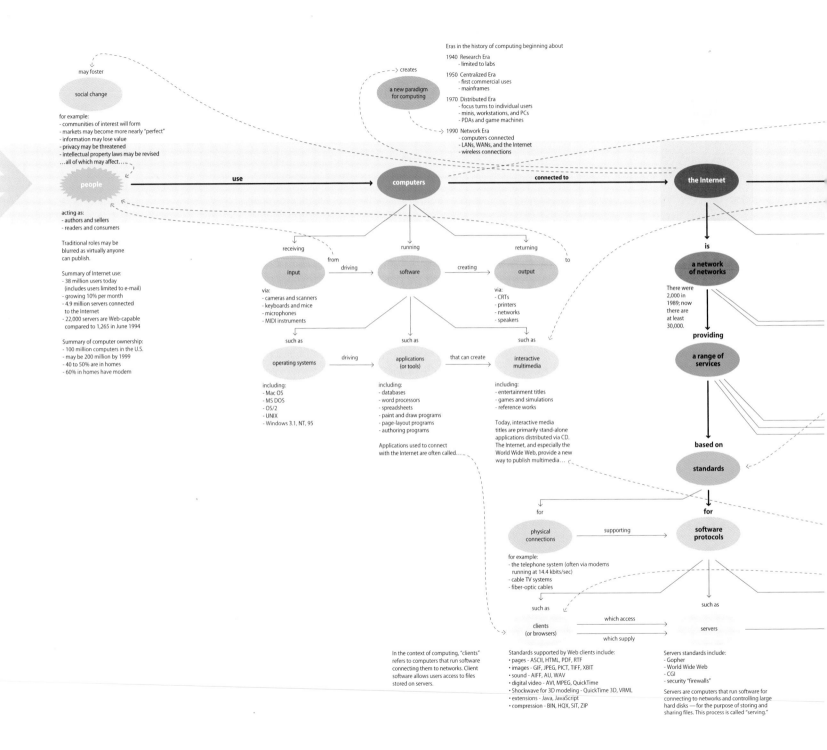

Eras in the history of computing beginning about

1940 Research Era
- limited to labs

1950 Centralized Era
- first commercial uses
- mainframes

1970 Distributed Era
- focus turns to individual users
- minis, workstations, and PCs
- PDAs and game machines

1990 Network Era
- computers connected
- LANs, WANs, and the Internet
- wireless connections

may foster

social change

for example:
- communities of interest will form
- markets may become more nearly "perfect"
- information may lose value
- privacy may be threatened
- intellectual property laws may be revised
...all of which may affect....

creates

a new paradigm
for computing

people

use

computers

connected to

the Internet

acting as:
- authors and sellers
- readers and consumers

Traditional roles may be
blurred as virtually anyone
can publish.

Summary of Internet use:
- 38 million users today
  (includes users limited to e-mail)
- growing 10% per month
- 4.9 million servers connected
  to the Internet
- 22,000 servers are Web-capable
  compared to 1,265 in June 1994

Summary of computer ownership:
- 100 million computers in the U.S.
- may be 200 million by 1999
- 40 to 50% are in homes
- 60% in homes have modem

receiving

running

returning

input

from

driving

software

creating

output

to

via:
- cameras and scanners
- keyboards and mice
- microphones
- MIDI instruments

via:
- CRTs
- printers
- networks
- speakers

such as

such as

such as

operating systems

driving

applications
(or tools)

that can create

interactive
multimedia

including:
- Mac OS
- MS DOS
- OS/2
- UNIX
- Windows 3.1, NT, 95

including:
- databases
- word processors
- spreadsheets
- paint and draw programs
- page-layout programs
- authoring programs

including:
- entertainment titles
- games and simulations
- reference works

Today, interactive media
titles are primarily stand-alone
applications distributed via CD.
The Internet, and especially the
World Wide Web, provide a new
way to publish multimedia...

Applications used to connect
with the Internet are often called...

is

a network
of networks

There were
2,000 in
1989; now
there are
at least
30,000.

providing

a range of
services

based on

standards

for

for

physical
connections

supporting

software
protocols

for example:
- the telephone system (often via modems
  running at 14.4 kbits/sec)
- cable TV systems
- fiber-optic cables

such as

such as

clients
(or browsers)

which access

which supply

servers

In the context of computing, "clients"
refers to computers that run software
connecting them to networks. Client
software allows users access to files
stored on servers.

Standards supported by Web clients include:
• pages - ASCII, HTML, PDF, RTF
• images - GIF, JPEG, PICT, TIFF, XBIT
• sound - AIFF, AU, WAV
• digital video - AVI, MPEG, QuickTime
• Shockwave for 3D modeling - QuickTime 3D, VRML
• extensions - Java, JavaScript
• compression - BIN, HQX, SIT, ZIP

Servers standards include:
- Gopher
- World Wide Web
- CGI
- security "firewalls"

Servers are computers that run software for
connecting to networks and controlling large
hard disks — for the purpose of storing and
sharing files. This process is called "serving."

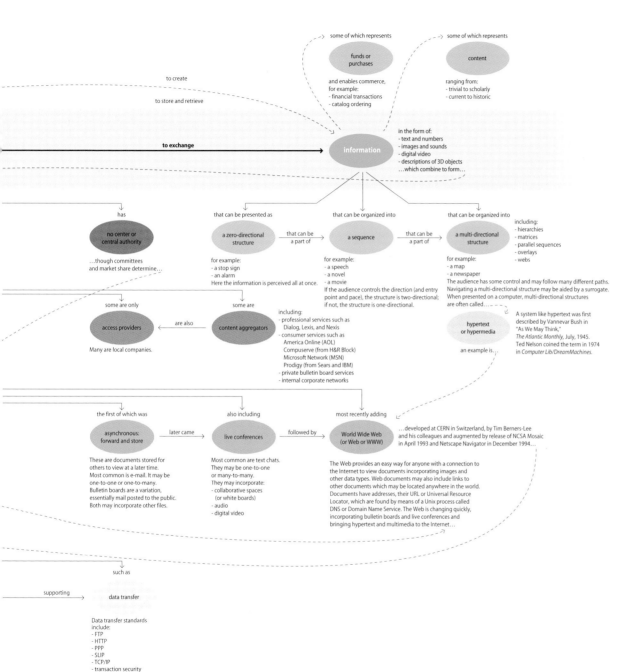

Concept Map of the Internet

This is Hugh Dubberly's evolving concept map of the Internet; it is one way of looking at the way information moves through the Internet.

Vertical box *defines main concept.*
Horizontal box *places main concept in a context.*
Ovals *contain major concepts linked in hierarchies, with broader concepts at the top.*
Linking phrases *connect the concepts.*
Dashed lines *connect concepts between hierarchies.*

some of which represents

funds or purchases

and enables commerce, for example:
- financial transactions
- catalog ordering

some of which represents

content

ranging from:
- trivial to scholarly
- current to historic

to create

to store and retrieve

to exchange

information

in the form of:
- text and numbers
- images and sounds
- digital video
- descriptions of 3D objects
...which combine to form...

has

no center or central authority

...though committees and market share determine...

that can be presented as

a zero-directional structure

that can be a part of

for example:
- a stop sign
- an alarm
Here the information is perceived all at once.

a sequence

that can be a part of

for example:
- a speech
- a novel
- a movie
If the audience controls the direction (and entry point and pace), the structure is two-directional; if not, the structure is one-directional.

that can be organized into

a multi-directional structure

for example:
- a map
- a newspaper
The audience has some control and may follow many different paths. Navigating a multi-directional structure may be aided by a surrogate. When presented on a computer, multi-directional structures are often called....

including:
- hierarchies
- matrices
- parallel sequences
- overlays
- webs

some are only

access providers

Many are local companies.

are also

some are

content aggregators

including:
- professional services such as Dialog, Lexis, and Nexis
- consumer services such as America Online (AOL) Compuserve (from H&R Block) Microsoft Network (MSN) Prodigy (from Sears and IBM)
- private bulletin board services
- internal corporate networks

hypertext or hypermedia

an example is...

A system like hypertext was first described by Vannevar Bush in "As We May Think," *The Atlantic Monthly*, July, 1945. Ted Nelson coined the term in 1974 in *Computer Lib/DreamMachines*.

the first of which was

asynchronous: forward and store

These are documents stored for others to view at a later time. Most common is e-mail. It may be one-to-one or one-to-many. Bulletin boards are a variation, essentially mail posted to the public. Both may incorporate other files.

later came

also including

live conferences

Most common are text chats. They may be one-to-one or many-to-many. They may incorporate:
- collaborative spaces (or white boards)
- audio
- digital video

followed by

most recently adding

World Wide Web (or Web or WWW)

...developed at CERN in Switzerland, by Tim Berners-Lee and his colleagues and augmented by release of NCSA Mosaic in April 1993 and Netscape Navigator in December 1994...

The Web provides an easy way for anyone with a connection to the Internet to view documents incorporating images and other data types. Web documents may also include links to other documents which may be located anywhere in the world. Documents have addresses, their URL or Universal Resource Locator, which are found by means of a Unix process called DNS or Domain Name Service. The Web is changing quickly, incorporating bulletin boards and live conferences and bringing hypertext and multimedia to the Internet...

such as

supporting

data transfer

Data transfer standards include:
- FTP
- HTTP
- PPP
- SLIP
- TCP/IP
- transaction security (encryption)

Lessons for Business

Work with Purpose

One of the most elusive aspects of working with the computing medium is defining a project's purpose. The completely new products – television watches, for instance – that media hybridization is generating are certainly fascinating, but their utility isn't always clear. Accomplishing a task requires defining a goal. Suppose a business wanted to establish a retail outlet on the Internet. What might its purpose be? To make money? To expand market share? To generate a perception that its developer is an innovator? To add onto an existing service? Each purpose has a significant impact on how the project is designed and implemented, and even whether it is implemented at all. A project's purpose could change to accommodate alterations in business strategy and vision, but whatever the purpose is, there would be no right or wrong way to implement it. Purpose is elusive largely because it can take any number of

The significance of industry convergence becomes clear when it's viewed in a historical context. The diagrams here are based on a series by Tony Oettinger that was published in a 1991 report from the Harvard Business School. Industry convergence has generated many products and businesses, and made a significant impact on social infrastructures. These diagrams are diagnostic tools to evaluate where technologies are going and what businesses must do to become serious players in their industries. They also serve as a framework for understanding the implications and the effects that technologies will have on the design of new computing experiences.

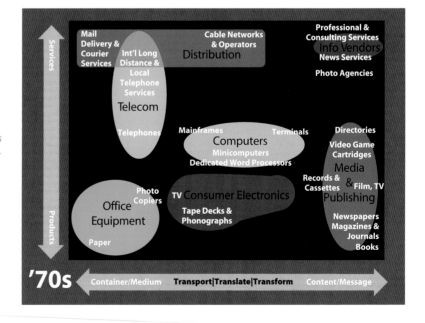

shapes. If Madonna wanted to become more famous, she could do it in any number of ways.

Digital technology hasn't changed the need to communicate, nor has it erased the characteristic human desire to put a mark on something. What digital media have altered are the ways we can go about expressing ourselves and conveying ideas, and the context in which we do so. Design will flourish as a discipline only insofar as it is understood that the computing medium alters the *process* of design, not its purpose. Purpose has to do with vision; design is an act that determines the expression of that vision, and even the extent to which it is expressed at all.

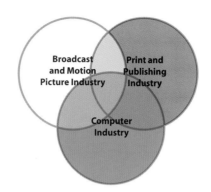

In the late 1970s, before the digital media explosion, print, broadcast, and computing were regarded in business as distinct industries. Nicholas Negroponte of the MIT Media Lab used three overlapping circles to show industry convergence and make a case for the metamorphosis of communication technologies. According to Negroponte, each industry's metamorphosis can be understood only when industry convergence is treated as a single subject, and each industry can advance properly only as a singular effort. The diagram resonated with technologists and also with corporate America. Soon everyone was drawing three-circle convergence diagrams to predict the future, with each diagram reflecting a different bias and orientation.

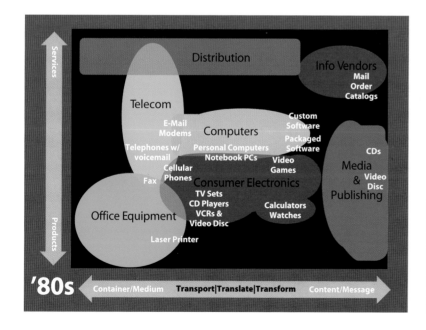

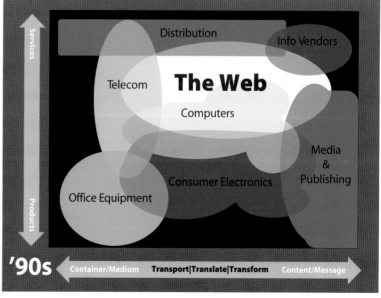

Milton Glaser, one of the world's great graphic designers, has observed that design executed without an explicit purpose is not likely to be good, and a design given minimal thought will have little cultural value in the long run.

Understanding a project's purpose helps define the problem it's meant to solve. A designer's role is to humanize and elucidate, contribute to the community, shape aesthetic values, and provide cultural resonance. Something that is well conceived and well designed has enduring value, whether it's the table of contents of a book or the graphical user interface of a software application. A well-designed object, inside or outside of its cultural context, will always be useful.

Visualize Information

Designers and businesses working in the computing medium must understand the nature of information and how to visualize it. More and more, designers and business people are finding themselves around a table with engineers and programmers, making drawings of circles and rectangles with lines and

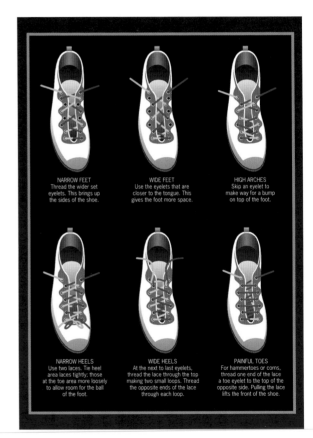

NARROW FEET
Thread the wider set eyelets. This brings up the sides of the shoe.

WIDE FEET
Use the eyelets that are closer to the tongue. This gives the foot more space.

HIGH ARCHES
Skip an eyelet to make way for a bump on top of the foot.

NARROW HEELS
Use two laces. Tie heel area laces tightly; those at the toe area more loosely to allow room for the ball of the foot.

WIDE HEELS
At the next to last eyelets, thread the lace through the top making two small loops. Thread the opposite ends of the lace through each loop.

PAINFUL TOES
For hammertoes or corns, thread one end of the lace a toe eyelet to the top of the opposite side. Pulling the lace lifts the front of the shoe.

Right: This information graphic, which Nigel Holmes designed for a sports magazine, shows shoe wearers how lacing their shoes in different ways can ease various podiatric discomforts. Facing page, top left: In this graphic, Holmes showed readers of American Health *magazine the advantages of using alpha hydroxy acids as an exfoliant.*

Conventional EXFOLIANTS get rid of dead skin cells one by one until the top layer has gone. This leaves the skin sore ...

... but AHAs dissolve the "glue" between the cells, allowing them to gently float away. This leaves the skin smooth.

arrows connecting them. Visualizing the abstractions behind a computer screen is a critical aspect of developing a product, no matter how much the interface finally reveals to the user.

Nigel Holmes, Richard Wurman, and Edward Tufte are among the people currently shaping our approaches to information. Holmes, who once created information diagrams for *Time* magazine, translates abstract concepts into understandable forms, not just by creating graphs and pie charts but by interpreting information. Holmes' work is not neutral; he imposes an editorial bias on it. His criteria for good information graphics are passion, thoughtfulness, and a journalistically true and accurate

viewpoint. Most information graphics are devised by formula, like those generated from spreadsheet software. Holmes adds a point of view to information, interpreting the subject matter. Information without a point of view is bland; it becomes valuable when it is given context, which Holmes does graphically.

Wurman takes a no-nonsense approach to information. An academic and author, Wurman bills himself as a seeker, the common man curious about subject matter most people are afraid to question.

"Graphics wiz Richard Saul Wurman . . . has finally figured out a way to make a nationwide road guide that's legible and well organized . . ." Condé Nast Traveler

RICHARD SAUL WURMAN'S NEW ROAD ATLAS

US ATLAS

ACCESS PRESS

Richard Saul Wurman

ROME

ACCESS

Nowadays, it's a necessary function he's fulfilling. Wurman has redesigned many commonly used reference tools, such as atlases. His Access Guide Series simplifies information on various topics, from dog breeds to football, in compact, understandable, approachable formats.

Holmes, then, interprets information; Wurman gives people the OK to question information; and Tufte shows us why it makes sense to pay so much attention to information in the first place. Information design has a rich and fascinating history, and Tufte has legitimized information design as a discipline. By making a connection between past and present, he gives us a way to understand the many ways in which information has been, and is, presented.

The task of designers and businesses making use of the computing medium is to visualize abstract concepts and then translate those abstractions into ideas or methods understandable to others. Design is for making ideas and information understandable and usable.

Use Design to Invent

Designing can be an entrepreneurial undertaking. The masses of information digital technology makes accessible not only pose challenges but create incredible opportunities. Computing technology moves information around in enormous volumes and at high speeds; if information is directed at everyone and no one in particular, it can easily be severed from origin and meaning. Without context and purpose, information is mere data. Information has become a product that requires designers who can give the narrative structure and context with social purpose and intellectual economy. Design's purpose is to create meaningful connections among people, ideas, art, and technology, shaping the way people understand their relationships with the new products of digital media.

We talk about how important information is, but few people spend the time to really understand it in the current context of computing. We tend to think of information as homogeneous clumps of data because that's the way computers treat it. But computers don't know what context is. Computers can't invent – only people can, and people who shape information into digital products and services must think like inventors. Designers and business people who can clarify purpose and context have phenom-enal opportunities.

Companies don't think twice about hiring a lawyer to unravel legal issues or a consultant to clarify any of countless other situations. Designers are also in the business of making things clear, and great products or services result when businesses package information in useful ways. Given the complexity of digital media, professionals skilled in deciphering intricate issues, simplifying processes, and designing frameworks that lead to understanding are more valuable to businesses than ever.

Design's purpose is always the same: inspire insight, evoke a response – transform thought into action. The success of a business depends on its ability to define design issues, prioritize them, and find some method or madness to give them a usable structure. Everything in business is designed. Design is the business of understanding at the most basic level.

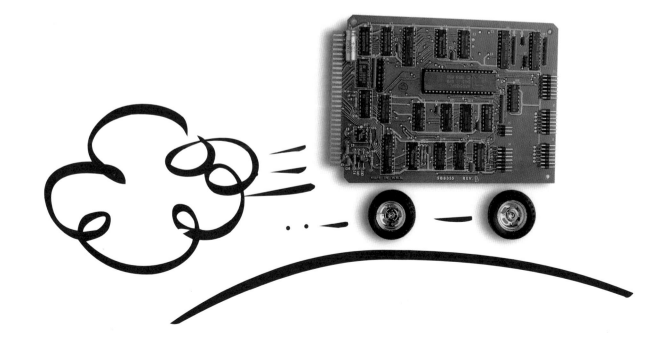

Models for

Designing Business

For as long as computing technology continues to cook at a rolling boil, industry will continue to serve up technologies du jour, and self-proclaimed experts will materialize to take advantage of the feast. What businesses should be looking for is designers who offer practical approaches to solving the problems that digital technology presents.

Many people think the sign of a "good" technology product is its ability to eliminate repetitive tasks. Software has automated some simple tasks, such as alphabetizing, only to replace them with

different tedium, such as batch file conversions, file formatting, and down sampling. Good products and services shaped from digital technology are the result of considerable planning followed by organized and efficient development. Businesses have many relevant frameworks at their disposal for staying properly focused. The two described here are the Eames Office Model and the Viable System Model.

The Eames Office Model

Ray and Charles Eames opened their "design" office in the early 1940s. Their background and training were in architecture, but their practice was an unorthodox combination of art and technology. They considered design a way to help people understand the world around them. The Eames were inveterate learners and experimented continually: to them, no problem was too big to solve. For the IBM exhibit at the 1962 World's Fair, they put together multi-image presentations using giant

From Charles we learned about the process of solving problems by structuring the information to be conveyed. We learned that no detail is too insignificant to be overlooked, and we learned that the quality in everything is what counts. We learned the difference between being forced to make compromises and the necessity to recognize constraints.
From the Introduction to *Eames design*

projectors – precursors of multi-imaging shows and multimedia. *Powers of Ten*, a remarkable film produced in 1968, takes the viewer on an adventure in magnitude and reveals the influence of point of view.

The Eames Office Model is aimed at making people's lives better within a business structure. The diagram that Charles Eames doodled captures the essence of their philosophy on designing a life and a business that would coexist. The diagram lays out the shapes of central business issues and of individuals' self-interest. When personal passions and interests coincide with a business's needs and wants, the individual is contributing maximum value to the business and the business performs at its best. This model represents a balance of personal, social, and business needs, and it works for both small design studios and large corporations.

Ray and Charles Eames

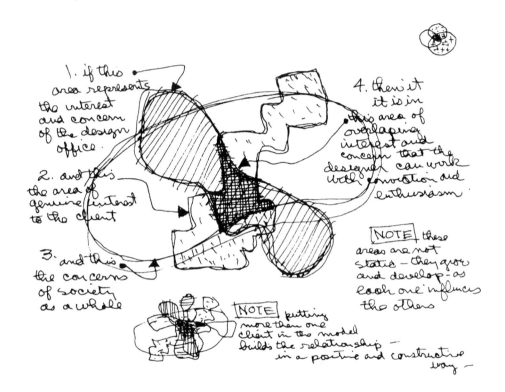

The Viable System Model

Stafford Beer developed the Viable System Model as a way to facilitate self-corrective behavior within an organization. The model gives an organization the ability to evaluate its current strengths and weaknesses as well as a way to make itself adaptable to future change and challenges. The Viable System Model is organic, made up of five integrated systems. An individual or a company must be in charge of all five systems. The foremost system, Identity, is concerned with the company's vision, giving shape, meaning, and purpose to the whole. The activities of the other systems are aligned to fulfill that purpose. The structure is infused with

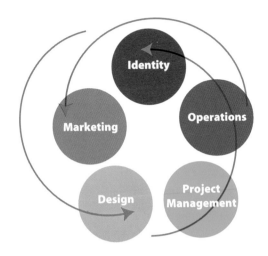

The Viable System Model, left, was created by Stafford Beer, one of only a few true experts in cybernetics. Cybernetics is a field defined by Stewart Brand, writer and provocateur-at-large, as "the discipline of whole systems thinking … A whole system is a living system is a learning system." Beer's insights go well beyond the realm of business in his 1974 book Decision and Control, where the Viable System Model is explained in great detail. On the right is a simplified version, designed to help convince the most stubborn of management teams of the system's equity and value.

non-judgmental receptors – labeled feedback loops, monitors, regulators, and scouts – that continually provide data on the activity and direction of each of the system's components and the system as a whole. For instance, as the Operations system copes with the present – the "inside and now" – a parallel recursion is always looking toward the future. The Marketing system constantly checks the external environment – the "outside and future," in its subtle ebb and flow as well as radical shifts and changes – for elements that affect the viability of the system as a whole.

Each of these systems can be defined in terms of roles and people within a corporation or any other entity. The Viable System Model has been applied to companies, communities, and in one case to an entire country. Skip Sagar, an organizational transformation architect, also translated and applied the model, creating a variety of diagrams that interpret how these various systems work together in decision making, collaboration, and self-regulation. The Viable System Model has enabled many organizations to better analyze problems and opportunities, regardless of the disciplines or specializations involved.

Putting Technology in Perspective

Computing is more than a set of tools for doing things faster – it's a medium people can use to create. Just as Michelangelo's contemporaries couldn't have foreseen abstract expressionism, we can't foresee how people will use the computing medium in the future. Technology's speedy pace may make it seem as if a long time has passed since "digital media" became part of our vocabulary, but the multitude of products, services, and technologies that the computing medium has generated up to now are only a small part of a history that will unfold over the next decades. It's easy to think, as Paul Saffo tells us, that the spectacle we're witnessing – the computers on the desks in front of us, the shapes and colors on our screens – is the main event. In fact, the main event has yet to come.

Along with hype comes skepticism; people are repelled or seduced by any new technology depending on the way they feel or imagine its impact on their lives. In the 1970s, when the first hand-held calculators were introduced, many people believed that from then on children would never learn to add or subtract. Skepticism is healthy – we need enough of it to keep technology from displacing values that are dear to us. In the end, though, there's no use either ranting or raving about technology because it's going to keep changing no matter what.

The only thing to do is to keep our sights on technology's future possibilities. Focusing on end results restricts our thinking, and the last thing anyone should do is approach this new technology with a narrow bandwidth – they'll miss every opportunity. The computing medium requires that design and business be addressed as processes based on a master plan that can change over time. Good ideas are expensive and difficult; it's almost impossible to get something worthwhile right the first time. Businesses need bridges they can cross back over, and it's by using the process of design that they can build those bridges.

The endless conflicts between the spiritual and material, between ends and means, form and content, form and function, form and facture, form and purpose, form and meaning, form and idea, form and expression, form and illusion, form and habit, form and skill, form and style need to be resolved.

It is the merging of these conflicts that determines the aesthetic quality of a painting, a design, a building, a sculpture, or a printed piece.

Paul Rand, from *Lascaux to Brooklyn*

Multiple Media | Multiple Disciplines

mul·ti·ple (mŭl′tə-pəl) adj. Of, having or consisting of more than one individual, part, or other component; manifold. –n. Math. A number that is divisible by another number with no remainder. [Fr. <OFr. <LLat. multiplum, a multiple: Lat. multi-, multi- + Lat. -plus, -fold; see pel-2*]

Me·di·a[1] (mē′dē-ə) n. See Pl. of medium. See Usage Note at medium.

me·di·um (mē′dē-əm) n., pl. -di·a (-de-e) or -di·ums. **1.** Something, such as an intermediate course of action, that occupies a position or represents a condition midway between extremes. **2.** An intervening substance through which something else is transmitted or carried on. **3.** An agency by which something is accomplished, conveyed, or transferred. **4.** pl. media. Usage Problem. **a.** A means of mass communication, such as newspapers or television. **b.** media. (used with a sing. or pl. v.) The group of journalists and others in the communications industry. **5.** pl. mediums. A person thought to have the power to communicate with the spirits of the dead or with agents of another world or dimension. **6.** pl. media. **a.** A surrounding environment in which something functions and thrives. **b.** The substance in which a specific organism lives and thrives. **c.** A culture medium. **7.a.** A specific kind of artistic technique or means of expression as determined by the materials used or the creative methods involved. **b.** The materials used in a specific artistic technique. **8.** A solvent for thinning paint. **9.** Chem. A filtering substance, such as filter paper.

dis·ci·pline (dĭs′ə-plĭn) n. **1.** Training expected to produce a specific character or pattern of behavior, esp. training that produces moral or mental improvement. **2.** Controlled behavior resulting from disciplinary training; self-control. **3.a.** Control obtained by enforcing compliance or order. **b.** A systematic method to obtain obedience. **c.** Order based on submission to authority. **4.** Punishment to correct or train. **5.** A set of rules or methods, as those regulating the practice of a church or monastic order. **6.** A branch of knowledge or teaching. –tr.v. -plined, -plin·ing, -plines. **1.** To train by instruction and practice, esp. to teach self-control to. **2.** To teach to accept authority. **3.** To punish to gain control or enforce obedience. **4.** To impose order on. [ME <OFr. descepline <Lat. disciplina <discipulus, pupil. See DISCIPLE.] – dis′ci·pli·nal (-ple-nel) adj. – dis′ci·plin′er n.

A parade of media: the digital choices for getting a message across.

1. *Online services*
2. *World Wide Web*
3. *Intercast (television on a computer)*
4. *Interactive television*
5. *CD-I titles*
6. *CD-ROM titles*
7. *Touch-screen kiosks*
8. *Pen-based computers*

Other media choices are television, radio, film, and print.

The world communicates in three main ways: through print, broadcasting, and, most recently, computing. This last phenomenon has acquired the label "multimedia," which people often think of as any pictures, sound, or video generated by a computer. However, the computing medium is much more than winking, blinking graphical user interfaces or virtual reality games. Its scope has expanded so far that it has permanently altered the older print and broadcast media. Almost all printing now is controlled by computers, and so are many aspects of broadcasting.

Designers and businesses now have to work in the computing medium, and it is the disciplines of identity design, information design, and interactivity design that the medium sets in motion most often. The practices and principles of these three disciplines embody what is necessary to produce "multiple media."

Print:

Information and

Cultural Currency

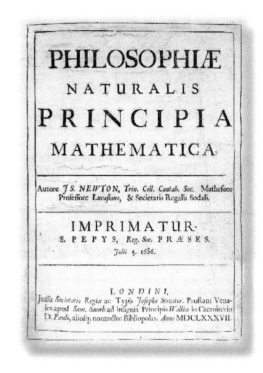

For the last five hundred fifty years, print has been the de facto currency of information and culture, and it will remain so for the foreseeable future. Printed material educates, informs, and facilitates the exchange of ideas. The stature of print has been established over the centuries as a result of its power to cause wars, reform churches, and build economies. Severe disruptions in society are frequently marked by the burning of books because books represent both the force of people and ideas. Print defines cultural heritage, and societies have measured themselves by what they have printed – until very recently.

The content of printed material has changed, and some of that change is related to what is on television; MTV culture, for instance, has given us not only a new set of values, but a new set of graphic aesthetics. Print is no longer the be-all, end-all medium of culture and information, and that change affects what we think is important.

Because of its age and maturity, print has the power to validate information; just about anything in print is readily accepted as genuine. Broadcasting and other screen media are not as evolved as print, so the methods used to judge the effectiveness, or rightness, of content aren't as established. The computing medium has made it possible for anyone to be an author, but it doesn't provide a framework or critical cycle for authenticating what is published. This "instant author" phenomenon has somewhat diminished the power of words.

Print is a rich medium of expression. A book, a brochure, or a train schedule instantly categorizes its content for readers simply through size, shape, and layout. Printed material can handle content with various orientations, like top-to-bottom-reading Japanese text or right-to-left-reading Arabic. It can hold words and pictures, and it can even convey motion (through diagrams and multiple pictures) and music (through notation). People adjust to the characteristics of specific types of printed material – in the Yellow Pages, for instance, people looking for a car know to look under A not C. Calendars are another remarkably rich print interface: despite their myriad shapes and sizes, calendars always behave the same way. The print medium also offers many formats, each with its particular interface and vocabulary; a dictionary has its own organization and structure, and so does an annual report. A book has a formal hierarchy of navigational clues – page numbers, chapter headings, bibliographies, footnotes, and so on – which define the relationships among its contents. The mixture of these elements gives the print medium its richness.

In the last ten years, the vocabulary of print has been reinvented and applied to the computer screen. The results are not the same. Some elements borrowed from the print medium, such as typographical hierarchies, may be appropriate, but most are not. Because the limits of the computing medium are unknown, which makes standardizing terminology for it impossible for now, people describe many of the computer's features and capabilities with metaphors from other disciplines. This phenomenon is symptomatic of any change – people build relationships with new things by imposing familiar values on them.

If a business publishes a printed annual report, it has complete control over the end result – size, shape, texture, and quality. But if a business puts up a Web site, its appearance will depend on the size and kind of monitor it's viewed on, the browser software used to view it, and possibly other factors. All these variables influence the message the business is trying to get across, so that what is intended is often not what is received. In print, color shades and

hues can be adjusted and fine-tuned; on a computer screen, identical pictures on a Mac and a PC look a little different because of variations in the way Macs and PCs display pixels and colors on screen. The computing medium renders slightly varied experiences; print renders an experience that is absolute.

The physicality of books is one of their strengths – it makes them widely accessible. Since the introduction of the book form in the third century, people have avidly collected books, and magnificent buildings have been constructed to house them. Some books have enormous value, and each of the various skills required to produce a fine book is an art form in itself. Now, five centuries after books became portable, millions of people carry them around daily, depend on them at work, use them to fill time during commutes, and take them to bed. However, people's attitudes toward books are changing rapidly. With the information age upon us, the next generation – children who are now ten years of age and younger – is likely to value books less as information sources and more as cultural objects.

Nonetheless, people will continue to record ideas and information primarily in the form of printed matter – until a certain piece of digital technology that can display physical objects on demand is developed. Most things still have to be documented on paper, including, ironically, multiple media projects. Right now, print is still the most reliable and accessible way to discuss and describe the new media.

Just what is it about print that makes it so important as cultural currency? And how can we give digital media the same legitimacy? Print is very good at creating kinesthetic experiences the computer world is as yet unable to provide. What's worth bringing forward, and what should be left behind? Consider people's attachment to things they collect and save. Will people collect software programs the way they save *National Geographic* magazines? Will they archive their favorite Web sites? Collecting is a way of making the world around us more comfortable, and in collecting and saving, people accumulate cultural values. Computer formats don't currently have the same level of cultural symbology as, say, postcards, but someday people will probably have cyber-shoeboxes for storing digital memorabilia.

Until recently, print has satisfied most of our communication needs. It can do just about anything, except process data – and that's why, over the next few generations, print will have to move over and share the stage with the computing medium.

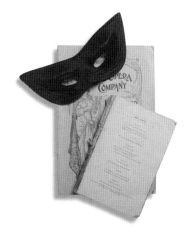

Broadcasting:

The Medium Is the Event

It was just a hundred years ago that broadcasting became the second media type to become significant in human communication. First came radio, and thirty years later, moving pictures; forty years after that, television reinvigorated the art of theater, and became an information source as well. If a medium is to be used as cultural and information currency,

people must be comfortable with it; for the past three generations, no other medium has made people as comfortable as broadcasting. Television, for instance, provides personal experience and intimacy, especially to many people who grew up with television as their babysitter; they find television so familiar that just having it on makes them feel as if someone else is at home. The broadcast medium is more accessible than other media because of the way it enhances the real world, providing a popular (and accepted) form of escapism. It requires the least amount of interaction for the perceived return.

The broadcast medium's greatest strength is its ability to deliver a single scheduled event during a specific period of time. In both television and radio, such events are designed and created with time, place, demographics, and psychographics in mind. Unlike books or other printed matter, moving-image media events are considered non-deferrable – they have to be seen in "real time." VCRs fundamentally changed this, but people are such creatures of habit that they schedule their own events around watching videos. Even television reruns are scheduled events. The broadcast medium has also become a social focal point – both as a commonly discussed topic and as a reason for people to gather together and socialize.

Digital technology has merged three time-based media inside the television box – television, video, and movies. The end product is still video, even though it's alternately described as movies, television, or video. Furthermore, by enabling multiple events to take place simultaneously, digital technology causes broadcasting and computing to overlap. People can experience Howard Stern on the radio or on television; the "Jim Lehrer NewsHour" is also broadcast either on television or on the radio. *The Wall Street Journal* is available in print, through cable syndication, and on the Internet. Each venue has its own following, which demonstrates that consumers consider such options important.

The identifying trait of broadcasting is that it conveys one message or a series of messages to a large group of people simultaneously. Broadcasting is a one-to-many medium, whereas computing can be a many-to-one medium; that is, it can be used to send many messages specifically to one individual.

Broadcasting is expanding as well as contracting because computing has allowed broadcasting to be customized, resulting in what might be called "singlecasting;" television now offers infinite choices, and it can be programmed to deliver specific types of information and entertainment to individual viewers. Instead of choosing from among predetermined broadcast events, a viewer can "order" events and information, tailoring them to his or her lifestyle, interests, financial portfolio, and just about anything else human behavior has engendered. Because broadcasting is time dependent, it is unlikely to survive as a medium on its own.

Appearances can be deceptive. What's broadcast through our television sets still feels like television most of the time, but it's beginning to look computerish, and some of it looks like something else altogether. On the television screen on the left, a story narrative occupies the screen completely; that's how we generally expect a television screen to look and behave. The middle screen, which shows a news-on-demand service, is a hybrid of television and computing – traditional television narrative shares the screen with a computer application interface. The screen on the right shows an online service that lets viewers search for and specify movie videos, view film clips, and order movies. The way interface and content are integrated in the third screen erases the differences between television and computing and results in a new kind of experience.

Computing:

The Chameleon's Chameleon

Computers can be or do practically anything. They can be visible or invisible, and they can simulate the appearance and functions of a variety of media. A computer can masquerade as a television or a calculator or a document. Computing is so flexible that it can even transcend visible forms, as it does in networking systems. Already the capabilities of computing seem far more expansive than those of print or broadcasting, even though computing has only been around for a short time and we still know relatively little about it.

What can we make of a device that can do anything from performing a quick calculation to bringing interactive "Monday Night Football" narration to our television sets? The territory that computers can cover extends well beyond the horizon of our understanding. In print and broadcasting, what is seen or heard – information or entertainment or art – is intended to be fixed, immutable. The computing medium can present absolutes, too, but it also allows users to act on those elements in an endless variety of ways.

Computers fool us. They can take on more forms and are more pervasive than most people think. Computers are generally thought to inhabit screens, but they are around us all day, every day – in our wristwatches, in our cars. The idea of having computers in suit-jacket lapels and belts is close to becoming a consumer reality – functioning like PDAs (personal digital assistants), such computers will serve as tracking and telecommunications devices. At the MIT Media Lab, researchers are exploring the concept of digital paper that is portable and capable of absorbing data into its surface. Other researchers are thinking about ways to integrate computers into the environment, so that a living room wall might become a computer. Such technologies abstract computing to yet another level – right out of its container; it removes

Some Computers Need Disguises...

...Some Don't

The screens on this page are manifestations of the computing medium that vary in depth of content and how a user can modify them. Such variation is an attribute of the computing medium's blurred character, which allows many functions to coexist in the same housing. The example above is a multimedia presentation. Though one can see a simulation of the various issues identified, the implementation is fairly one-dimensional, not unlike a slide show. Its functions are limited to allowing a user to choose, select, and receive a predetermined set of texts, pictures, and data, rendering a relatively passive experience.

Apple's QuickTime Starter Kit is essentially a digital video projector that lets a user run a collection of animated shorts and film clips; it's a VCR or a Super-8 on a computer. Even though the content projects sound and movement, the experience it renders is still relatively passive and one-dimensional because the content does no more than present itself. The user cannot control or modify it.

ATMs and online services now offer more than just banking services. Here the computer takes on the role of mediator between one system (the user) and another (the banking system). Even though the graphics are flat, the system appears to be "thinking" as it mediates between the user and the bank.

This prototype of an online shopping service has the same level of functionality as an ATM, but in three-dimensional form. View the CD-ROM to experience the interaction.

This prototype of a cyber-theme park displays an environment that "surrounds" the user; the experience is immersive and lifelike. The interface gives the user freedom to explore a space, interact with the objects in it, and participate in events.

Over its five-and-a-half-century history, print has grown into an enormously rich medium of expression. Broadcasting revived the oral tradition of storytelling only a hundred years ago. Because it's so much younger than print, broadcasting's lexicon isn't as highly developed or as widely understood – relatively few people try to write screenplays, for instance, compared to the number who try to write books. And compared to broadcasting, the computing medium is primordial ooze. A complaint often heard from designers who practiced their profession before computing is that the capabilities of computers are limiting creative output. Architecture, for instance, used to reflect the hand-drawn renderings that architects made, now building design reflects the limitations of CAD software.

computers from their familiar gray or beige plastic boxes and places them in another dimension. These ideas may seem far-fetched now, but the computer's capabilities have repeatedly soared above and beyond their imagined limits.

At the moment, a three-dimensional presence is the one characteristic that printed things can be said to have which digital things don't. But the sensory experiences virtual reality produces call even that distinction into question. Telepresence (the result of combining telecommunications with computing power) can essentially take anyone anywhere to experience anything – sitting in a cubicle, wired up to sensory devices, a person can directly experience any kind of world. Telepresence creates portable reality – people don't have to "go" anywhere. At Imax theaters, people can "fly" over the Grand Canyon, for instance. As computers acquire more multisensory capabilities, the computing medium will gain a real advantage over print and broadcasting. Imagine, for example, exploring the human chest cavity: walking through a heart the size of a house and hearing the blood surging through the aorta with a thunderous din. That kind of sensory experience could be a valuable tool for medical students – before they actually picked up a scalpel.

The three-dimensional form a computer takes isn't its reason for being – hardware is just a shell for the computing activities of calculating and moving data from one place to another. Print and broadcasting are little more than containers for what people put into them; they display information or entertainment or art in a finished state. A computer's purpose, on the other hand, is to perform work. Suppose a business is producing a brochure that has many color illustrations. Printing in color used to require many separate mechanical steps once the design had been specified. Now, though, because computer scientists have figured out how to describe color using mathematical equations and because software can express images in computer code that "calculates" color, the design process absorbs all those separate mechanical steps while still producing the same

Regardless of a medium's physical or digital properties, its products can be placed along a spectrum between tools and titles. In the print world, tools include phone books and airline schedules, and titles include novels and coffee table books; guidebooks fall somewhere in the middle. In the digital world, tools are what we understand as applications, such as database and word processing programs, and titles include interactive CD-ROMs. Intuit's Quicken software is an example of digital tools and titles merged into one.

Tools ◀┈┈┈┈┈┈┈┈┈┈┈┈┈┈┈┈┈┈┈┈┈┈┈┈▶ **Titles**

Print

Reference Source

Non-Fiction

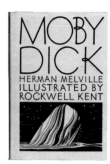

Novel

Broadcasting

Instructional Video

Documentary

Movie

Computing

Application

Tool/Title

Digital Entertainment

brochure. This increase in efficiency can be compared to the difference between fastening one's sneakers with shoelaces or Velcro.

Computing's essential function of processing is not easy to grasp. Paradoxically, though, it embodies the shift that business and industry need to make. Now the payoff will come not from focusing on an end result but from paying close attention to the way things get done.

The computing medium is so different from all other media that nothing can be assumed about it. Its extraordinary transformational behaviors and

powers make any attempt to label it an exercise in futility. People who work directly with the computing medium know that making assumptions about where it will lead wastes time and can result in unsound business decisions. We still think of computing in terms of how similar or different it is from familiar things. What is really different about it, however, is not how it gets us from point A to point B, but how it has merged point A with point B.

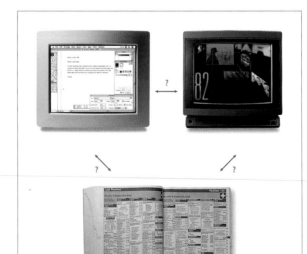

As digital media become more pervasive, the relationships between broadcasting, print, and computing are becoming less distinct.

Content

Understanding and structuring the relationships
between broadcasting and computing is currently a
major business concern. The constant flux between the
two media makes this relationship difficult to decipher.
As content from non-screen-based media – print, music,
telecommunications – is being forced into digital format,
it takes shape as hybrid forms of media on a spectrum
of applications between tools and titles. Businesses must
consider the entire process, including every functional
aspect of each hybrid and the context appropriate for
each type of content.

What Next?

As print, broadcasting, and computing are transforming and merging, so are the industries and professions that deploy them. The more technology changes the goods and services produced, the more those goods and services change our lives. In turn, the more our lives change, the more we demand that businesses respond with appropriate goods and services. The proliferation of digital technology is resulting in a new two-way relationship between business and consumers.

Ten years ago, a magazine called *Computer Life* was unthinkable. A life with computers? How ridiculous and boring, if not incomprehensible! Now, not only do we have personal computers on our desks at work and at home, the very values we live by spring from possibilities that didn't exist before computers. The growth of home-based and freelance businesses, the spread of telecommuting, and the trend toward outsourcing are largely based on digital technology. The general availability of "desktop publishing" tools has encouraged many to try their hand at what used to be practiced only by experienced craftspeople. The Internet, now a powerful force in business, has

This diagram shows a way to look at industries in terms of their core competencies and how they relate to other industries. The industries depicted here are the front-line soldiers in the media revolution.

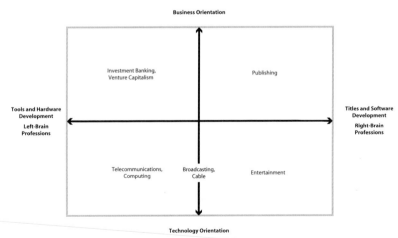

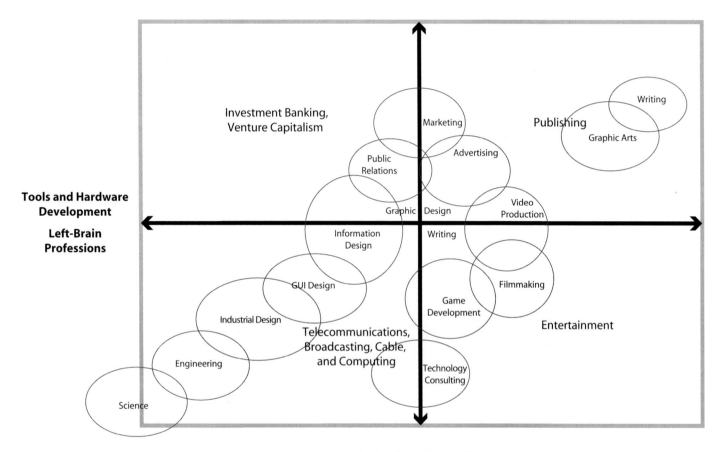

Business Orientation

Investment Banking,
Venture Capitalism

Marketing

Publishing

Writing

Advertising

Graphic Arts

Public
Relations

**Tools and Hardware
Development**

**Left-Brain
Professions**

Graphic Design

Video
Production

**Titles and Software
Development**

**Right-Brain
Professions**

Information
Design

Writing

GUI Design

Filmmaking

Industrial Design

Game
Development

Engineering

Telecommunications,
Broadcasting, Cable,
and Computing

Entertainment

Science

Technology
Consulting

Technology Orientation

*This diagram shows the professions most closely
associated with the front-line industries. View the
CD-ROM for a complete explanatory overview of the
overlaps among industries, media, and disciplines.*

NETSCAPE

Potholes on Wall Street: The computing medium is jarring financial models. On the day of Netscape's initial public offering, before it had ever made a profit, the company's stock skyrocketed from 27 to 78. By the time it was released two months later, the Netscape Navigator browser was fast becoming an industry-wide standard. Months later, Yahoo!, a popular Internet search site, had a greater initial percentage increase than Netscape, although Yahoo! provides a service, not a product.

It's not just through stock that computing is changing business, though. An online search for "salsa" shows that a microeconomy has sprung up in specialty salsa sales over the Web.

Such bizarre business activity is making it more difficult to predict the value of a stock portfolio, not to mention foresee business trends.

leveled social and corporate hierarchies. And the availability of shareware is a challenge to capitalism itself, based as it is on the idea that everything on the Internet – information, graphics, software – should be free and universally accessible.

By decentralizing access to information and promoting individual empowerment, digital technology is wreaking havoc on established business conventions and making companies – from blue chips to startups – behave in unpredictable ways.

In the consumer market, the shift to the computing medium is resulting in products and services that are "neither fish nor fowl." Fax

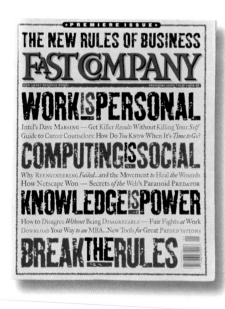

machines, printers, scanners, and copiers are collapsing into a single device, and businesses from banks to publishers are sprouting new products and services over the Internet. A day doesn't go by when products based on digital technology aren't in the news. Consumers are being offered more choices all the time, but not all of them are meaningful ones.

Technological changes are hitting so fast that people and businesses don't really have time to grasp them. On the other hand, people who disregard technological megaleaps are likely to end up feeling disenfranchised. Worse, once a person falls behind in the endless race to know and understand new technology, it takes tremendous determination and stamina to catch up. The way to adapt to the pace of change is to be constantly aware of new developments, but it's time consuming, difficult, and frightening to try. The only way we have to judge the usefulness of what results from this spreading and merging is through the application of design disciplines.

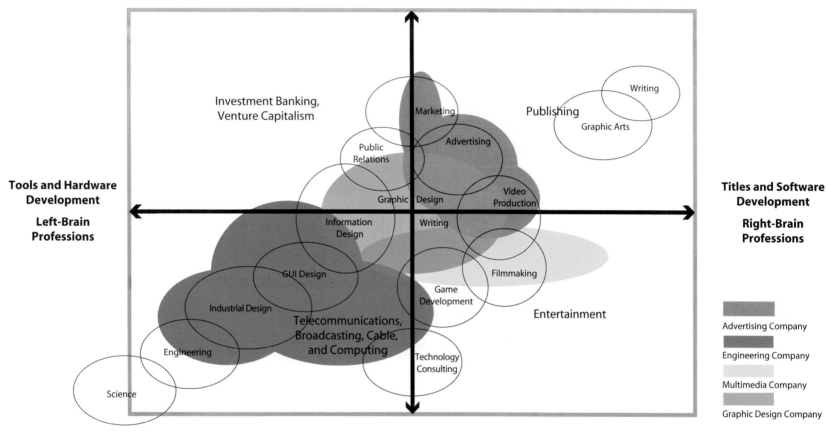

Business Orientation

Investment Banking, Venture Capitalism

Publishing

Writing

Graphic Arts

Marketing

Advertising

Public Relations

Graphic Design

Video Production

Tools and Hardware Development

Left-Brain Professions

Information Design

Writing

Titles and Software Development

Right-Brain Professions

GUI Design

Filmmaking

Industrial Design

Game Development

Telecommunications, Broadcasting, Cable, and Computing

Entertainment

Engineering

Technology Consulting

Science

Technology Orientation

Advertising Company

Engineering Company

Multimedia Company

Graphic Design Company

The left side of this diagram shows that "left-brain professions" such as hardware and software engineering are tool makers in both the physical and digital worlds. The skill sets depicted in the diagram change from technical on the left to artistic on the right, and the colored areas show different design practices and professions overlaid on the industry framework. It's important for businesses and designers using the computing medium to understand who the industry players are, where they are going, and what they are evolving into. Companies are developing new services to accommodate new business needs, and as designers and business people take on projects in the computing medium,

they need a way to examine what kinds of skills are required. Products and services that communicate marketing ideas require different skills from technically oriented projects; professionals in public relations agencies, for instance, don't know how to design code for computer games any more than engineers can devise strategies for selling them. This diagram is a way to determine the nature of a business: designers can use it to figure out a company's needs, and it can help businesses understand what to look for in a design firm. *View the CD-ROM.*

Identity Design:

Synthesizing

Say "identity design," and the first thing people are likely to think of is a logo. A company uses a logo to identify itself in the same way a person uses a signature. However, a logo is not a company's identity any more than a signature is a person's identity. A logo is the entry point to people's view of a

company – it's usually the first impression the company makes – and sometimes it's the only impression, which is why its design is so important. Nonetheless, logos aren't the only way companies express themselves. There are many manifestations of identity design, and they're not all graphical.

The identity of telecommunications giant MCI derives largely from the character of the company's presence on television. MCI's logo appears at the end of its television commercials, but what people remember about MCI isn't its logo as much as the irreverent tone of MCI's challenge to AT&T. A company's behavior, from its advertising messages to its customer service, supplies a tremendous amount of information about who it is and what it does.

Identity is the expression of a company's vision and intent. A designer's job is to express that vision and intent in a pure, efficient form. That's what logos, advertising, press releases, and online service icons are all about – they're visual cues that invoke

Content as identity: CMCD sells royalty-free photographic images. The functions and value of its products are designed right into the packaging, which displays the entire content of each CD on the back.

Business Orientation

Investment Banking, Venture Capitalism

Marketing

Publishing

Writing

Graphic Arts

Advertising

Public Relations

Tools and Hardware Development

Left-Brain Professions

Graphic Design

Video Production

Titles and Software Development

Right-Brain Professions

Information Design

Writing

GUI Design

Filmmaking

Industrial Design

Game Development

Entertainment

Engineering

Telecommunications, Broadcasting, Cable, and Computing

Technology Consulting

Science

Technology Orientation

The arrows in this diagram indicate that identity professionals are moving out of their familiar territory onto new industry turf. Advertising and design agencies traditionally are viewed as identity design specialists. The way communications and products are melding is forcing agencies to think hard about ways to extend identity consulting services. View the CD-ROM.

bigger thoughts. They distill and express a company's values.

Identity design synthesizes all the elements that make up a company's interaction with the rest of the world. It's an analysis of all the information about a company's products or services – the way the company behaves, who its customers are – and how the company interacts with other entities. Through identity design, a company can articulate its goals and character consistently. The identity design process builds a framework for a company to find a cohesive voice, whether it's expressed in a logo or an advertisement.

The computing medium's pervasiveness, limitless forms, and unpredictable behavior are a new aspect of identity design. What place does identity have in the context of dynamic, interactive, two-way environments? Consider Microsoft Network's retail software area, where consumers can buy products from companies other than Microsoft. Multiple brands of hardware and software have coexisted for years, but the idea of one business using another's storefront to sell its goods – the way Microsoft's logo and, say, Adobe's logo appear together in the same space and context – is an important design factor.

What is the relationship of a product's identity to its parent company? To a Web site's graphical interface? Is identity just a way to recognize sponsorship or is it something more? How can the labels on different products and services reinforce the value of a given brand *and* whatever other brand is sharing the same space? Good identity design answers those questions.

Logos are only the front portals of a business's identity. A company's business cards, benefits manual, inventory network, online support, the impression its customer service representatives leave on callers – everything about a company's products, its physical and online locations, and its employees – are all part of its identity. Identity design is a way to capture a living organization and how it accommodates dynamic behavior while reflecting cultural, social, and business changes.

Hewlett Packard provides thousands of products and services to the technical, medical, and computer industries worldwide. One of the services it offers is equipment leasing. To spread the word about the advantages of HP Express Financing, the company issued a variety of collateral materials, including an interactive "test drive" disk that provides interested customers the ability to run "what-if" leasing scenarios. The expressions of Hewlett Packard's identity, in both print and digital form, are consistent in appearance without being rubber-stamp repetitions. They're complementary, not repetitive.

Information Design:

Providing a Context

The discipline of information design isn't specifically about promoting or selling, although when people understand an idea they may feel inspired or compelled to respond. Information design makes information understandable by giving it a context. It analyzes, defines, and structures the relationships between ideas and the way the ideas are visualized.

Because information design brings focus and order to content and the media used to express it, today's digital quicksand makes this discipline more relevant than ever. Computing's power to target information from many sources toward individuals makes information design a useful tool – it highlights disparate bits and pieces of data and collects them into a structure that gives them meaning. Incorporating information design into a process increases efficiency, too, by guiding a project toward a focused end.

The recent explosion in the availability of information has given information design new prominence as a discipline, although it's not a new idea. Everybody already knows what information design is, whether they realize it or not. Its end products are navigational structures – page numbers, tables of contents, buttons. An information designer evaluates where information will reside – on packaging, on a CD, online – and then decides what form – text, still or moving pictures, music or audio – best illuminates the information's overall structure and the relationships among its components. Information design is taken for

Multiple Media | Multiple Disciplines

Investment Banking, Venture Capitalism

Marketing

Publishing

Writing

Public Relations

Advertising

Graphic Arts

Tools and Hardware Development

Left-Brain Professions

Graphic Design

Video Production

Titles and Software Development

Right-Brain Professions

Information Design

Writing

GUI Design

Filmmaking

Industrial Design

Game Development

Telecommunications, Broadcasting, Cable, and Computing

Entertainment

Engineering

Technology Consulting

Science

Technology Orientation

The arrows in this diagram indicate new horizons for information designers. Practitioners of information design are primarily graphic designers and industrial designers because of their work in semiotics, cognitive science, and information services; because cyberspace is a three-dimensional model, environmental designers are also entering the fold. View the CD-ROM.

granted because until now the world has been very physical, which itself imparts a sense of context. In the computing world, context is elusive and changes constantly.

Information design builds new relationships between thoughts and places. A subway system is a good analogy for the way information design works. Like the space on a computer monitor, a subway system is somewhat confined; it lets travelers ride on the A line or the B line or the F line. And, like software, a subway system's usability is based on the veracity of its signage system. What gives that system structure and context are its interim points – what people find interesting and relevant as they travel from point A to point B. In the case of subway systems, visualization is used to build hierarchies in a three-dimensional environment. In cyberspace, the way to work is to transfer navigation and structural concepts from the real world.

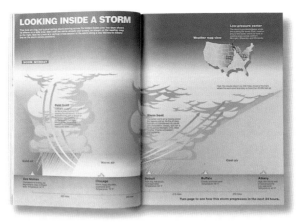

Information design isn't restricted to graphs, pie charts, and maps. This information graphic by Richard Curtis shows how a storm moves across the country. The diagram constructs a visual narrative, giving the reader a sense of time and space, and thus a context in which to interpret the data.

These few bars of music from Georges Bizet's Carmen *are designed information. Composition and annotation are two of the information arts a composer employs. Those who can read and understand music know that the Brandenburg concerti are finely structured designs.*

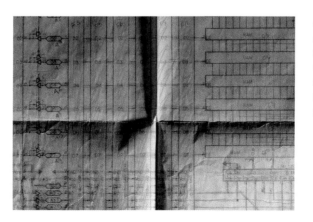

Circuit board design is information design requiring an understanding of mathematics, physics, binary logic, and chemistry. The principles behind the Pentium chip and the PostScript language are beyond most people's grasp, but people who understand computing and what it takes to construct great code see such computing architectures as beautiful examples of information design.

Interactivity Design:

Facilitating and Mediating

The discipline of interactivity design isn't new, but it has only recently been recognized outside of exhibition work and the video game industry. The advent of computing and its ties to business opportunities have quickly raised the status of interactivity design.

Interactivity design involves examining two systems and then creating a way for those two systems to work with each other. For instance, cellular phones are a complex telecommunications system that interacts with the human "system." Interactivity design facilitates or mediates the interaction between the two.

Interactivity design determines the quantitative and qualitative behavior that a product or service has to accommodate. When personal computers were first introduced, designers and engineers, looking for ways to make them understandable to people, used the familiar typewriter keyboard as a model for the insertion of characters. That kind of transference is not foreign to designers; as a matter of course, designers appropriate models and drop them into new contexts to make them behave differently .

Interactivity design makes it possible for the human system to interact with another system. In the world of industrial design, interactivity design is sometimes a key component of ergonomics design, which is based on the study of how and why a specific thing functions. Dashboard design

Business Orientation

Investment Banking,
Venture Capitalism

Marketing

Publishing

Writing

Graphic Arts

Public
Relations

Advertising

Tools and Hardware Development

Left-Brain Professions

Graphic Design

Video Production

Information Design

Writing

Titles and Software Development

Right-Brain Professions

GUI Design

Filmmaking

Industrial Design

Game Development

Entertainment

Engineering

Telecommunications, Broadcasting, Cable, and Computing

Technology Consulting

Science

Technology Orientation

The arrows in this diagram show the areas where interactivity design is flourishing. The practitioners of interactivity design are primarily in the industrial design and video game development fields. Many self-appointed interactivity experts are now working with computing systems because they are knowledgeable about computers, not because of their expertise in interactivity design. View the CD-ROM.

is concerned with positioning particular elements where they will best accommodate driving behavior – putting the wiper switch where it can be reached easily, for instance. A similar interactivity lexicon is just beginning to develop for computer screens. People can now deploy multiple applications on screen, engaging in many different activities at once. This increase in functionality complicates the designer's task.

Designers now need to understand what kind of interactivity is appropriate for each application in order to determine at which points interactions between a computer and a user, and content and a user, should take place. However, human-computer interaction can be observed and software can be user tested, which makes interactivity design relatively quantifiable compared to identity and information design.

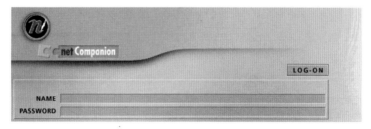

Net.radio is an Internet radio station that provides an application, NetCompanion, that lets listeners customize programming. This proposed interface is based on the familiar metaphor of a car radio so that users don't have to take the extra step of figuring out how to work it. The graphical user interface changes to reflect the time of day.

Media Hybrids

The mind-boggling number of media choices available for just about every product and service, along with the many versions of those products and services, creates unparalleled challenges for everyone working with new technologies. It is important that advertisers, marketers, and designers who have to reckon with these new projects consider fresh business propositions: what looks on the surface like a simple advertising project might actually require a publishing effort with staffing and a substantial operating budget.

We are already familiar with multipurpose hybrid objects and tools in the physical world, such as combination scanner/faxes, phone/message machines, and Swiss Army knives. New technology makes it possible to "multipurpose" content, which results in mongrel communications and products. Just a quick look at what's on the World Wide Web can reveal a gallery of strangeness on par with the Ripley's Believe It or Not Museum. For example, the Internet address www.yahoo.com is the company Yahoo!'s Web site, its directory service, and its search application – in essence, company and product identity all rolled into one. There are virtual graffiti sites where users can share their innermost revolutionary thoughts on the walls of a digital community backlot; cyber fashion runways with slinky models flaunting the latest from Gucci, Pucci, and Fiorucci; and a fictional episodic Web site where people can hang out with friends and interact with serial Web site soap operas. The computing medium makes possible adaptive response and mass customization, as well as one-to-one communication.

New hybrid technologies include CD-ROMs, a combination of print and digital media; the Internet, a combination of computing and telecommunication media; and Intercast, a relatively new combination of broadcasting, computing, and the Internet. These hybrids put human activities into new contexts – it lets people watch television on a computer, for instance. What does this mean for viewers, advertisers, networks, and the billions of dollars they represent?

Each medium is good at expressing a certain voice: particular kinds of information are clearer and stronger in print than on television. How can these differences be reconciled in the computing medium, which might present a broadcast model and a page model on the same screen? Are they one and the same? How are decisions made about which is dominant? Many digital technologies can solve these problems. Businesses have to look carefully at what's being created (the rules and con-straints imposed by the ideas), then at the rules that govern technologies (the information containers), and, finally at the rules that people follow.

To design in this new hybrid arena, one has to have a firm grasp of a variety of disciplines and media. Interactivity and information design are inter-dependent disciplines in the design process; other design disciplines – identity, publication, graphic, broadcast, advertising, software engineering, and strategic planning – can also be components of the design equation in structuring information. The aggregate of these interdisciplinary interactions is the framework for identity, information, and inter-activity design.

Ready, fire! aim.

Hit and run seems to be the modus operandi of high-tech culture. People involved in marketing communications – designing brochures and advertisements – know that the nature of their work is immediate and transient: what's said today becomes outdated in a relatively short time. Planning is, of course, essen-tial in marketing communications, but a different kind of planning than that required for product development. Now that industries are converging, the line between a piece of communication and a product is often indistinguishable. That makes it necessary to devote more time to the planning process. At the same time, spontaneity is the means and the end in the computing world, so a system has to be planned within a framework that allows for improvisation. Flexibility and real-time interaction are important considerations in analyzing any working system. Careful planning – from projects to systems – is absolutely necessary in the computing world because of the number-less possibilities the technology presents; the underpinnings of every technology used in a specific project have to be fully understood before that project can begin. Thus, a computing project requires much more lead time than work in the known media of print or broadcasting.

Intra-activity:

Collaborative Disciplines

The intra-activity model is an attempt to address the issues many business people and designers face when working with digital media and defining the multiple skill sets required to make a project successful. Even designers with experience in this collaborative arena will admit that it is terrifying to commit anything to paper. On the surface, intra-activity might seem like applied cybernetics, which is the theoretical study of control processes in electronic, mechanical, and biological systems. In this context, it refers to the overlapping areas of the identity, information, and interactivity design disciplines.

As print, broadcasting, and computing media are converging, so are the design disciplines associated with their execution – identity, information, and interactivity. The term "intra-activity" is a way to refer to the process of collaboration by professionals from various disciplines, a process that in the context of computing requires every professional to bring multidisciplinary knowledge to a project; intra-activity provides the intelligent framework in which to do so.

The intra-activity concept is based on the Viable System Model (see page 20). It creates a framework for the iterative nature of the design process, which is frequently lost when companies become larger and conformity seems necessary to maintain control. The speed and multiplicity of the computing medium's development makes computer programmers and engineers integral to the design equation, and it pushes everyone, businesses and clients both, into uncharted territory – companies must bring together and match internal and external agendas and integrate them into their creative processes.

Hiring specialists may seem to be a logical way to save the time it takes to bring together a well-trained staff. However, consultants come with their own values and intentions, which are manifested in the way they set priorities and define quality. Furthermore, most professions don't rely on collaboration to a great extent – compare engineers and designers to, say, filmmakers, who have always worked within the boundaries of collaboration. Imagine that a design firm is working with an engineering company to develop a way to clarify a company's complex databases. The design studio's task is to synthesize the data and put it into an accessible computer environment. Even though each part of the team is working toward the same goal, their problem-solving approaches may be completely different; they may have similar intentions, but the value each perceives in what they see on paper or on screen may be different. The engineers will probably think in terms of solving a technical problem; the designers will probably think the issues are in communication; the corporate VPs likely will walk the fine line between the two while staying focused on the original intent behind the project.

In product development, mediation is as necessary as compromise. Businesses need a way to integrate all the parts of the process, a common language for discussing all the facets of a project, and a definition of quality everyone agrees on. Only after a business has established such a system for people to work within should it bring in specialists. To work together and complete tasks within an appropriate time frame, people need a structure. Collaboration is the act of working within that structure.

There are old and new ways of accomplishing particular tasks, and a transition phase between the two. We are all in this transition phase, and the tension is high. Some people get frustrated with the continuous learning process, hoping that eventually the technology will resolve crises by superseding them. These conclusions aren't based on poor judgment, they're just another route through the obstacle course that technology sets before us. In fact, it's precisely at the point when things get most confusing that a business can use the intra-activity model to learn from experience.

Adding value to a product or service gives business a competitive edge. In the computing medium, businesses have to design a new kind of value. In business, design needs to be focused on building a dynamic system rather than grouping

static parts. When the pace speeds up in a business, people tend to get more small things done, but that results in disconnected pieces – more of the same, not something better. It's working with the whole that adds value.

Computing projects have the complexity of buildings. A building design doesn't just consist of sketches of what the door frames will look like; or even finished models. Buildings have plumbing and electricity and other systems that contractors need to be hired to install. Digital technology introduces similar levels of intricacy to the processes of product design and running a business.

Building with a Design System

What can business people, designers, and engineers do when they find themselves caught in the web of converging industries and overlapping media? The four phases described here give businesses a common framework for successful collaboration.

DADI: Definition, Architecture, Design, Implementation

Each of these phases involves editing, which is the process of making choices. Editing is selecting the most appropriate way to express a thought or an idea, as measured against defined goals. Design is the enhancement of an entity; it gives an entity form through the processes of addition and subtraction.

Overall, it is by understanding a project's purpose and following through with it that a business makes a successful product or service. There is a difference between saying "I want to make a lot of money by selling this product" and "I want to create a terrific product and make a lot of money." These two very different purposes determine how the scope of a project is defined, structured, designed, and implemented. A project needs both an internal and an external focus, and the two must not contradict each other. An internal focus might read this way: "I want to learn a lot about filmmaking while I'm working on this multiple media project." A corresponding external focus might read like this: "With this project I can create a terrific portfolio piece, and learn a lot in the process." The way focus is articulated in the context of business is called an agenda, and designers must reconcile companies' agendas with their own.

The DADI process creates a framework that (1) defines a project; (2) creates an architecture that explains the process and, if necessary, the technology platform; (3) defines who does what; (4) defines the time frame and budget; and (5) establishes efficient communication among all the players. This process keeps any project focused on its purpose by preventing progression from one step to the next if the purpose is not understood.

> Design is inherently a messy process. It's ironic that the end result is about creating order. Tom Mecklen

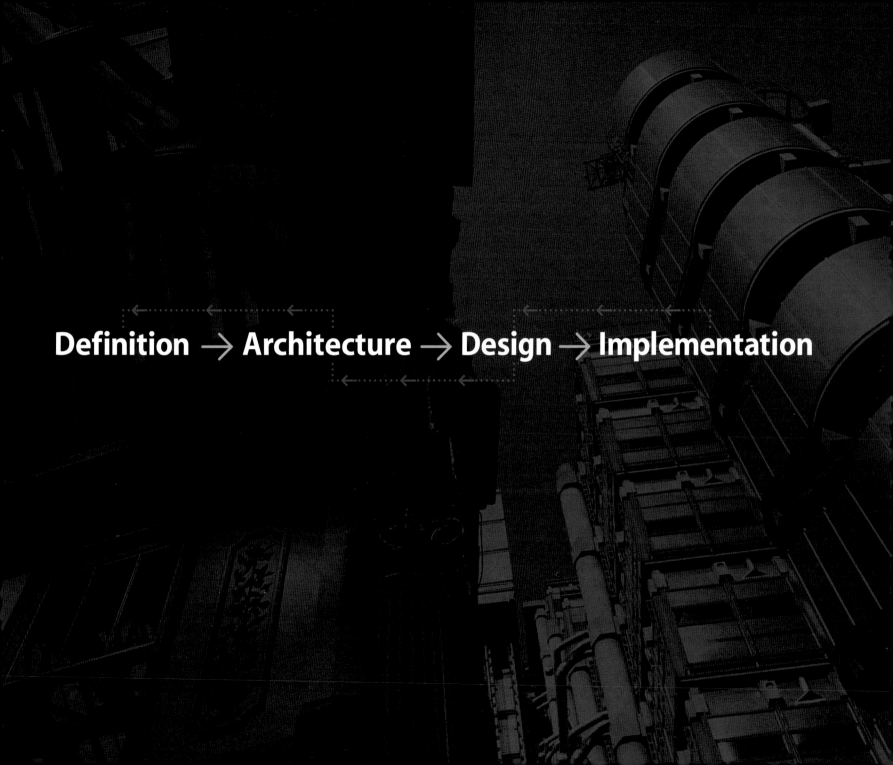

Definition $\rightarrow$ **Architecture** $\rightarrow$ **Design** $\rightarrow$ **Implementation**

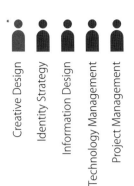

Creative Design
Identity Strategy
Information Design
Technology Management
Project Management

Definition

In this phase, a project team collects and analyzes information, then identifies objectives and considers them in the context of practical parameters such as budget and time frame. The scope and depth of a project begins to materialize during this phase.

CHECKLIST: DEFINE THE CONTENT

- Determine the objective of the project. What needs to be accomplished?
- Understand the competitive scenario. What kind of business does the company do, and what companies will it be competing with?
- Identify the project's content. What does the company want to sell, promote, or provide?
- Define the types of functionality. What kinds of features are desirable? Chat rooms on a Web site? Commercial venues?
- Establish the demographic and psychographic profile of the company's customers. Who are the customers?
- Identify the execution medium (or media). Is the project an identity package? A Web site?
- On interactive projects, explore the technology issues. What browsers or operating systems need to be supported?
- Determine the time line. What is the deadline for the project, and what is driving that deadline?
- Determine the budget. How much does the company want to pay, and what determined that budget?

The length of the definition phase can vary from a one-hour meeting to months of research and interviews.

*Red indicates the lead activity/activities in each phase of development.

Creative Design
Identity Strategy
Information Design
Technology Management
Project Management

Architecture

In this phase, information design is implemented. Is all the information gathered in the definition stage relevant? Does it all have high priority? Will the structure for the information be easy or difficult to build? In this phase, the designer determines where different parts of the information will fit into the structure and which media to use to express them. Prototypes and models fall into this phase because they are a way to analyze, prioritize, categorize, and interpret information gathered in the definition phase.

CHECKLIST: ASSESS THE CONTENT
• Define the key messages.
• Define the information types and functionality.
• Define logical relationships.
• Define links between information types.
• Brainstorm and conceptualize.
• Perform any required research and development related to advanced technologies.
• Test the functionality of the information architecture and navigation.

• Identify specialized resources required to complete the project.

CHECKLIST: GENERATE DELIVERABLES
• A proposal to design or implement the project.
• A technology platform agreement.
• A proposal to create specialized resources, such as a custom program or prototype.
• Positioning statements, naming, and marketing and communications plans.
• A time line for designing or implementing the project.
• Maps, thumbnails, storyboards, or roughs as required to communicate the architecture.

The architecture phase provides the framework on which the project's look and feel will be built. This phase can consist of one simple brainstorming session to determine the hierarchy of information on the front panel of a package, or an elaborate six-week Web site mapping exercise. In either case, the architecture phase should provide concise analysis of the content and complete mapping of the information. The designer's work in the architecture phase should be checked against the business's expectations. If there are differences between what is being delivered and the expectations of either the company or the designer, the cause must be identified before the process moves on to the design phase.

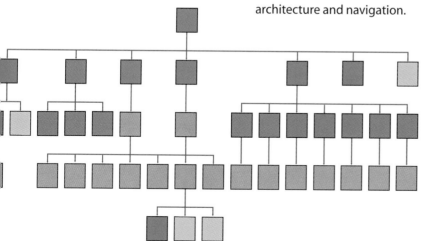

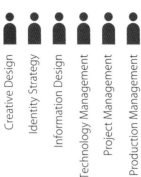

Creative Design
Identity Strategy
Information Design
Technology Management
Project Management
Production Management

Design

In this phase, the project takes on form in colors, shapes, and other audio, visual, or textual elements that bridge the parts of the project developed in the definition and architecture phases. It is in the design phase that a project acquires look and feel. This is not the only phase in which design plays a part, but it is where the creativity that gives the project its personality is employed, and where the visual metaphors that support and enhance the architecture of the information are devised.

CHECKLIST: ACTIVITIES

• Create or supervise the creation of illustrations, photography, and writing.
• Perform customer testing if necessary.
• Perform beta testing and proofreading.

CHECKLIST: GENERATE DELIVERABLES

• A proposal to implement the project.
• Photographs, illustrations, animation, and copywriting.
• A proposal to create or supervise the creation of illustration, photography, and writing.
• Comps or prototypes.
• Analysis of customer research.

The design phase maximizes the results of creative time by following the information structures defined in the architecture phase. Properly implemented, the definition and architecture phases create a solid foundation on which to build a functional and memorable look and feel.

Creative Design
Technology Management
Project Management
Production Management

Implementation

In this phase, the project becomes "real" as the project team synthesizes the ideas, activities, and deliverables developed in the first three phases. Testing takes place during this phase because implementation is concerned with making sure that the project has the desired effect on people. Because the design process continues in this phase, it should not be considered "the production phase," even though it's when deliverables such as mechanicals and HTML code are produced; production work and creative direction take place as necessary in executing the design. The implementation phase is when architecture is manifested in look and feel.

CHECKLIST: ACTIVITIES
- Implement the design as specified in the design phase.
- Extend the system across multiple components or platforms.
- Perform beta testing, proofreading, and press check.

CHECKLIST: GENERATE DELIVERABLES
- Mechanical files.
- HTML templates.
- Complete Web pages.
- Photographs, illustrations, animation, and copywriting (as required to extend the project).
- A proposal for printing, manufacturing, or producing variations on the design.

The implementation phase facilitates the execution of projects across large systems or across various media types and platforms or browsers. This phase also provides a system for proofing and testing work before the project is completed.

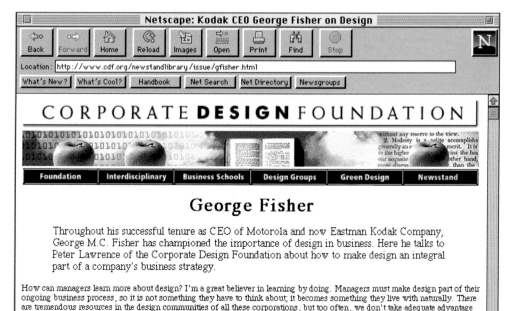

Netscape: Kodak CEO George Fisher on Design

Back | Forward | Home | Reload | Images | Open | Print | Find | Stop

Location: http://www.cdf.org/newstandlibrary/issue/gfisher.html

What's New? | What's Cool? | Handbook | Net Search | Net Directory | Newsgroups

CORPORATE **DESIGN** FOUNDATION

Foundation | Interdisciplinary | Business Schools | Design Groups | Green Design | Newsstand

George Fisher

Throughout his successful tenure as CEO of Motorola and now Eastman Kodak Company, George M.C. Fisher has championed the importance of design in business. Here he talks to Peter Lawrence of the Corporate Design Foundation about how to make design an integral part of a company's business strategy.

How can managers learn more about design? I'm a great believer in learning by doing. Managers must make design part of their ongoing business process, so it is not something they have to think about; it becomes something they live with naturally. There are tremendous resources in the design communities of all these corporations, but too often, we don't take adequate advantage of what's there. The reason is "out of sight, out of mind."

These examples of digital media projects are the results
of accepting new challenges and carrying them forward
into products and services. Each one is a valuable lesson
in design, business, and collaboration, and a new understanding of the strengths and weaknesses of digital
media. It's important not to be paralyzed by the volatile
nature of the computing medium and the confusion
it creates.

Identity Design

i·den·ti·ty (ī-dĕn ′ tĭ-tē) n., pl. -ties.
1. The set of characteristics by which
a thing is recognized or known. **2**. The
set of behavioral or personal traits by
which an individual is recognizable
as a member of a group. **3**. The quality
or condition of being the same as something else. **4**. The distinct personality of
an individual regarded as a persisting
entity; individuality. **5**. Math. a. An equation that is satisfied by any number that
replaces the letter for which the equation
is defined. **b**. Identity element. [FR. identite < OFR. identite < LLat. identitas < Lat.
idem, the same < id, it. See i-*.]

de·sign (dĭ-zin ′) v. **-signed, -sign·ing,-
signs**. –tr. **1.a**. To conceive or fashion
in the mind; invent. **b**. To formulate a plan
for; devise. **2**. To plan out in systematic,
usu. graphic form. **3**. To create or contrive
for a particular purpose or effect. **4**. To
have as a goal or purpose; intend. **5**. To
create or execute in an artistic or highly
skilled manner. –intr. **1**. To make or execute plans. **2**. To have a goal or purpose
in mind. **3**. To create designs. –n. **1.a**. A
drawing or sketch. **b**. A graphic representation, esp. a detailed plan for construction or manufacture. **2**. The purposeful or
inventive arrangement of parts or details.
3. The art or practice of designing or
making designs. **4**. Something designed,
esp. a decorative or an artistic work. **5**. An
ornamental pattern. **6**. A basic scheme or
pattern that affects and controls function
or development. **7**. A plan; a project. See
Syns at plan. **8.a**. A reasoned purpose; an
intent. **b**. Deliberate intention. **9**. A secretive plot or scheme. Often used in the
plural. [ME designen <Lat. designare, to
designate. See DESIGNATE.]

Identity design articulates a company's vision; it encompasses a company's messages, its goods

and services, and the ways in which it does business. Identity design is not a clever advertising

campaign on television, or the thoughtfulness behind a packaging system, or a spiffy new logo,

or a major business or communication initiative. It's the consistent expression of all those parts.

Great companies know this and live by it. Identity issues arise from new contexts and problems,

and unpredictable business conditions that cannot be neatly packaged in a graphics standards

guide. Identity is a living, breathing organism, and its graphical constructs have to be flexible

to accommodate the changes the digital world imposes on

business. Designers must bring traditional design principles

into new media contexts, and then determine how those

principles apply to new business conditions.

Left: Stanford Stadium before the 1985 Superbowl, which was sponsored in part by Apple Computer. Right: FedEx's lucid vision is responsible for its success, because from that vision a distinct character and sense of purpose has emerged. The company's rapport with its customers shows in the ease with which it was able to change its name to FedEx after the company's former nickname became business slang, as in "I'll FedEx that to you today." The trust FedEx has built has been reinforced by its Internet effort, which allows customers into the same package-tracking database that FedEx itself uses. That aspect of the company's vision has also realized fiscal benefits: the tracking software saves money and improves the company's image by allowing customers to do some of the work and feel good about it.

Guarding the Vision

Just as architecture is concerned with the spaces between walls and ceilings as much as the walls and ceilings themselves, identity is concerned with a company's actions and culture as well as its logo, graphic design system, and graphics standards manuals. Graphic representations are only visual amplifiers of data points – they themselves are not a company's vision.

Given the unpredictability that digital media are imposing on the economy, it's critical for a company to maintain a clear vision. Clarity of vision offers the best context for business practices, from hiring to product development and marketing strategies. It helps a business keep pace with the competition, and it keeps a company from having to reexamine its goals every time there's a

merger, an acquisition, or re-engineering. It also makes incongruities and stress points that the company must attend to easier to recognize. The level of complexity digital media has added to the way a company can articulate its vision makes clarity of vision more relevant than ever.

The Guardian

Who should guard the vision, and why it must be guarded, are important considerations. The guardian of a company's vision should be the founder or the CEO. The CEO may delegate the task to another executive, such as the vice-president of marketing, but whoever does the job has to have a firm grasp of its responsibilities. The guardian's task is to make sure everyone in the company understands the vision – why it is doing business in the Far East, or why it is developing one product line and not another – and the value system behind it. Without that company-wide understanding, it's much harder to realize the full potential of a marketing program, an identity system, or a product. It is the way a guardian defines and propagates a company's vision that makes it possible to convey an effective identity.

The role a guardian plays in the business world now is directly affected by the speed and multiplicity of digital media's development. In a way, this book is expressly for guardians surveying the possibilities of

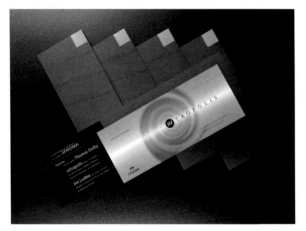

Icons, t-shirts, party invitations, corporate signage, industrial product design, poker chips, and graphical user interfaces for software are not the items companies focus on when putting together an identity design. They are nonetheless an expression of the values of a company and how it conducts business. These expressions matter a great deal, but they are not the identity or the vision.

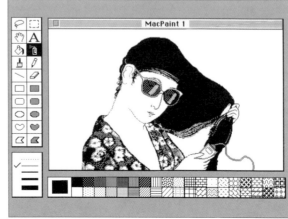

Graphics standards manuals explain in minute detail how to implement a company's identity in all the media used to convey it. It's a way for companies not to have to reinvent the wheel every time a logo is used. A company with many international divisions would distribute manuals to every office so that catalogs or brochures out of, say, Denver would look similar to material from the London office.

In the past, the size of a graphics standards manual has been proportionate to company size; some are massive, and, in general, they are expensive to produce, difficult to maintain and update, and frequently take a year to publish.

Companies still need graphics standards manuals, but now the way they are maintained and updated can accommodate the mobility of a company's identity and take into account that more people shape corporate communications. Some companies have replaced their forty-pound graphics standards manuals with

simple pamphlets updated on a quarterly basis, making them available to everyone in the company. Digital technology has spurred streamlined, direct communication, and some companies have dispensed with printed manuals altogether by distributing graphics standards and artwork electronically – making updates instant and universal.

new media. A guardian must be conversant with the many options a company has for orchestrating its actions and broadcasting its image, as in the choice between implementing a print advertisement or a direct-mail program, or targeting customers with e-mail. A guardian must understand the relevant technology's power and options before initiating a design development process. Before computing, delivery points for communications were familiar and comparatively few. Now, "also" is the key word: all the conventional media plus new ones. A guardian must be aware that the characteristics and behaviors of those "alsos" may be in his or her blind spot.

A guardian in a large corporation should be able to manage the education of VPs and other

executives both inside and outside the core organization. In a smaller company, a guardian must translate the vision into tactical and practical terms, and then turn it into action. For instance, the guardian of a company with aspirations to work within both Mac and PC environments would want to lead the firm to platform agnosticism.

It's especially important for a guardian to make sure that the marketing and creative service departments comprehend the vision. In most organizations, those departments are the designated "design police," but the real responsibility of each department is to help implement the vision – not create it – by maintaining the company's graphic identity. Too often, a graphic identity is policed by marketing groups as if it were the vision.

It's everywhere! Identity manifests itself in small and seemingly insignificant places, such as elevator buttons.

What Consistency Really Is

Many people have definite ideas about corporate identities, assuming, for instance, that if a graphics standards manual says a logo is blue, it must always be shown in blue, or that if a logo is specified in a certain size and shape, it must always be shown in that size and shape. No one, and especially the guardian, should fixate on any graphical aspect of an identity. Many business professionals think that consistency is the cornerstone of an identity system. Consistency, though, is not about rubber-stamping a graphical element; it's concerned with tone. Whether identity is brought to life in a brochure or a corporate headquarters building, it's the tone of the company's voice that reflects its vision. MTV's identity, for instance, has a strong voice and vision, which has earned it a distinct presence in broadcasting even though it doesn't look the same from day to day or week to week. Like MTV's identity, most successful identities evolve over time, changing with business conditions and company priorities. A common pitfall for designers, marketing departments, and business people is thinking that consistent use of graphic tricks or trends can clarify an identity.

The identity for Omnipage is evident in the consistent look of its packaging letterhead, etc. Below: The interface for Photodisc's service has a consistent look, but its identity is further enhanced by the actions revealed by the interface, which produces "feel." The Photodisc interface displays the same behavior in the both the Internet and The Microsoft Network versions.

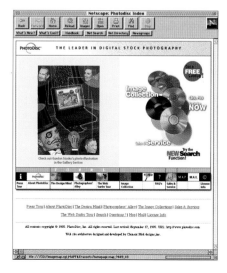

Identifying the Vision

in a World of Pluralities

Because of the mesmerizing variety of options for delivering products and services, achieving consistency of tone – the hallmark of a good identity system – is becoming more than a little elusive. Businesses used to have the relative luxury of creating identities with a secure knowledge of everything a product or service did and who its consumers were. That security is now a thing of the past. The ever-widening diversity of digital media has had dramatic repercussions that affect all aspects of business, making it harder to translate raison d'être into graphic form. An identity system's basic elements must be rethought frequently simply because of the increasing number of ways to communicate and express identity.

Scenario: A traveler is flying at 35,000 feet over the Grand Tetons in a commercial airline. All the seats are connected in a local area network, with flat-panel display screens mounted on the backs of the passenger seats. Attached to the underside of each armrest

is a contraption that is both a mobile phone and a video-game controller. The screen's main menu offers a variety of services – a transcription service that allows a memo, note, or letter to be dictated over the digital cellular phone, then faxed anywhere in the country within a few hours; a suite of video arcade games costing five dollars for the duration of the flight; numerous toll-free numbers for transportation and lodging reservations; dial-up access to stock quotes, sports, entertainment, and hometown news; and a substantial gift catalog with products and services from businesses offering clothing, gadgets, and floral delivery. This device – a phone, an electronic catalog, a video arcade game, and a news wire service rolled into one – is not science fiction or fantasy. It's real technology and it's available today.

To take the scenario one step further, imagine that our traveler gets bleary-eyed looking at the screen and picks up the in-flight magazine. Inside is a catalog insert for the same gadget company that made its products available through the in-flight online service, but the insert shows different products and a different toll-free number. How can the traveler know which number to call to place an order? That duality of market presence should be a concern for many people at the gadget company, including the guardian, the marketing department, the design department, and the sales staff.

Identity in Motion

The expression of an identity is not just a graphical communications issue. A company can express itself with combinations of products and communications media on screen. Apple's Macintosh interface, for instance, is an expression of Apple's voice.

The challenge for identity designers is not merely creating an adaptable identity, but inventing a process that ensures adaptability. Such a process includes a re-evaluation step and a feedback loop, so that whenever an identity is updated, re-evaluation is already built in. That step is in the form of imposed continuity – whether rules for that continuity have been established or not. "Continuity" can take the shape of a specific person assigned to review an identity's focus, or simply an extra item added to the agenda of a company's weekly meeting. Maintaining an identity used to be a matter of creating a style guide; now it can be a full-time job.

The concept of identity in motion, although it isn't new, is fast becoming an integral part of identity design strategies. An identity in motion retains an appropriate state and context no matter what medium is used to express the identity. Because it's adaptable, it can reflect the multitude of changes a company undergoes.

Being Everything to Everyone

The problem of relating each of a large corporation's products and services to a single identity – one thought, one brand expressing the whole – is not a new problem in identity design. It dates from the time companies began diversifying, segmenting, and localizing their customer bases. What is new is the exploding array of media that identity can be expressed through, as discussed

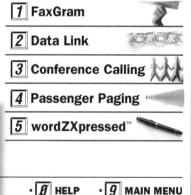

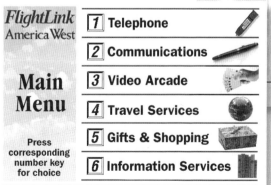

Data networking is one of the new industries that can't be seen or easily defined. Companies that provide networking products and services have to go beyond the usual abstraction of a corporate mark in order to convey their identity. For instance, 3Com, known for its hubs, switches, and adapter card products, wanted to extend company brand awareness beyond the traditional networking market. The company found a novel way to let its existing and potential customers know that it was involved with the community: it associated its name with the local major league ballpark. Doing so linked 3Com to broader, more substantial values than baud, speed, and feed.

earlier – and also the number of shapes it can take, especially in products without physical form. Take banking, for instance, in which identity is expressed at the local branch by how friendly the tellers are and how tastefully the interior is decorated; the identity is also expressed in the ATM and online banking service interfaces. Banks must now build many new and different kinds of relationships for a single account.

Part of the promise of computing is its ability to accommodate diversity by allowing businesses to customize messages. Designing for plural consumer relationships within an identity, however, doesn't mean accommodating the lowest common denominator. Technology may provide access to a worldwide audience, but that access shouldn't be translated into an everything-to-everyone-at-once identity. People are still people, and they have different values in different parts of the world.

Today, a company can customize a message by country, gender, age group, or any other demographic. Some international companies have homogenized identities, expressing their presence in a different country by language change only. Other companies may need to adapt their graphics at a local level to accommodate cultural aversions to certain colors (as with the color white, which is associated with innocence in England, but which connotes death in China). Until a few years ago, the

restrictions of print made it difficult, and expensive, to customize identity. Because the computing medium is malleable, it can take on alternative forms to accommodate usage patterns, time of day, or myriad other variables.

Identity in the Global Village

Now that companies can communicate instantly with millions of individuals around the world, they are finding it more difficult to evaluate whether an identity is appropriate. What does it mean to have an identity that is global, or international, when there are only a couple of mouse clicks between Microsoft North America and Microsoft Japan? Are they the same? Should they be the same?

An international company may only have an address in the country where it is doing business, but a global company has entirely separate operating units. IBM U.S. and IBM Japan are managed very differently, and their products accommodate the preferences in those markets. In certain countries where people are particularly health-conscious, McDonald's serves salad-like foods; in France, it serves wine. These are truly global companies because they accommodate regional and local needs.

What will become of identity now that computers are allowing businesses to accommodate so many differences? Because locale is conceptual in the digital world, the minute a company goes online it becomes, by default, an international company. The advent of the global marketplace has given paradoxical significance to the environmental mantra of the 1970s: "Think globally, act locally."

Identity in Real Time

Service sector companies know very well that identity comprises human activity and culture. The identities of companies like Nordstrom and FedEx are built around interacting with customers in real time; those identities can be expressed in a sales clerk's tone of voice, the intelligence of a reply to a query, and speediness of service. Product sector companies, on the other hand, are one step removed from those kinds of realities; they are used to expressing their identities in controlled third-party environments, such as print and broadcasting. Customer support is important to the success of many product sector companies, but it isn't second nature to them.

When MCI customers access their long-distance service, they hear a recorded, but pleasant, voice intone "MCI." That's one example of a company using digital technology to communicate one on one with customers in real time. As interactive

The Republic of Tea's teapot logo anchors the company's numerous expressions of its identity to its vision. The company markets its teas by variety and by tea drinkers' preferences, personalities, and the time of day they drink tea. It promotes its teas by creating a unique ambience: product information, for instance, is presented in a letter from the "Minister of Tea." The teapot logo can take various forms, with the steam issuing from its spout implying different personalities and moods. Shown here (top to bottom) are logos for morning tea, afternoon tea, and nighttime tea.

PowerTV

A company with a product identity for an invisible technolgy: PowerTV develops operating system software for digital set-top applications – in other words, software that enables cable modems to talk to network servers.

television and the Internet push businesses further into the interactive areas of news and movies on demand, we'll see more and more company-customer interaction conducted through digital interfaces. Technical support and interface usability are growing identity issues for both the product and service sectors. Because service sector companies already understand how to take care of customers in real time, they have some advantage over product sector companies; what isn't yet second nature to either, however, is supporting that same proposition through computers, without personal contact. How can a company communicate with customers through a computer interface and still leave them feeling like royalty? Widget makers take note: the transition won't be easy.

Never Underestimate the Value of Brand

Understanding the value of brand and building brand recognition are going to be more important as we move further into a world of pluralities. The value of a brand is built over time, with good experience built on top of good experience. When a company merges with another or is acquired or reconfigured, divisions are spun off, which changes the very nature of the business. With little time to nurture new customer relationships, maintaining the value

of a brand while finding a way to express it in terms of the company's new goals is likely to be a challenge.

As a large company diversifies its product line or enters a new business altogether, a familiar brand can help or hinder acceptance of a new product in a particular market. Take Texas Instruments, which is well known for its pocket calculators. Most people don't know that Texas Instruments also manufacturers computers, voice recognition software, and military defense technology. When a company sells products as different as defense satellite technology and pocket calculators, it needs a complex image structure to pull all those concepts together into a coherent identity; the complexity is amplified when "invisible" enabling technologies are added to both products. Digital technology can simplify the identity confusion this variety of product creates because its flexibility allows companies to smooth out the rough edges that incongruous ideas present. Putting pocket calculators and voice recognition technology together in the computing medium is perfectly fine.

However, the forcefulness of digital technology has swayed some companies to compromise their identities. In taking their products or services online, some companies go out of their way to "accommodate" the medium, abandoning crucial parts of their

Farallon provides local area network products that simply and economically connect networks of PCs, printers, notebooks, and workstations, as well as software that monitors, sends, receives, and shares documents. Farallon products handle data from both the Internet and intranets. The nuances of this company's products and identity are endless; all its products are either invisible or reside in a closet. Visualizing the abstract nature of Farallon's products is an ongoing challenge. At left is one of several editorial drawings from Farallon's original packaging that depicts the different functions, activities, and steps involved in managing a network remotely.

identity such as service, logo, established tradition, and name. Businesses must make the medium work for them, not the other way around.

Making the Invisible Visible

Networking is a multibillion-dollar industry that produces hardware and software for transporting data packets to and from computer systems. A significant percentage of the networking industry produces "enabling" technology – technology that enables other technologies to work – that has no physical form. Telecomputing, for instance, allows a computer user to watch and modify a document on someone else's computer 3,000 miles away.

So networking is networking is networking, right? Wrong. When companies that make complex products fail to acknowledge that complexity, they end up creating meaningless, oversimplified identity statements. Communicating about things we can't see or hear is a challenge, but it isn't impossible. Designers and businesses have encountered this kind of communication problem before, and they use metaphors to great effect. Take the telephone or insurance business, whose products and services are just as "invisible" as networking products and services. For years, those industries have translated that invisibility and made it understandable and compelling.

What makes communication about products like networking hardware and software a new challenge is that no one has ever seen electronic pulses. Designers articulating and shaping a visual language for this kind of technology realize it is not a trivial undertaking. Yet a company can't afford to gloss over the nuances that differentiate a net modem from a fax modem. In the enabling technology industry, identities must be designed within a broad framework that illustrates the different acts of connecting people.

Context Media is an Internet publishing and software development company whose proprietary web-based software filters, organizes, and contextualizes vast amounts of information. The company builds customized information delivery platforms for corporate clients as well as external and internal Internet applications. Essentially, Context Media's founders created a new software genre to respond to the information overload. View the CD-ROM.

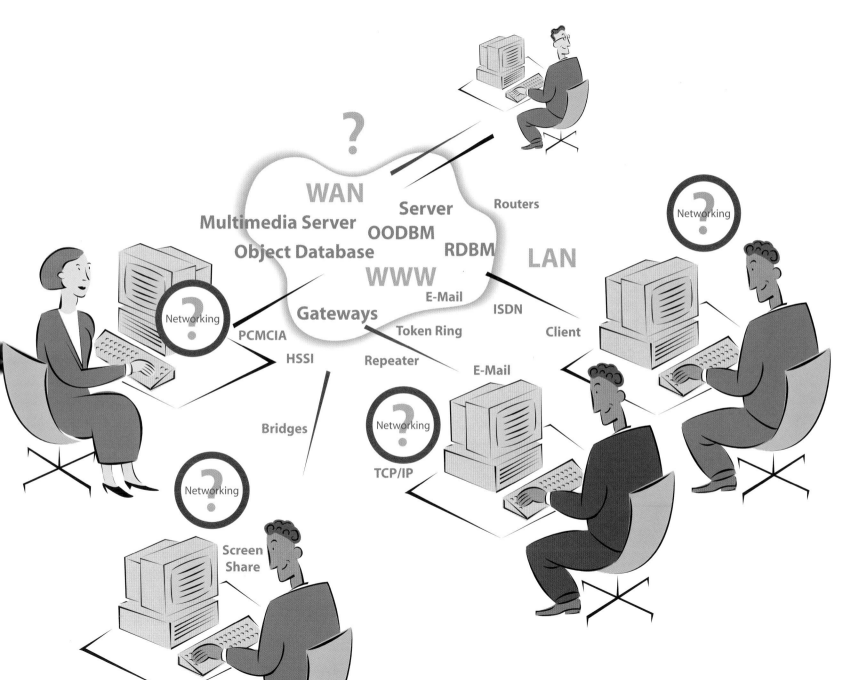

Asking the Right Question

The objective of the 24 Hours in Cyber-space project was to collect and publish stories about the computing medium and how it changes people's lives. As the project got under way, the team led itself off track, both stymied by technological limitations and mesmerized by the array of new technologies that theoretically could be implemented. In dealing with technological options, the questions to stick with are: if a new technology is implemented, who will use it? How will they see it? Does using it defeat the purpose of the project? Technology is seductive; if it's not used purposefully, a project team can very quickly find itself off course.

Unless a company goes through a merger or an acquisition, it will move in an evolutionary way, not a revolutionary one. The nature of an identity problem changes incrementally, so that an organization must repeatedly revisit the questions raised by each project it undertakes. It's no real surprise that after several years the ongoing debate over health care reform hasn't been resolved: no one agrees on the definition of the problem. Businesses, too, often set out to solve a problem only to find that it's a symptom of a larger one. Where identity is concerned, a business needs to define problems clearly before beginning the planning and organization stages of any project, and such clarification is best accomplished in collaboration with design consultants.

One way to check whether anything has happened to change an identity problem once it has been defined is to revisit the Definition, Architecture, Design, Implementation process (see pages 54-59). After the Definition phase, the checklist should be gone over. Are all the items on the list still relevant to the problem? Go over the checklists after each subsequent phase; are all of the items still relevant? Forgetting to ask these and other questions as a project progresses can result in knotty situations. When Adobe decided to develop a new Web site, it wanted to take advantage of the unique capabilities of Netscape's Navigator 2.0 browser. In the rush of development, however, no one asked the "when" question. When Adobe's CEO took a look at the finished product, he didn't miss a beat in informing the project team that version 2.0 of the browser hadn't been officially released yet.

A word of caution: defining an identity problem can be rather simple; the tricky part is staying focused on the problem. Digital technologies appear so benignly flexible that when new ones are introduced, as they frequently are, designers and clients alike can easily be lured away from their goal toward ever-more-attractive possibilities. Staying focused on a goal is harder than dreaming, and not as much fun, especially for people whose work style tends toward the organic and instinctive. Spontaneity is important in design, but in the context of the endless distractions that technology spews forth, it must be balanced with attention to a project's focus and schedule.

"Tell me again what problem we're supposed to be solving?" Eastman Kodak's Motion Picture division asked a design firm to create a graphics standards manual. After the design firm asked questions about the division's relationship with the rest of Kodak's products and services, it became apparent that the problem was bigger than resolving inconsistent logo placement on products – it had to do with naming conventions. Some product titles were preceded by the name "Kodak," some by "Eastman Kodak," and some titles included neither. The inconsistency made developing a standards manual impossible; the relationships between Kodak and its products and services first had to be remapped, as in the chart at right. What was initially considered an identity standards problem evolved into an examination of product naming and division repositioning.

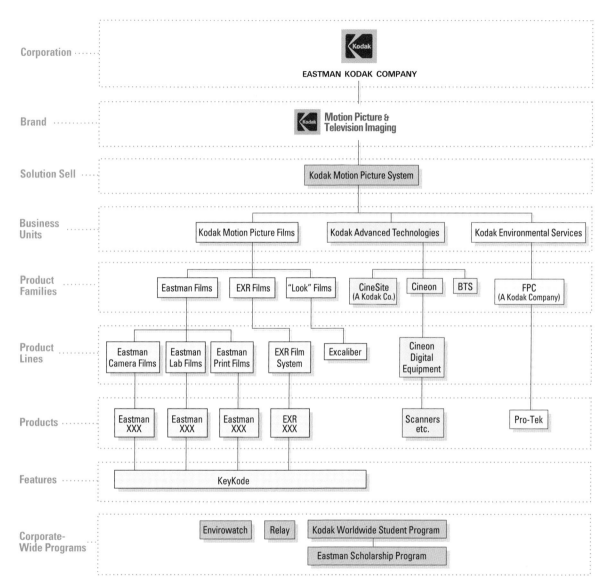

Defining Priorities

Defining and staying focused on an identity problem is one aspect of maintaining a project's direction; defining priorities is another. Priorities are important because of the many distractions thrown in the path of a project in digital format, the number of different groups of people that can be involved in a project, and the paralysis that can set in when digital technology breaks down. One way to define priorities is to put down – on paper, e-mail, somewhere – all the elements a project encompasses. When priorities are established, ideas can be flushed out and given shape and form.

At the beginning of a project, when all its parameters are in flux, making a wish list can give individual tasks realistic dimensions. Then the project team can discuss goals and time frames or the importance of implementing a complex task. This process is a simple procedure that not only provides a currency for agreements but gives a team a way to determine a project's scope and depth.

It used to be that the marketing department approved a designer's sketches and storyboards, and that was that. Now, digital technology involves more people with different skill sets in a project. Visualizing project dimensions helps everyone understand the problem the project is meant to solve. Only through a common understanding can priorities balance art and technology, design and business, sales and marketing, engineering, and client or service management. The design process can help businesses find that common ground.

How can people from different disciplines grasp a common understanding of an idea? Visual expression seems to be the most widely understood language for expressing ideas, and the more ideas a designer can articulate in visual form, the better the chances of a project's success. Maps and diagrams serve quite well in conveying complex ideas; they allow design concepts from the most abstract to the most vivid to be neatly integrated into logical, sequential terms. It's always been a designer's job to give form to ideas; digital media make it a designer's job to express ideas in terms that engineers and technicians can work with, too.

The nature of digital media sometimes deceives us into thinking that basic common-sense approaches don't apply to the issues it presents. It may help to remember that even though the physical context that orients people working in print and broadcasting is missing in digital media, the fundamental procedures of defining priorities and creating an identity are the same as if the project were printed on paper or broadcast on radio.

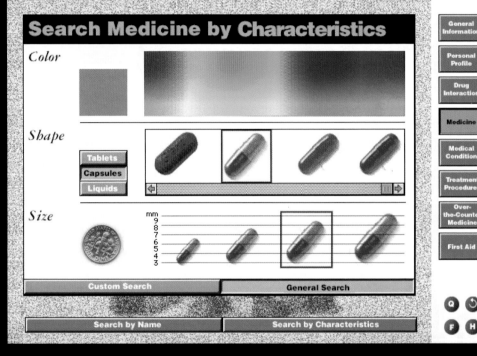

Medicine Search

Search Medicine by Characteristics

Color

Shape

Tablets
Capsules
Liquids

Size

mm
9
8
7
6
5
4
3

Custom Search   General Search

Search by Name   Search by Characteristics

General Information
Personal Profile
Drug Interaction
Medicine
Medical Condition
Treatment Procedures
Over-the-Counter Medicine
First Aid

Q ↺
F H

Honing in on the nature of the identity problem resulted in a successful interface for the Family Pharmacist CD-ROM, which was based on content licensed from the publisher of a comprehensive prescription drug reference. After extensive research, it was decided to base the title's functionality on patient needs (medical history and condition, medication, adverse drug reactions, and so on) rather than list the information alphabetically. The Medicine Search function lets a user search for medicine by size, color, or shape, so that if Johnny swallowed several pink pills, they could be quickly identified.

Company Identity, Brand Identity, Product Identity

Articulating company identity requires an understanding of why a company exists and how it sustains itself. The way a company is organized – its divisions, services, and technologies – is manifested in company, brand, and product identities.

A brand articulates a family of products with a collective identity that is based on similar values. New products added to a brand line can take advantage of the reputation of existing products. Company, brand, and product identities are distinct but interrelated and can overlap, as do Yahoo!'s company and product identities. They can also shift, as when Levi Strauss' blue-jean product identity grew so successful that it overtook company identity.

Brand *identity* represents an organization or product visually through advertising, packaging, product design, and graphic elements. An effective brand identity is based on visual metaphors that support, shape, and deliver a carefully crafted message. Brand *image* represents all the impressions that customers, competitors, employees, and the public form about an organization or product. An ingredients mark represents a component product. Ingredients marks are created for one very important reason – to extend the power of a company's identity to its products. The familiar ingredients mark for wool connotes quality and helps visualize both a concept and a brand: it's used internationally, and it boosts the identity of any product it appears on. The ingredients mark for the PostScript technology from Adobe Systems lets customers know that visual and text information are in a compatible format and will be displayed and printed accurately from monitor to monitor and printer to printer. Ingredients marks give visual form to abstract concepts.

Consistent Identities

In some cases, brand image is consistent with corporate image, and that connection casts a favorable light on the brand by reinforcing common themes. Motorola, a forward-looking company with many communication divisions that were generated over seventy years, wanted to create a branding strategy for their wireless products group, which include PDA's, PCMCIA modems, and a range of software offerings.

Motorola engaged a design firm to help the wireless products group determine the best way to

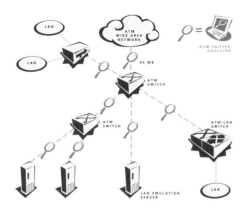

This diagram, created for Network General, shows the functions of the company's network management software and the relationships that it establishes among the components of a network.

Adobe

SONY.

PURE NEW WOOL

Adobe PostScript

It's a Sony

Certain companies often license "enabling" technology from another company for use as a component of a product. When an enabling technology contributes to or can be perceived as contributing to the value of a product, the marketing advantage that the technology provides dictates that the technology be made visible to potential customers. An ingredients mark – a small, mobile graphic that can be expressed through multiple media – acts as a kind of roving ambassador for a parent company, embodying a company's identity.

OneServer™

SANCTUARY WOODS

The universal symbol for databases is the cylinder because of the stack of hard disks on which the database resides. OneServer is a database technology and its logo makes visual reference to that symbology. Sanctuary Woods is in the business of interactive game titles. The company logo is depicted as an animated arrow cursor. A good way to visualize a concept for the computing medium is to use inherent symbolic references.

approach branding strategy. For some people, Motorola represents just televisions – not cellular phones or pagers, let alone new wireless devices. The first question was whether the corporate image said things that were consistent or inconsistent with the desired brand image for the wireless products group. After some preliminary studies it became obvious the best way to present the new wireless division's products was to leverage the image of quality the parent company had established – the wireless group should take advantage of Motorola's established reputation to maximize awareness of its products.

To visualize the wireless concept, it was necessary to take a good look at where the wireless products group resided within Motorola and to what extent the group's identity should reflect the identity of other parts of the company. Diagramming all the parts of the company helped define this part of the identity problem and clarify the issues. At what level in the corporate hierarchy should the building of the brand be invested. Did they want to be known as the best PDA vendor, or as the purveyor of the best wireless products, or in the larger picture, as the ultimate source for mobile communications? An eye chart was created to compare variations for the logo design of the wireless products group, ranging from logos that strongly associated wireless products with the Motorola name to logos that created more distance between the parent company and the new brand. This gave a feel to the expression that would be most comfortable and credible for Motorola's distributors and customers.

This animation sequence was first used in the demo for Connect Inc.'s bulletin board service. As the logo implies, Connect sells telecommunication products.

CONNECT

Identity Design

Understanding the relationship between the organization of a company and its product is critical in determining not only the identity of the organization, but also how the organization behaves. Behavior is what defines the identity/persona of a company.

What You See Is Not
Everything You Get

Just as print and broadcasting products have look and feel, so do products of digital media – but with an important difference: there's no one-to-one relationship between feel in traditional media and in digital media.

The visual and physical manifestations of an identity are its *look*. In print, for instance, look has to do with graphics, paper, and size. The way a product's physical parts work together (or don't work together) to create an impression about the product – that's the product's *feel*. To take the print example further, imagine what happens when people pick up a magazine and thumb through it. What they see and feel in their hands are all the aspects of a magazine's look: the style of the graphics, the quality of the paper, the tone of the headlines, the subjects of the photographs. A magazine's feel comes from the overall impression those elements make. But there's another aspect of feel. As a reader looks through the magazine, little interactions take place: pages make crackly noises as they are turned, the reader sometimes tears out subscription information and perfume ads.

Subtle and ephemeral though they may seem, those aspects of feel are important clues in the course of our interaction with three-dimensional objects. Products manufactured in digital media don't offer the same kind of built-in interaction; they don't behave the same way. That difference makes it essential for anyone developing software to think about feel very carefully.

Because they're used to the physical dimension that print identity resides in, marketing departments and designers often settle for giving a product a look without first addressing its feel. But feel has everything to do with the way we think about and use digital products and services. The CD-ROM market is flooded with shovelware, which is the result of digging up a printed piece or a video and dumping it into digital format without paying attention to feel. A company might launch a Web site that offers online customer support, but if it doesn't assign enough staff to field queries received through the site, it would be ignoring an important aspect of feel.

Mac

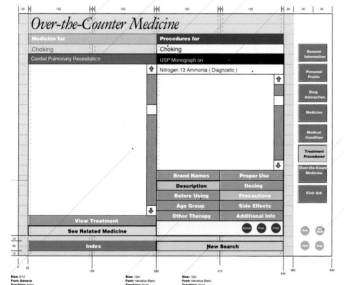

Type
TYPE · SPECIMEN

Size: 36/40 pt.
Font: Garamond Three Italic
Tracking: -40
Position: U&LC
Flush-Left Ragged Right
Display: Anti-alias
Color: Black

Size: 10pt.
Font: Helvetica
Tracking: None
Position: U&LC
centered on all sides.
Display: Bit-Mapped
Color: Black

Size: 12 pt.
Font: Helvetica Black
Tracking: None
Position: U&LC
Flush Left/Ragged Right
Display: Bit-Mapped
Color: White

Size: 10pt.
Font: Helvetica Black
Tracking: None
Position: U&LC
Centered on all sides.
Display: Bit-Mapped
Color: White

Size: 10pt.
Font: Helvetica Black
Tracking: None
Position: U&LC
Centered on all sides.
Display: Bit-Mapped
Color: White

Size: 10pt.
Font: Helvetica Black
Tracking: None
Position: U&LC
Flush Left/Ragged Right
Display: Bit-Mapped
Color: Black

Over-the-Counter Medicine

Medicine for — Choking — Cordial Pulmonary Resesitation

Procedures for — Choking — USP Monograph on — Nitrogen 13 Ammonia (Diagnostic)

General Information
Personal Profile
Drug Interaction
Medicine
Medical Condition
Treatment Procedures
Over-the-Counter Medicine
First Aid

Brand Names | Proper Use
Description | Dosing
Before Using | Precautions
Age Group | Side Effects
Other Therapy | Additional Info

View Treatment
See Related Medicine
Index
New Search

Admin. Prob. Print.

Helvetica Regular
ABCDEFGHIJKLMNOPQRSTUVWXYZ
abcdefghijklmnopqrstuvwxyz
1234567890 !@#$%^&*()_+=?<>,.

Helvetica Black
ABCDEFGHIJKLMNOPQRSTUVWXYZ
abcdefghijklmnopqrstuvwxyz
1234567890 !@#$%^&*()_+=?<>,.

Garamond Three Italic
ABCDEFGHIJKLMNOPQRSTUVWXYZ
abcdefghijklmnopqrstuvwxyz
1234567890 !@#$%^&*()_+=?<>,.

Geneva
ABCDEFGHIJKLMNOPQRSTUVWXYZ
abcdefghijklmnopqrstuvwxyz
1234567890 !@#$%^&*()_+=?<>,.

Size: 7/10
Font: Helvetica Black
Tracking: None
Position: U&LC centered on all sides.
Display: Anti-alias
Color:
Black (active mode)
White(passive mode)

Size: 7 pt.
Font: Helvetica Black
Tracking: None
Position: U&LC centered on all sides.
Display: Anti-alias
Color:
Black (active mode)
White(passive mode)

Size: 9/10
Font: Geneva
Tracking: None
Position: U&LC flush-left ragged right
Display: Bit-Mapped
Color: Black

Size: 10pt.
Font: Helvetica Black
Tracking: None
Position: U&LC centered on all sides.
Display: Anti-alias
Color: Black (active mode)
White(passive mode)

Size: 10pt.
Font: Helvetica Black
Tracking: None
Position: U&LC centered on all sides.
Display: Anti-alias
Color: Black (active mode)
White(passive mode)

Many aspects of specifying typefaces and type sizes in screen media are the same as in print; some type elements can be standardized on the screen just as they can be in print.

Being Explicit

Because digital media aren't just another way to say the same things that are in print, designers making the transition from print to digital media have to leave their biases behind. Print has very high resolution; on-screen resolution is low. In print, type and graphics can be aligned on tight, rigid grids; on screen, they often can't, and frequently it's not appropriate to do so. And when elements can move across a screen as fast as they can be read, some graphical boundaries and typographic distinctions become moot. Digital media have aesthetics of their own, and trying to "correct" those aesthetics using the standards of another medium is a mistake.

There isn't yet a very robust visual vocabulary and language for digital media; conversely, digital media cannot always support the language nuances and subtleties of other disciplines. The meanings that photographic symbols and sound effects have in other media are frequently lost when these data types are dropped into graphical user interfaces. Print and film are richly expressive media, and the subtleties that can lend sophistication and beauty to content do not automatically carry over to electronic media. It's important for designers to be aware that articulating a simple idea in digital graphic form can be more difficult than anticipated. Complicating that basic premise is the fact that users or viewers have varying ideas, expectations, value systems, and even computer monitors. Being explicit in the graphical interpretation of ideas is an important design consideration.

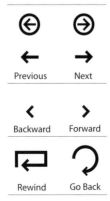

The top two pairs of symbols have been used to convey the concepts of previous and next; the middle pair is often used to convey the same concepts as well as backward and forward; and in the last pair, both symbols are used to convey the concepts of rewind and go back. Rewind and previous are two very different concepts, although their symbols here look similar. As simple as these concepts are, it's easy to be confused by their symbols. Designers need to be explicit in expressing ideas visually. When in doubt use words or audio to reinforce a concept. Mind-reading is not a feature – it's a bug.

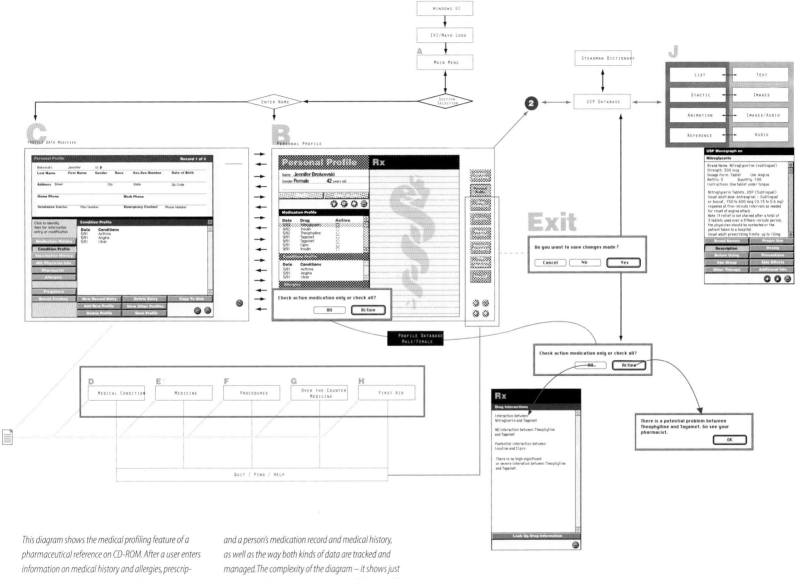

This diagram shows the medical profiling feature of a pharmaceutical reference on CD-ROM. After a user enters information on medical history and allergies, prescriptions, age, and sex, the program supplies prompts such as the titles of other references on disease or illness or alert messages about conflicts between medications. The designer dictated the behavior of the product by specifying every relationship between the program's database

and a person's medication record and medical history, as well as the way both kinds of data are tracked and managed. The complexity of the diagram — it shows just one feature of the title — is an expression of the value this particular company places on its product. It also illustrates the kind of programming that can be required to create feel.

Feel and Identity

The convergence of the look and the feel of a product on a computer screen affects company identity and the processes a company uses to implement identity. MTV and Nickelodeon took advantage of the way the broadcast medium facilitates animation when they created their look and feel. The success of their strategies shows in the way the look and feel of those channels sets them apart from the rest of the television market. Even with the sound off and without looking at channel numbers or logos, a television viewer clicking through the channels easily recognizes either station.

Banks are beginning to sell stamps through ATMs, and they may someday sell movie tickets. Such functions are unlike any other aspect of banking, and they raise questions for banks and designers. Would the average person be comfortable with the idea of buying movie tickets at an ATM? Maybe, maybe not.

Marketing departments and designers are familiar with the process of developing and keeping a consistent look. It's far more difficult to keep the feel of a product or service displayed in digital media under control because digital media require mediation between a consistent identity and the complex nature of the technology. At an ATM where movie tickets are sold, the ATM screen might display some kind of movie promotion. How consistent should

that promotion's behavior be in terms of the rest of the ATM interface? Which movies should be promoted, and what kind? X-rated ones, for instance? Up to now, decisions like this haven't been considered to be in the realm of identity design, but the computing medium changes that.

Getting more people visiting an ATM system to see an Arnold Schwarzenegger trailer isn't the idea; some marketing and advertising criteria might be fulfilled, but the communication program wouldn't be a success in terms of supporting the bank's identity. ATM design should be focused on providing a comfortable interface that directs people toward specific tasks. If the reason for a particular activity is not made explicit and there is no logical relationship between the interface and the core competencies of the business, a feature meant to create feel will not further business goals, and it might even damage a company's identity. When look and feel converge, that convergence affects the criteria for evaluating a design. It's companies that create effective identities by incorporating the capabilities of digital media into the process of identity design that harness the power of digital media.

Your bill payment request
is being processed.

Remember, any payments you
schedule on a non-business day
will be automatically
rescheduled for the next
business day.

Please wait for your
on record.

To schedule a payment, enter payee #
using the keypad below, then press OK.

#
Payee
Amount
Send date   Type

From which account would
you like to pay bills?

*Available balance

Cancel

Please remove your card.

nking at
RGO

Please remove your cash
and transaction record.

Enter the amount using the decimal point,
then press OK.

OK

Cancel

*Beginning of a
cash withdrawal
sequence.*

From which account?

Primary Checking

Primary Savings   Credit Card

Primary MRA / MMA   Line of Credit

Other Accounts

Investment

What would you like to do?

Withdraw Cash

Express Cash   Print a Statement/
                      Account Balance

Deposit   Bill Payment Service

Transfer/   Buy Stamps

                      Direct Deposit Advance™/
                      More Choices

Transaction choice screen.

Please enter your Secret Code,
then press OK.

OK

Cancel

Para
Español

Please insert your card.

Welcome to
WELLS FARGO
EXPRESS

*Touch-screen keypad.
When buttons are selected, they confirm
the customer's choice by appearing to depress.*

*To access accounts, the
customer clicks through
introductory screens, at which
point a transaction can
be chosen.*

Please remove your transaction record.

Would you like to do
another transaction?

Yes   No

Please take your stamps.

Using Science Fiction

to Propagate a Vision

Apple Computer produced a "vision video," the Apple Knowledge Navigator, to supplement a keynote speech that former CEO John Scully gave at the 1987 Educom Conference. The video's purpose was to explain Apple's multimedia strategy and show how people could use multimedia products in practical ways. The video showed a variety of scenarios, sketched out by a small team in the marketing department, that described ways people might use multimedia products at work and play and to communicate with each other.

In the video, what-if scenarios were acted out by a nerdy professor and his digital agent "Phil" in the year 2000. The dramatization showed Phil helping the professor prepare a lecture and work on a research project with fellow professor Jill Gilbert; Phil also reminded the professor to call his mother. Although the video was never meant to portray realistic possibilities but only to create an impression of Apple as a forward-looking company, it introduced into the public mind new concepts of what technology – and engineers – could do. Apple's expression of such a bold vision captured the

This famous television commercial announcing the introduction of the Macintosh used the Orwellian vision presented in the book 1984 in an anti–Big Brother message. The feel of the commercial distanced Apple from other computer manufacturers.

This screen from the Apple Knowledge Navigator vision video shows the professor directing "Phil" to do research on deforestation in the Amazon and global warming.

imagination of the entire computer industry; the video's obvious utility in creating the impression of a clear company goal led other companies to produce their own vision videos.

Using drama and science fiction to explain ideas may be a step outside normal business practice, but vision videos can inspire valuable ideas about where a company is going and what it wants to accomplish. Companies have been born around far-out concepts, and many of the scenes envisioned in vision videos a few years ago are now realities. In 1987, talking to computers and sketching on flat-panel devices were science fiction scenarios. It's not necessary to look too far back in technological history to find an imagined model that is now a product.

It's digital technology's wonderland of possibilities that makes an identity based on dramatization and science fiction believable. AT&T based its "You Will" campaign on that principle, positioning itself as a company with its pulse on the future, capable of bringing fabulous technologies to everyone, even if they didn't exist yet. The science fiction genre ranges from fantasy-possible to fantasy-maybe to fantasy-impossible. "Star Trek," tame by science fiction standards, continues to be a model for people learning to create user interfaces.

The idea for the Wildfire system – a smart digital telephone operator that keeps track of a user's work and social habits, sets priorities, and acts as a private secretary, returning calls and making appointments – came directly from "Star Trek." On the starship *Enterprise,* no one ever picks up a phone, but crew members can always talk to each other, whether they're in sick bay or on the transporter deck. Wildfire was built on the premise that current phone technology, which is based on a keypad model, represents the scientific limitations of the 1940s, whereas current technology makes it possible to mediate communication with voice. Digital technology brings imagination into the realm of reality.

This vision video for IVI Publishing shows how people can take responsibility for their own health care decisions when they have access to appropriate medical information. The video was created to show prospective investors the possibilities of a medical online service that IVI was planning. View the CD-ROM.

Information Design

in·for·ma·tion (ĭn′fər-mā′shən) n. **1.** Knowledge derived from study, experience, or instruction. **2.** Knowledge of a specific event or situation; intelligence. **3.** A collection of facts or data: statistical information. **4.** The act of informing or the condition of being informed; communication of knowledge for the information of our passengers. **5.** Comp. Sci. A non-accidental signal or character used as an input to a computer or communications system. **6.** A numerical measure of the uncertainty of an experimental outcome. **7.** Law. A formal accusation of a crime made by a public officer rather than by jury indictment. – in′for·ma′tion·al adj.

de·sign (dĭ-zīn′) v. **-signed, -sign·ing, -signs.** –tr. **1.a.** To conceive or fashion in the mind; invent. **b.** To formulate a plan for; devise. **2.** To plan out in systematic, usu. graphic form. **3.** To create or contrive for a particular purpose or effect. **4.** To have as a goal or purpose; intend. **5.** To create or execute in an artistic or highly skilled manner. –intr. **1.** To make or execute plans. **2.** To have a goal or purpose in mind. **3.** To create designs. –n. **1.a.** A drawing or sketch. **b.** A graphic representation, esp. a detailed plan for construction or manufacture. **2.** The purposeful or inventive arrangement of parts or details. **3.** The art or practice of designing or making designs. **4.** Something designed, esp. a decorative or an artistic work. **5.** An ornamental pattern. **6.** A basic scheme or pattern that affects and controls function or development. **7.** A plan; a project. See Syns at plan. **8.a.** A reasoned purpose; an intent. **b.** Deliberate intention. **9.** A secretive plot or scheme. Often used in the plural. [ME designen <Lat. designare, to designate. See DESIGNATE.]

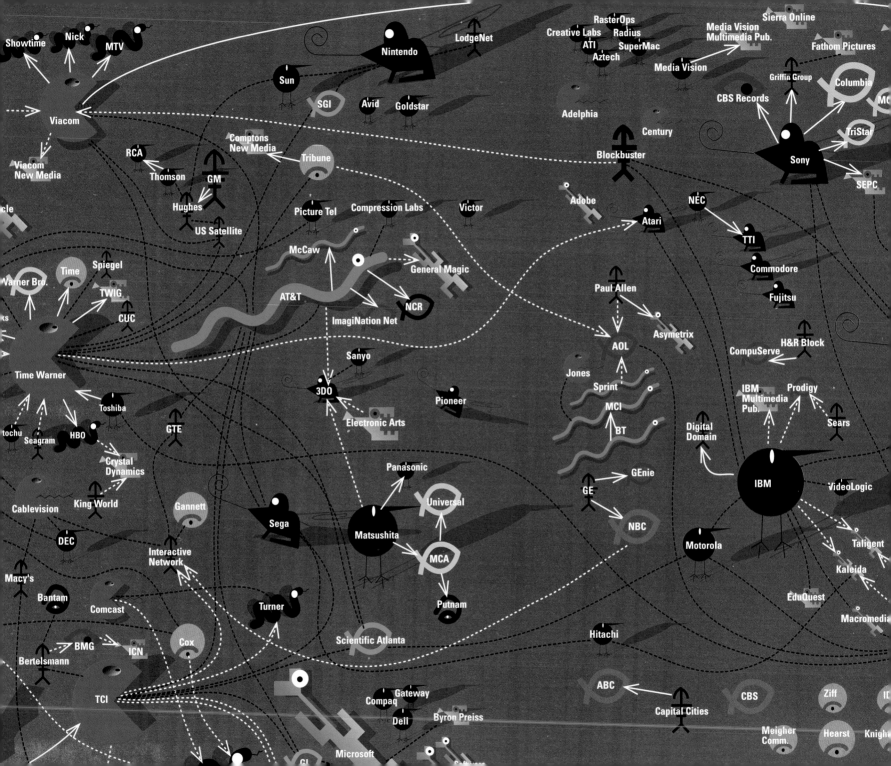

The economy is now based on a vast system of knowledge created by the merging of technologies, information, and media. In the past, knowledge systems were in the domain of information services managers and information scientists (otherwise known as librarians) whose professions weren't highly esteemed because of their focus on organizing data, rather than creating it. Now, small chunks of data appear in huge high-speed conglomerations, and they're often unedited and have no identifiable connection to original sources. It's little wonder the media explosion perplexes people.

Information architecture, the meaningful organization of information, is becoming an important discipline because it concentrates on deciphering data and giving it shape within the complex structures behind the computer screen. The Edward Tuftes and Richard Wurmans of ten or fifteen years ago were correct in their prediction that people would begin paying close attention to information science.

Today, information is a product. When information is in the right hands, it can be translated through design into powerful products and services – and successful businesses.

It looks like information, it feels like information, but is it information? This poster, designed for New Media *magazine, originally illustrated in an article covering the strategic alliances, joint-venture partnerships, and deal making in Silicon Valley. It was so popular that it became the focus of the magazine's marketing promotion.*

Visualizing Information Structures

Charles Altschul, an educator in new media studies, explains the nature of information by deconstructing the definition of the Pythagorean theorem: "The square of the length of the hypotenuse of a right triangle is equal to the sum of the square of the lengths of the other two sides." The entire statement is an accumulation of information pieces, each of which can be considered an information point. Each noun in the sentence, for instance, has a specific, learned meaning. In turn, each word is composed of a series of letters, each of which is also learned. Points of information grouped together form larger points. As we read the definition, we think about one idea at

Information graphics and information design have a rich history, beginning with pictures and diagrams of hunts on cave walls and including the notebooks of Leonardo da Vinci. Music annotation and computer programs are kinds of information design.

The formalization of information design as a practice is relatively recent, but in its current form information design seems to touch on almost everything because its arts are tied so closely to the pervasive disciplines of graphic design, interface design, media studies, and linguistics. Each of the information arts is a craft on which the practice of information design is built. Information architecture is

a time: first the square of a length, then the hypotenuse of a right triangle, and so on. This flow of information, from one point to the next, is a line of information. A point of information is immediately comprehensible; a line is only understood over time.

the integration of the structures underlying a system. The challenge for an information designer is to create an architecture that reveals a system of knowledge.

Every display of information has a framework that supports the structure of ideas, thoughts, and principles; a display of information could be an online shopping network or the portrayal of weather patterns on television. The framework behind intelligible information displays is often taken for granted because our early language training automatically supplied the myriad connections between ideas, thoughts, and principles.

People working together on a design or business project require a common language to describe ideas and processes. They need a mutual understanding of verbal and written signs as well as a common vocabulary for visual elements. We learn our visual vocabulary from familiar structures such as picture books, where sequences of images create narrative by carrying ideas from page to page. Comic books are a good example of a visual medium with a unique language; comics readers know that "POW!" means that one comics character is punching another in the jaw. We pick up thousands of undocumented visual cues from television and books. The visual arts are so varied, however, that their language is more difficult to analyze; yet some people have an innate gift for understanding the inexplicable.

Information Architecture

The assembly of the collective whole,
or the integration of technological applications.

- globe
- book
- software application
- musical
- exhibition
- template
- annual report
- transportation system
- Web site

Information Design

The organization of the products of information
arts, or the arrangement of information structures.

- map
- paragraph
- programming subroutine
- music score
- painting
- layout
- financial reports
- signage system
- Web page

Information Arts

The thoughtful arrangement of data.

- schematic
- sentence
- numeric model
- sound
- image
- sketch
- bar chart
- sign
- CGI script

Main Menu

Section 4

Section 3

Section 2

Section 1

A B C D E

Taylor Marries Again!
For the second time!

Dog Bites Man
on the Knee and Lives!

Financials

Consolidated net sales

Consolidated net income

This diagram shows how information is built up from data into a complete architectural system. Information design is based on comprehending information and the relationships among its parts. An information designer evaluates the behavior of different kinds of data and then organizes principles and thoughts on the basis of that evaluation. When structures are arranged to form a cohesive system, information architecture results.

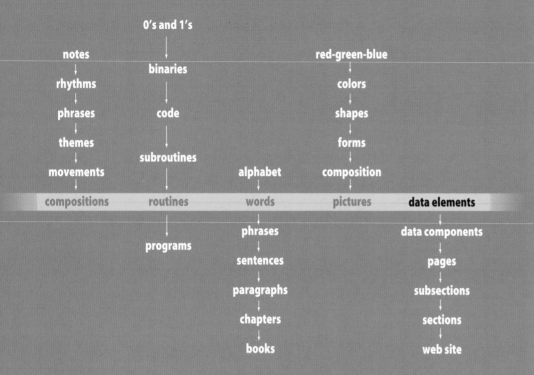

```
                          0's and 1's
                              │
        notes                 │                      red-green-blue
          │               binaries                        │
        rhythms               │                         colors
          │                 code                          │
        phrases               │                         shapes
          │                   │                           │
        themes                │                         forms
          │              subroutines                      │
       movements              │          alphabet      composition
          │                   │             │             │
      compositions         routines       words       pictures     data elements
                              │             │                           │
                              │          phrases                   data components
                           programs         │                           │
                                         sentences                     pages
                                            │                           │
                                         paragraphs                  subsections
                                            │                           │
                                          chapters                    sections
                                            │                           │
                                           books                      web site
```

The nature of information. These hierarchies show how various art forms might be built, beginning with the lowest common element. The first step in practicing information design is understanding the relationships among various elements: whether they are similar or different, whether they have comparable levels of complexity, or whether the relationships between them are one-way or two-way. The basic idea behind designing information structures in interactive computing is introduced here with the yellow strip that indicates the integration of information produced within different disciplines, and in varying degrees of complexity.

Unlike the study of written language, the study of the language of visualization is not an integral part of educational curricula. It is confined to art and drawing classes, most of which teach skills such as drawing and mixing paint. Curricula include little formal instruction that might further students' understanding of visual organizational principles or methodologies. Such principles are learned mostly through ad hoc channels.

A major aspect of design involves the search for behavior patterns, and then refining those patterns until they perform efficiently. People who follow the stock market use groupings of like data as a means of understanding: market trends are information patterns that can be plotted on x and y axes to represent increments and values. Just as patterns indicate the way a complex system is built in the physical world, they can also help construct frameworks in the computing medium. Looking only at patterns as a source for design direction, however, is not always the best approach; certain projects defy all the rules but still possess great systematic richness. Buildings that have survived from the gothic and romanesque periods acquired additions over centuries, merging into structural hybrids. They appear to us as wonderful singular objects, when in fact, they are a cluster of contradictory values and beliefs.

Abstract modeling principles are often used in working with raw data. Depending on the profession using them, these principles are called comparative analysis, cluster diagrams, or Cartesian coordinates. No matter the name, plotting *x* and *y* coordinates defines the ranges and constraints of the features a designer wants to apply; the *x*'s and *y*'s track and plot information paths. This formula is especially useful when working with the computing medium because of the unpredictability of digital data. The *x* and *y* axes can be assigned to any type of data or process; understanding *x* and *y* ranges enables information designers to create context.

In the physical world, when a third axis is introduced – the *z* axis – a project takes on spatial characteristics. In the computing medium, the *z* axis indicates complexity rather than space; the computing medium's "alsos" and "manys" are beginning to make the *z* axis a familiar design element. For example, a company selling Shaker furniture through a Web site is a model with *x* and *y* axes. If the company also began offering its products through interactive television, that added complexity would be the *z* axis.

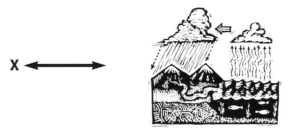

Morph

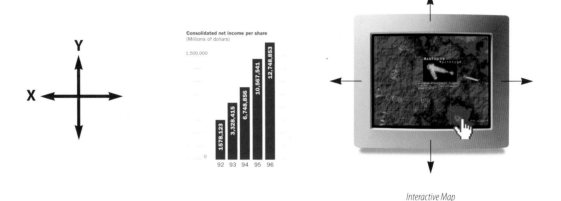

Interactive Map

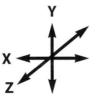

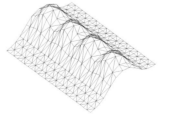

3-D Puzzle

This chart shows how the x, y, and z axes apply to graphic representations, and then to the computing medium.

Information Arts

Information arts are the thoughtful arrangement of data. A chapter title in a book, for instance, is a composition of word data. Information arts have many functions, but the function most relevant in the context of the computing medium is supplying navigation mechanisms. The print medium has pagination, divider pages, display heads, pull quotes, and captions – all are conventions that help the reader navigate through a book or magazine's content, and each is a highly evolved information art form. Our familiarity with the book form makes the comprehension of its information arts, and their use as navigational mechanisms, second nature; anyone who picks up a book knows where to find the bibliography, the index, and the table of contents.

The digital equivalent of such a vital art form does not exist. Because digital media have no tactile depth, we have a limited understanding of the size of a body of work or the amount of information on a CD-ROM or behind a screen – whereas in the print medium, we just have to leaf through a book or magazine to get that information. In this early stage in

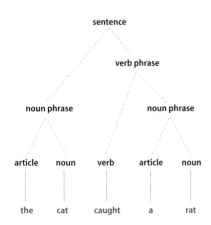

the development of information arts for the screen, we still lack a comprehensive vocabulary for expressing concepts, such as sequences. Some conventions – icons, directional arrows, and main menus – have already become established in the digital lexicon, but others – morphing navigation bars and virtual 3-D spaces – are too new to make the list.

One reason our digital wayfinding vocabulary is scant is that the so-called screen real estate available for displaying information and navigational cues is limited. In print, organization of and navigation through content are intrinsic to form and function. No one wonders whether the numerical data on a printed page are prices or page numbers; the data's location and context determine meaning. Digital media are some distance from attaining the clarity of the print medium, but one way to work toward resolving navigational problems and accommodating content in digital formats is to understand how information is organized.

Organization Models

Although named differently in linguistics, music, and the visual arts, the seven universal data organization models – linear, hierarchical, web, parallel, matrix, overlay, and spatial zoom – underlie the structure and presentation of ideas. They support five data types: text, audio, music, pictures, and moving pictures. These models can be used as diagnostic tools

Organization Models

Linear

Slide Show

Interactive Art Gallery

Hierarchical

Babushka Dolls

Biographical Family Tree

Web

Reference Source

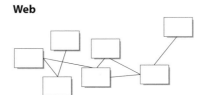

Interactive Game

Parallel

Television Guide

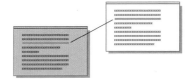

Closed-Caption Television

(diagram continued)

for examining the behavior of data types in the computing medium; they help decipher the function and form of data, determine whether structural models are transformable and transferable to other media, and indicate the context for the information after it is translated into a new data type. Rarely are the seven principles applied singly to any structure; integrated systems in both the physical and digital worlds generally are based on a combination of several models.

It is the purpose of any project that determines which information arts will be applied (in the form of data types or organization models). The specific purpose of a dictionary, for instance, determines its function and organization model; the linear model would be the wrong one to use to format a dictionary, but it would be the right one for a novel. For every purpose, there is an organization model that will facilitate its function.

A dictionary has a rule-based design system, which means that the parameters for arranging the data are fixed – altering the organization model results in a dysfunctional dictionary. Introducing a dictionary format into the computer medium requires that a bridge (in the form of computer code) be built between the engineer and the user. The software engineer creates the code for the dictionary application using database structures such as inverted indices, hash tables, and hardware access metrics; these structures have little relevance to the potential dictionary user – who only wants to look up a word – but are essential for the dictionary to function properly.

The computer code, which optimizes the performance of a system and the use and display of content, can't be seen by the user, but its effects are perceptible. An information designer bridges the gap between a user's cognitive model and an engineer's database structures by creating an interface that deploys familiar organization models, corralling data into groupings and perceptible hierarchies.

The unlimited possibilities resulting from combining organization models change data relationships, especially when these models are transferred into digital form. A designer must define and quantify the potential functions of organization models – choosing one or another set of features for a product or service. Through compromise, information designers create balance among portions of data – making the decisions that transform the data residing in organization models into meaningful work.

Bingo Card

Matrix

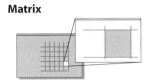

Interactive Thumbnail Index

X-ray

Overlay

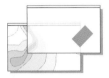

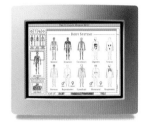

Interactive Anatomical Reference

Magnification

Spatial Zoom

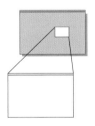

Virtual Art Gallery Tour

Information Design

Application	Linear	Hierarchical	Web	Parallel	Matrix	Overlay	Spatial Zoom
Print							
Dictionary	●	·	●	•	•	·	●
Encyclopedia	•	·	•	•	•	·	●
Phone Book	·	•	·	·	•	·	•
Almanac	•	·	•	•	•	·	•
Library	·	•	•	●	●	•	●
Thesaurus	·	·	•	●	•	·	•
Textbook	●	●	·	·	•	·	•
Brochure	●	●	•	•	•	·	•
Journal	•	●	•	•	•	•	•
This Book	•	•	•	•	•	·	•
Broadcasting							
Toll-free Number	●	●	·	·	·	·	•
Infomercial	●	•	•	•	·	·	•
Teleconference	●	•	•	•	·	·	•
Documentary	●	●	•	·	·	·	●
Interactive TV	●	●	●	●	•	•	●
Computing							
CD-ROM title	●	●	●	●	●	●	●
Internet	●	●	●	●	●	●	●
Intranet	●	●	●	●	●	●	●

This matrix shows how strong an influence each of the seven organization models has on the basic structure of familiar applications in different media. The larger the dot, the stronger the influence. The structures at the bottom are applications that the computing medium has made possible. The potential of the technologies those applications are based on has not yet been realized; although that makes it impossible to determine definitively how the organization models might influence those applications, it's likely that the influence of all the models on all such applications will be great.

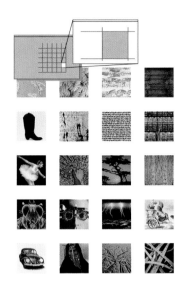

Left: A matrix built with pictures. Each of the seven organization models is flexible and can be manipulated to accommodate any data type. A matrix, for instance, can hold either thoughts or patterns, and can accept endless types of data, thereby giving rise to many different experiences. Matrices are familiar forms in print: they show one set of values along one axis and another set along the other, with hybrid instances in between. In the matrix here, the hybrid instances are displayed – the matrix structure is self-evident.

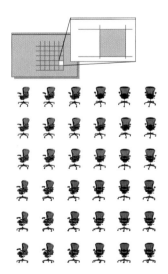

This interactive demonstration of Herman Miller's Aeron chair is an extravagant use of the matrix structure. Fifteen hundred photographs of the chair were taken from various angles. Each photograph was placed in one frame of an interactive QuickTime movie. (QuickTime technology allows for the storage of movie frames in a matrix as well as a linear sequence; see page 222.) On screen, the perspective from which the chair is viewed changes as the user moves the mouse pointer around the screen, giving the illusion of motion. What makes this application of the matrix model so unconventional is that the matrix can't be seen: the structure isn't revealed to the user.

Information Design

Information design begins where all other design disciplines do: with a specific purpose. Information design is the arrangement of organization models to provide context and meaning for the information. Once the purpose of a project is specified, whether it's to sell vintage jazz recordings over the Internet or provide stock market tips on CD-ROM, the design of the information – the way data types (text, pictures, moving pictures, audio, or music) are organized into structures (linear, hierarchical, web, parallel, matrix, overlay, or spatial zoom) – can begin.

Our perception of how data and content are built changes once these elements are transferred to the computing medium. An example of this is the seemingly simple function of mouse clicking on a computer. When a user clicks to get around the parts of a program, it has a different implied meaning than clicking to summon data. The difference is barely discernible, but critical to an understanding of the way the computer perceives information. If a user clicks to go to a screen, a place, or a page and the information at the starting and end points is similar in weight, this could indicate parallel construction within the program. However, if the weight of the information at the destination is different, another type of organization structure might be implied. If the user clicks and the information is brought forward, a nested thought within the broader context of the structure is implied. Even though both clicking options provide access to the content, the user gets distinct ideas about the arrangement of information from each. Information structures that employ the clicking function have to be carefully designed because of its implicit behavior.

The nature of a project's purpose also affects how much influence each organization model has on the content. A shopping community on the Web requires a different organization from a comparatively simple online catalog. The two-way communication at ATMs is structured in hierarchical sequences similar to those of push-button telephone services: the user makes one choice, then another, then a third.

The process of information mapping (see case study, pages 150-159) helps determine how to integrate organization models into the digital format. Information mapping begins with identifying the type and volume of information, and the information's intended use. The designer puts ideas and intended forms and functions down on paper and begins looking for similarities, disparities, and patterns among the various elements.

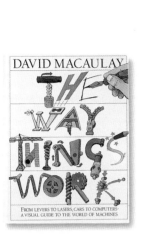

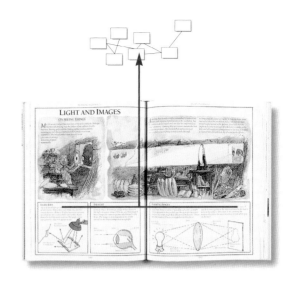

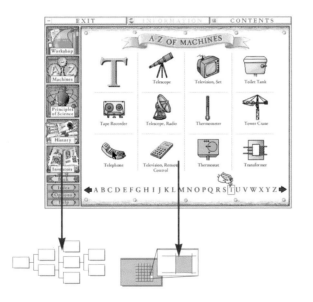

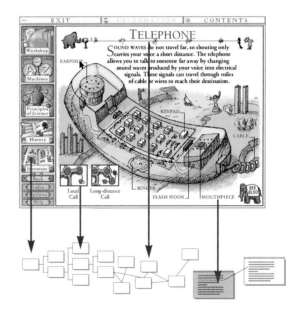

Top: The organization models that apply to the printed book version of David Macaulay's book The Way Things Work. Bottom: The organization models required to make the CD-ROM version of the the same text.

Designers creating Web sites face the problem of designing navigation through content at the same time that browser applications impose their own navigation controls, such as the forward and back functions. It is possible, though, to design a Web site that allows direct access to information without insisting that the user take an extra "go back" step every time he or she wants to reach a new level of information. This kind of problem can be solved with creative processes such as parallel navigation, which is an integrated system of navigation and content – it can reveal the structure of a site and the selected path through it so that a user never has to think about what "going back" means.

In working with multiple media, a designer's objective is to shape a harmonious whole. A designer's ability to create breakthrough crossovers, such as using parallel navigation to reflect the underlying computing structure *and* enhance the content – makes the difference between a good multiple media project and a great one.

Third and Fourth Dimensions

The seven organization models described previously are all two-dimensional. When information designers are working in the computing medium, however, they also have to reckon with the third and fourth dimensions of space and time. Every discipline has its own unique methodology for defining data's absolute and relative relationships to people, time, and space. Architects and filmmakers work with time and space as a matter of course, and designers working in the computing medium can learn a great deal from them.

TIME   Great design systems accommodate time very well. The monuments in Washington, D.C., for instance, appear beautiful during the day, and they are just as impressive at night. Online community chat rooms, which are accessible to virtually anyone,

The Netscape Navigator browser application uses a page model that has a forward and back mode, which doesn't accommodate complex structures of data. The design of this Web site is based on parallel navigation to clarify the hierarchical nature of the information organization.

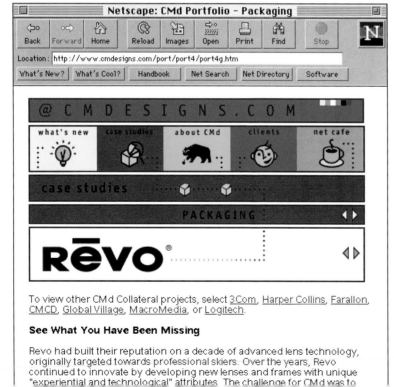

To view other CMd Collateral projects, select 3Com, Harper Collins, Farallon, CMCD, Global Village, MacroMedia, or Logitech.

See What You Have Been Missing

Revo had built their reputation on a decade of advanced lens technology, originally targeted towards professional skiers. Over the years, Revo continued to innovate by developing new lenses and frames with unique "experiential and technological" attributes. The challenge for CMd was to

| **Intent** | + | **Organization Model** | + | **Design** | = | **Solution** |

Farallon's packaging system was designed in 1989 to communicate the breadth of the company's product offerings and how they are related to one another. The construction of this system required the use of the matrix and web organization models.

+

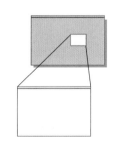

+

=

In 1992, after the distribution requirements for Farallon's products changed, a new packaging system was designed to accommodate the popularity of the product line and consumer demand for specialized products. The structure of this system was based on the spatial zoom organization model.

Information Design

anywhere, at any time, are the digital equivalent of adaptability to the time element.

Although time doesn't take on physical form, it has an expressive visual lexicon in the quantitative display of information. Clocks and calendars are constructed consistently, and their meanings don't change no matter what the context. In the computing medium, it's difficult to provide context for real time. The telephone system's ubiquitous and flexible infrastructure accommodates the quirky aspects of human communication, letting people talk any time, wherever they are. Computer networks use the telephone infrastructure to transport data; telephone systems, however, cannot distinguish data from voice signals so computer systems have no way of detecting what kind of data is being moved around.

SPACE   Designers have interpreted and transformed many different concepts of space into screen environments, but two of them are especially relevant in the context of information design. One definition of space is a container in which people design communication and house information; an example is an electronic document. This kind of space has constraints: how big is the container? how much can it hold? The other definition of space incorporates a metaphorical understanding of environmental surroundings and the rules of human behavior in those surroundings. The electronic document is contained, and has definite parameters; the office building is also contained, but its parameters – shape, size, divisions, sequences – are determined by what people do in office buildings. Office buildings aren't designed to accommodate ballroom dancing because people don't go to office buildings to dance.

These two very different spatial modes can cohabit, for example, in an art exhibition: people move around in the bigger space (a museum) to look

This chart shows the contexts in which communication can take place. Communication can occur in either of two modes. Synchronous communication – conversation in person or by telephone – takes place in real time. Asynchronous communication is delayed in time and disconnected in space; letters, voice mail and e-mail messages, and online chats are all communications in asynchronous mode.

Place	Real Time	Delayed Time
Same	Conversation	Yellow Sticky
Different	Telephone Teleconference Fax	Voice Mail E-Mail
Any	Cellular Phone PDA Internet	Wildfire® System 1-700-Number

placed in a store – deciding whether to play elevator music or classical music in a restaurant, or whether a cappuccino bar would be a success in the lobby of a medical building. Such experiential decisions are common retail practices, and they are just as relevant in the computing medium, where retail needs aren't different but have to be translated from material space to computing space.

at what's contained in smaller spaces (the paintings). Most spatial systems, however, function independently. In the computing world, on the other hand, just as media and disciplines are converging, so are the two spatial modes. The computing medium can be used to design a virtual place where users can explore, create, work, and play outside the constraints of physical space; that place is both an information container and a destination.

Computers can also be a place where users browse through merchandise and make transactions. Successful retailers and merchandisers in both the physical world and cyberspace know where and how to place products, what kinds of products sell, and the proper amount of information to supply about each. In the physical world, retailers who don't quite comprehend information design rely on their instincts and knowledge about merchandising and display to orchestrate where certain products are

Navigating Through Information

People, time, and space – how do they all come together? Information designers need to know how people move through spaces and what they do in those particular spaces. One of the most important issues in information design is determining how to

navigate through a designed space. When information designers identify the particulars of time, space, and place, they can create familiar structures and syntax that help define the paths which people, or – in the case of computing – information will move along to get from point A to point B. Navigation is a system in itself, and there are many ways to design navigation in cyberspace so that people can visit places, buy things, or play or work with each other. If people are engaged in those activities in the computing medium, how does the information designer build an underlying navigation system? One way is to use the architectural model of signage.

A subway station is a good analogy for what users are trying to contend with in the computing medium. People using a subway system generally have a limited understanding of how large the system is, but signage cues tell them whether they can reach a destination by moving "up" (ahead) or "down" (back) or left or right. Signage systems incorporate a vocabulary that helps people go where they want to go. That doesn't mean that designers should apply subway signage metaphors to everything they design for the computing medium – there are many other efficient navigation systems. Tables of contents and color coding are navigation systems we use all the time quite successfully. Subway signage is just an especially pertinent example of a navigation system with established conventions. The computing medium has few accepted conventions, so designers must practice information design as a way to begin building a core vocabulary for use in cyberspace.

This experimental, interactive information environment was created at Murial Cooper's Visual Language Workshop at MIT. Designed by Lisa Strausfeld, this information system uses three dimensions to volumetrically represent a sample portfolio of seven separate mutual funds. Graphical and spatial design techniques (transparency and dynamic objects) focus the user's attention on particular subject areas. We can grasp information in this kind of space in the same way we decipher it in the physical world: by compiling many simple elements and actions. Navigation through this experimental information space makes use of the three-dimensional structure to provide the multiple contexts the depth of the information requires.

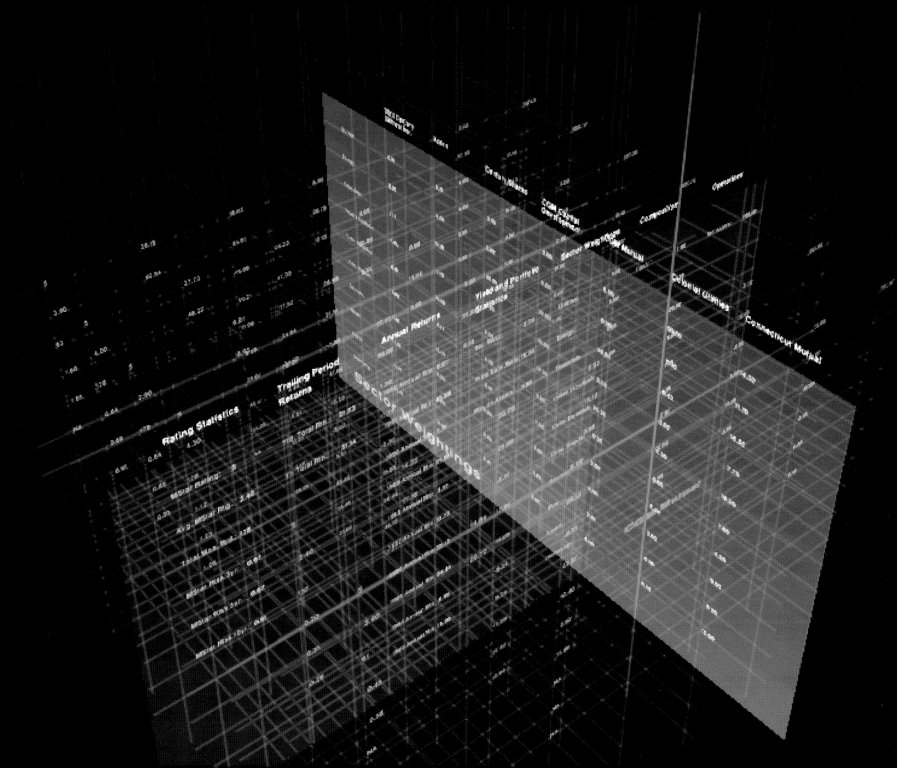

Thank You, Mr. Beck

Mapping is a set of conventions that explains geographical concepts and the idea of place; it is a visual construction with the capacity to embrace the complexity of language itself. The London Underground map embodies a visual language that we can apply to the understanding of the way digital systems operate. A map is quite visceral – if people don't understand it, they get lost. The London Underground map is considered a diagram because it does not actualize the surrounding geography; however, it easily accommodates the diversity and complexity of the railway system. A look at the evolution of the London Underground diagram reveals many similarities to the evolution of the computing medium in terms of the creation and definition of language.

The London Transit Authority's first maps showed the actual railway routes in and around London. These first maps appeared to make sense because of the contextual relationship between the railway system and the actual area it covers –

it seemed that riders using this kind of map would know exactly where they were. People nevertheless got lost in the subway, and as the system grew, riders became more and more confused.

The diagram proposed in 1932 by Henry Beck, a 29-year-old engineering draftsman, contained only what was essential for riders to understand in order to get around inside the system. He abstracted routes and edited out what was not necessarily helpful to the riders' perception of where they were in the system, emphasizing the Underground's connections rather than its surrounding geography. In the end, the only contextual element Beck used was the River Thames. The rest of his diagram, made up of a network of vertical, horizontal, and diagonal lines, was purely functional: he compressed the outlying portions of the routes, which made room for the enlargement of the central district, with its complexity of interchanges and stations. To abstract the map into a diagram, Beck himself had to have a very good working knowledge of the railway system and its environs. Underground riders quickly adapted to the diagram.

People get lost in cyberspace too, and just as the art of mapping helps railway riders find their way, so too can it illustrate links within structures and crossovers between media and data types. Mapping is a prerequisite for smooth navigation through cyberspace. Once someone on a project team gets all the thoughts and ideas about the project down on paper, the designer can use that material to map out the project's requirements. Once those requirements are mapped out the team can begin the scripting, programming, and graphic design. It may help an information designer mapping out a project to imagine designing Grand Central Station: where should the portals be? the different gates? where should they lead? In other words, how accessible should the elements of a project be? Mapping is the process of creating a framework, just as diagramming a sentence helps define the nature and scope of language. In the context of business initiatives, mapping is a terrific exercise for understanding the exact nature of a problem. Mapping can clarify many problems that seem nebulous at first glance.

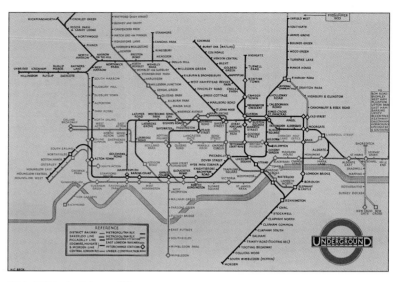

Original 1932 London Underground Diagram

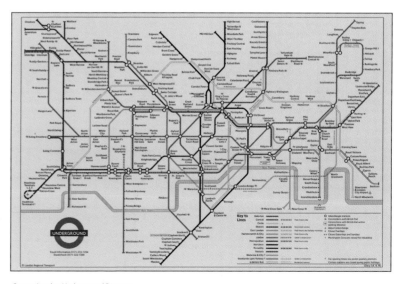

Current London Underground Diagram

If Mr. Beck Had a Computer

What Mr. Beck did was visualize the kind of information riders needed to get from Victoria Station to Regent Park. His diagram for the Underground was the solution to a problem; it was also the end product of his work. In the computing medium, a solution is generally not something as absolute as a hand-held diagram; instead, it's a process. Mr. Beck was working with physical realities the computing medium doesn't offer. Designers used to design nouns; now they design verbs.

How can an information designer go about mapping complex systems and concepts to create a usable system? One way to determine the design parameters of complex information spaces and solve the design problems they present, is to understand what a user, viewer, or customer needs or wants to accomplish. The structures that underlie language are excellent diagnostic tools for those needs and wants. Language is a formal, universal framework that is common enough to encompass most structural problems, but most importantly, it is people-centric. Designers can use basic conversational language to build diagnostic tools, and language is an ideal structure for an information framework.

In one example, a design firm was asked to create an electronic reference resource library for a large medical institution. It took many months of research and development to examine all the aspects of the content and determine the system's optimum functionality. At this juncture, the challenge was to determine what kind of disciplines would be required to take the project forward. Is it the software engineering or the various medical specialities. Who should be doing what?

The designers used sentence diagramming to solve the problem. The simple sentence "Show me what I need to know about the heart," represented all the functionality the system required. The designers dissected each word and its meaning in the sentence to uncover its alternate computer function. "Show," for instance, meant present and display. "What I need to know" translated as information the computer had to identify and match. Once the project's basic functions were understood, the sentence diagram model was translated into the computer model, matching functions, knowledge levels, age, learning levels, etc. Language helps diagnose and identify the nature of a problem, and match needs with appropriate solutions.

Bubble diagrams are another way for designers to create frameworks for efficient processes. Architects use bubble diagrams to organize people's movements through particular spaces in a specified order; as in determining how to accommodate the activities of people in a cafe and a bookstore, for instance. Designers need such visualization techniques to define navigation and interactivity.

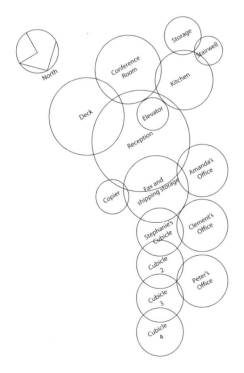

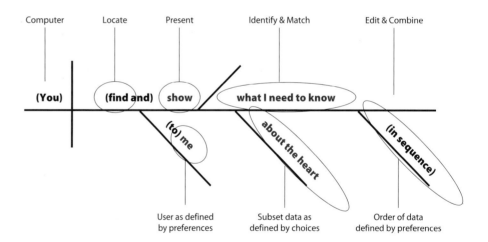

Show me what I need to know about the heart.

Information Architecture

The architectural model is apropos to the computing medium because architecture is concerned with the relationships among people, time, and space – architects design and create systems to move people in time and space. The kinds of materials architects use to define space are cinder blocks, wooden beams, and copper pipes. In the computing medium, designers create systems by plotting structural and data type information as x and y axes; when different media are factored in, the z axis is introduced; and so is the equivalent of three dimensionality in cyberspace – complexity.

Consequently, spatial models are important to designers building models that represent relationships in the digital environment. Working with spatial models may be a stretch for many designers, since in general, designers have limited experience working with the spatial dimension.

The architecture of an operating system is the organization of data instructions and computer code that indicate the way information should be passed along. Few designers have taken information structures to the level of spatial depth (see page 115). Most information in cyberspace is still two-dimensional; depth of information in cyberspace is detailed information.

Designers have much to learn from architects. Just as an architect wouldn't go forward with a blueprint for a convention multiplex if the proposed site were on swampland, a designer shouldn't begin planning huge information systems before understanding the system's technological underpinnings. This doesn't mean that designers have to be computer engineers any more than architects have to be geologists, but they do need to know what the relevant technology does and who will be using it. A current, renowned example of construction on digital swampland is the Orlando project, which was supposed to bring interactive TV to homes – the alliance partners for this venture went ahead with the technology without reconciling the social wants and needs. Projects that are well designed only *look* simple because designers and others have spent countless hours making them look that way.

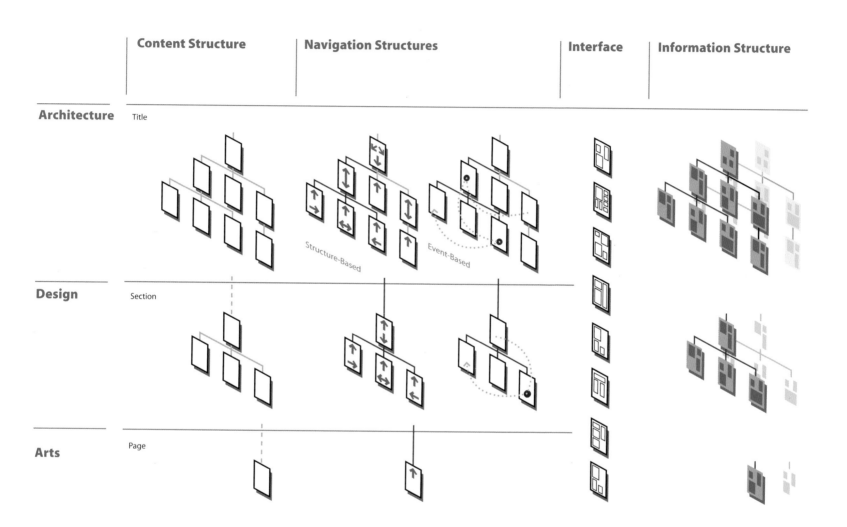

	Content Structure	Navigation Structures		Interface	Information Structure
Architecture	Title	Structure-Based	Event-Based		
Design	Section				
Arts	Page				

This graphic schema represents how content,
navigation, and interface design combine into
an integrated information structure. This
deconstructed view shows the progression from
the simplest art to a complete architecture.

Data to Concept

Creating the database and operating system architecture for a multifunctional corporate Web site, for example, require that everything seen and used in the computing environment relate to the systems within. The diagram is not just information architecture, but an integrated view of the elements required to create that architecture. The gold represents right-brain professions and the blue, left-brain; that is, artistic and scientific. The lower levels of the diagram require the skills of scientists and computer programmers, while the top layers demand serious abstract design talent; right now, the most sought-after professionals are those who have the ability to mediate between the two worlds. *View the CD-ROM.*

INFORMATION ARCHITECTURE

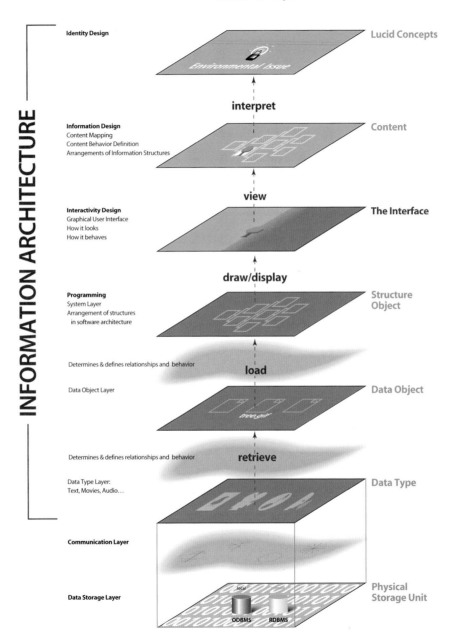

Identity Design — Lucid Concepts

interpret

Information Design
Content Mapping
Content Behavior Definition
Arrangements of Information Structures — Content

view

Interactivity Design
Graphical User Interface
How it looks
How it behaves — **The Interface**

draw/display

Programming
System Layer
Arrangement of structures
 in software architecture — Structure Object

Determines & defines relationships and behavior — *load*

Data Object Layer — Data Object

Determines & defines relationships and behavior — *retrieve*

Data Type Layer:
Text, Movies, Audio… — Data Type

Communication Layer

Data Storage Layer — Physical Storage Unit

ODBMS RDBMS

Daisy chain

Star

Ring

Bus

Hierarchy

These configurations (see communication layer, left) represent the way information is passed along through networks. See William Mitchell and Malcolm McCullough's in-depth study in Digital Design Media.

Information Design

Interactivity Design

in·ter·ac·tive (ĭn′tər-ăk′tĭv) adj.
1. Acting or capable of acting on each other. **2.** Comp. Sci. Of or relating to a two-way electronic or communications system in which response is direct and continual. **3.** Of, relating to, or being a form of television entertainment in which the viewer participates directly. –in·ter·ac′tive·ly adv.

de·sign (dĭ-zīn′) v. **-signed, -sign·ing,- signs.** –tr. **1.a.** To conceive or fashion in the mind; invent. **b.** To formulate a plan for; devise. **2.** To plan out in systematic, usu. graphic form. **3.** To create or contrive for a particular purpose or effect. **4.** To have as a goal or purpose; intend. **5.** To create or execute in an artistic or highly skilled manner. –intr. **1.** To make or exe- cute plans. **2.** To have a goal or purpose in mind. **3.** To create designs. –n. **1.a.** A drawing or sketch. **b.** A graphic represen- tation, esp. a detailed plan for construc- tion or manufacture. **2.** The purposeful or inventive arrangement of parts or details. **3.** The art or practice of designing or making designs. **4.** Something designed, esp. a decorative or an artistic work. **5.** An ornamental pattern. **6.** A basic scheme or pattern that affects and controls function or development. **7.** A plan; a project. See Syns at plan. **8.a.** A reasoned purpose; an intent. **b.** Deliberate intention. **9.** A secretive plot or scheme. Often used in the plural. [ME designen <Lat. designare, to designate. See DESIGNATE.]

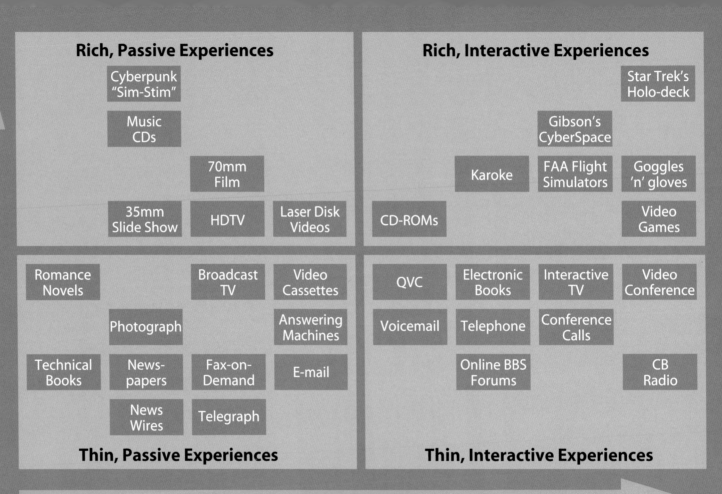

This diagram, from a 1991 Harvard Business School Report, shows what is on the market in the way of interactive products. It's a way to evaluate each product's "interactiveness." Hybrid media are popping up everywhere, making it possible to design new kinds of interactivity with increased richness and directed orientation.

The word "interactivity" has become a computing world buzz word, but it has a meaning that illuminates an ultimate goal: to create a totally immersive experience. It takes several disciplines, each difficult to manipulate, to compose a successful interactive experience, and everyone who uses digital media to communicate is searching for guidelines and ways to achieve it.

Like information design, interactivity design is not new, only a new focal point in media studies – but the recent popularity of multimedia has fostered many attempts to formalize it as a discipline. Interactivity design borrows many concepts and models from the study of ergonomics, semiotics, artificial intelligence, cognitive science, and theater. The computing medium is quickly absorbing the principles behind those disciplines and art forms, which is making it possible for visual, sensory experiences to materialize on screen. The interactivity arts can transform those experiences into meaningful, humane communication.

Interactivity Arts,

Interactivity Design,

Interface Design

Unlike identity and information design, which are manifested in specific physical forms, interactivity design results in the display of actions. Interactivity design itself, however, is not an activity, though the slight differences between interactivity design and interface design might make it seem so. As different as look and feel, or appearance and behavior, these two "inter"disciplines are often viewed as one, but judging each one requires distinctive criteria.

Just as the application of information arts collectively forms an information design, it is the collective application of interactivity arts that results in interactivity design. In the digital domain, each interactivity art results in a directed action that generates cognitive responses or captures a process that reveals an action. The most basic function of an interactivity art is providing a cue for a specific action. Interactivity arts emerge through an interface as bells, a blinking cursor, or a pointer that changes shape as it moves around the screen. When these arts are strung together as a series of actions, the result is the process of interactivity design.

Theater and filmmaking are analogous to interactivity design. Where the application of book arts – papermaking, bookbinding, writing, editing, illustration, and typesetting – results in something people can see and hold in their hands, what an actor does – the application of theater arts – results in an *impression,* not something that can be seen and felt like a book. Interactivity design deploys many of the same skills and tricks actors practice.

The way interactivity arts are implemented depends on the media they are being applied to. Imagine the actions involved in browsing on television, and compare them to the actions employed while browsing through a book: one involves pressing a button and invoking a linear sequence of images; the other is the physical activity of opening a book and turning its pages, which sometimes results in a non-linear sequence of text and pictures.

So far, in the early stages of the computing medium, many of the attempts at providing a way for the highly adaptive human system and a machine to conduct cogent discourse have been primitive and feeble. Successfully designing any kind of inter-activity in the computing medium requires balancing technological feasibility with the integrity of the content. If a Web site is to be designed so that users can browse, make transactions, and play games, each of these actions must be coordinated and then integrated into a system; interactivity design comes into play when the paths of these actions intersect. The quality of an interactive experience is determined by how well the designer crafts the transitions at the intersections. A good interactive piece has invisible construction and an effective graphical user interface; it maintains integrity in the experience it generates by providing and reinforcing context. A designer must integrate interactivity design within a content structure; without content, interactivity design is just a parade of winking, blinking shapes.

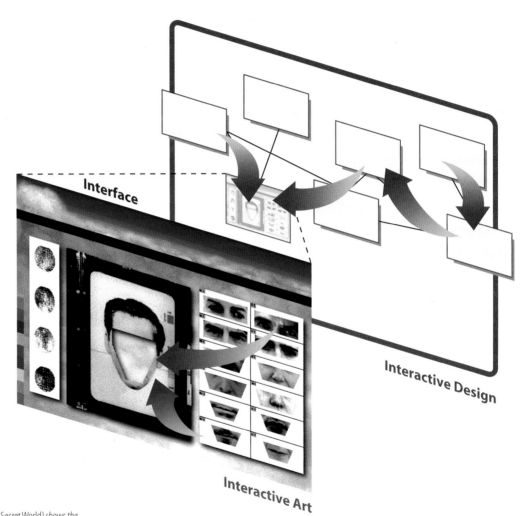

This diagram (the screen is from the CD-ROM Peter Gabriel's Secret World) shows the components of interactivity design. The arrows on the interface indicate actions that a designer has created, that is, interactivity arts. The other arrows indicate actions that give a user access to different parts of the CD. The sum of all the arrows or actions is the product's interactivity design; the interface mediates and facilitates the actions.

A graphical user interface, or GUI, is where interactivity and interface design intersect. An interface is only a visual manifestation of "inter"activities – only an aspect of interactivity design, not the interactivity design itself.

Moving Targets

Early user interfaces – those created before graphical interfaces were developed – required that a user work on the computer's terms. For instance, a single specific action, such as FIND, required a complex series of commands – *find/relativity*print* – the user had to instruct the computer where to begin the search, what it needed to look for, determine the criteria, and then tell the computer to display the

information. In short, every action and subroutine the computer was to perform had to be specified. Nowadays, the FIND command not only delivers the result after character input and a simple mouse click, but it delivers it in multiple quantifiable and qualifiable data formats. Further complexity has been introduced to other single actions, such as COPY – when a user activates the COPY function, a dialogue box appears with an animated graphic showing the status of the copying procedure.

Enabling technologies, such as C++ programming languages and operating system software, incorporate a series of commands and subroutines that allow one command to invoke many actions. The sophistication of those technologies requires

This IBM personal computer had a text-based screen. It limited interactivity to text prompts – yes, no, up, down, and cursor blinking, simple interactivity arts.

Icons and graphics were introduced with the Xerox PARC screen, the grandfather of the Mac. It had two types of one-way input devices: the keyboard and the mouse. At the same time, the system had graphical elements that provided the blinking of text, highlighting of icons, and features such as zooming. The metaphor for the desktop was first used here, and along with the coinage of the term "graphical user interface."

The Macintosh's quirky icons gave it a distinct voice, and its interface was the first to be endowed with an identity with personality. It was at this point that identity design became intertwined with interactivity.

a high level of interactivity, which isn't feasible without graphical user interfaces. Graphical user interface designers are people who know how to string together a complete set of interactivity and information arts and synthesize them within a context. How well a designer orchestrates a series of interactivity arts and an interface design is what determines the richness of the user's experience.

In personal digital assistants, such as the Newton or the Envoy, the placement of icons and the way they move and blink provide functionality and feedback on what is happening inside the digital assistant. The synthesis of the icon appearing, blinking, and disappearing creates context and meaning.

Interactivity arts and interactivity design are frequently lumped together under the label of GUI design, which seems to have an ever-expanding definition. When a business comes to a design studio requesting a GUI, it can mean many things: does the business want an application, a title, or a tool? will the medium be a hybrid? what level of user interface does the business desire? is it a cosmetic overhaul or a structural overhaul? does the business need a complete system from end to end. A graphical user interface can be as simple as a blinking icon or as complex as a department store on the Internet. Because of the broad implications the term GUI has assumed, even something as intricate as Microsoft's online network is called a GUI system.

The identity of the Windows operating system displays its personality through its business-like conventions and graphics.

MagicLink and other personal digital assistants extrapolate on the metaphor of a desktop by incorporating multiple metaphors into their interfaces: around the desktop are a rolodex (which the user can click on to call up an address), a filing cabinet, and so on.

The room or spatial metaphor is the operating model that Microsoft's Bob interface is based on. Bob lets users choose from different "rooms" as their "desktop;" each room has a distinct feel.

The online service e-world uses a town square model, taking the room spatial model one step further.

What makes things interactive? CD-ROM titles, Web sites, online transactions – even television and games – are classified as interactive. Many titles are called interactive simply because they're on a CD-ROM; perhaps it's because users click on a button instead of turning a page.

The four C's – Control, Consistency, Context, and Corroboration – can be used to evaluate whether a project is interactive at all and, if so, whether its interactivity design is successful. First, users should have some level of Control over an experience – where they are going, how they get there, and how easily they can stop and start. Second, the look and feel of behavioral elements – what's on the screen, and audio or music as well – should be Consistent. Third, the interactivity should have a Context. Is it related to the information around it? Fourth, the interactivity should reflect the nature of the content – that is, it should Corroborate the content. If there's video on a Web site or a CD-ROM, is the video conducive to understanding

Within any industry, people have a common way of defining a GUI depending on where they are on the technical curve. In the computing and software industries, the term is rather specific and means windows, icons, and menus; publishers and broadcasters interpret it as a complete set of attributes, such as the look and the behavior of buttons and the entire presentation of a product, including audio, video, and other media. A GUI is not always a moving target, but what different industries expect from a GUI is.

GUI Metaphors

The definition of a GUI has expanded considerably. At one point GUIs were menus and icons on the computer – purely functional. Then along came applications like Myst, Bob, e-world, and the Imagination Network, and GUIs broke away from the desktop and into the more complex organizational structures of rooms and towns.

Currently, CD-ROM and World Wide Web interfaces are littered with GUIs based on the document-

the content? Or should that material be in the form of text?

The best projects have all four C attributes, but the minimum requirement for successful interactivity is Control along with one other attribute. The success of a project's interactivity diminishes as the number of C attributes decreases.

and-desktop metaphor, with left- and right-hand pages, tables of contents, title pages, and other elements in an attempt to mimic printed material. In GUI design, there are as many models to work from as there are real-life situations. If a project is driven by the metaphor model, is that the GUI? Or is the model just a metaphor applied to the GUI? Mall and town square models, for instance, behave very differently from each other, and their behaviors are structured using a variety of media to reveal the characteristics of those environments.

If the overall metaphor model for a GUI is a town square, or a mall, the corridors and buildings in those places have to be endowed with specific features. Working from semiotic and cognitive models in the real world to create GUIs is no different from the way design is practiced by theme park designers or architects; designers in the physical world, however, have a more extensive view than that provided by the microscopic world of the desktop. Understanding human needs and impulses is the key to creating usable GUIs.

The city is another metaphor model challenging the overall concept of GUI design: its look and feel, integrated with functionality, encompass ideas that are more far-reaching than mere malls. Creating an interface for such an intricate model is a colossal task because a city is a fusion of several smaller systems – each with inherent content structures and navigation requirements. Although information design is necessary for the simplest interface, projects such as the development of a city GUI have to be *based on* information design. Interactivity design and information design are now married together like a drive-through Las Vegas chapel (no metaphor intended).

GUI Rules and Renegades

Strange and quirky rules have been imposed on GUIs even as the definition of GUI is shifting and changing. GUI principles (see pages 134-139) remain the same, but the conventions and standards their usage is based on are about as solid as quicksand.

Some manufacturers and software engineers attempt to dictate how GUIs should look and behave, imposing standards such as representing "function" with icons that look like "buttons" – rectangles with beveled edges and drop shadows. Despite their efforts, though, many interesting innovations are finding their way into GUIs, mostly introduced by non-technical people who are able to look at the underpinnings of an interactive project and take it where it seems to want to go. A mouse pointer, for instance, originally was used to point to and select items; its function is a single action, no more, no less. In some products, the pointer acts as a sensor, so that the proximity of the pointer to a defined area of the screen evokes a predetermined series of actions – displaying a picture, playing an audio file, or a combination of the two. The pointer can also

serve as a counter and a tracker, remembering where the user has been and logging those actions.

Some people believe that pointers should evoke cause and effect. Now, instead of making the pointer display a graphic, many applications allow the pointer to change shapes and purpose, as when it indicates that a program is loading so that a user knows to be patient. Many people are not abiding by established GUI conventions and are using the pointer for purposes far from its original one; sometimes they make the pointer perform, but more and more it's used to reveal.

At some point in the not-so-distant future, the pointer will develop more of the characteristics of a personal servant, not only traveling from program to program but guiding, answering, querying, and performing other kinds of personal services in the realm of artificial intelligence. Like everything else associated with the computing medium, GUIs are changing and merging, in this case with structure and content. The task of designers and businesses alike is to build a design framework that can adapt to every new breakthrough in GUI behavior.

GUI Terminology

The terms "platform" and "standard" have taken on meanings that are quite different from their original definitions. In the early 1980s, platform implied hardware; later it referred to operating systems; then its meaning shifted again from hardware to software

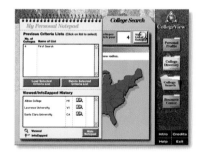

This combination interactive reference tool and title was produced to help high-school students find colleges that meet their specific criteria. College View has appropriated many metaphors, including notebooks, folders, and maps. To make the experience of looking for the right college more enjoyable, the designers created digital tipster-agents which climb around the notebooks pointing out and highlighting the application's features.

operating systems, and now platforms are frequently referred to as applications. Microsoft, Lotus, Adobe, and Netscape have raised the bar, making their software the lowest common denominator – the platform. Microsoft Word and Netscape Navigator are referred to as platforms. The term platform has been migrating toward the user level, and applications are now considered platforms, some of which have become standards. Netscape Navigator, an application, has become a platform and a standard.

These standards have implications for the GUI. Operating systems and the GUI embody the voice and character of an entity, and evoke the image-making aspects long recognized in print as valuable. This is an important concept because computing and interactivity can shape a customer's perception of what a company is and what kinds of products and services it provides. The sophistication possible in the computing medium can marry brand issues with a company's voice, making the GUI a vehicle for defining and positioning a brand, as well as for establishing company value. The Lifetime cable channel has positioned itself as a women's channel by virtue of its programming content. Its GUI – in this case, animated computer graphics and a female voice-over – has the persona of a caring sister, serving as a guide and advisor. That focus has

generated a brand element and identity, and the strength of Lifetime television's voice is likely to carry its viewers into interactive television and onto the Internet.

Companies that are not media-centric can also extend brands by establishing themselves on the Internet. If Clinique, which sells cosmetics, takes its products online, it would become a guidepost for a large number of customers previously unfamiliar with the Internet. In turn, Clinique's presence online would generate a progressive image which would gain it an entirely new audience. The computing medium would also provide a vehicle for Clinique to communicate with its customers. Interactivity and GUI design combine many of the techniques a company uses to manipulate and orchestrate its image, as well as its behavior.

GUI Principles

There are many ways to create interaction. In this book, the interactivity arts are applied in the broader scope of the identity and information disciplines. Interactivity design uses the skill sets of identity and information design, contextualizing and utilizing those skills to do the work. These kinds of actions are cumulative – similar to combining nouns and verbs.

The interaction and interface in any project must possess certain attributes. Ten different functions measure the usability and success of an interactive experience.

PREDICTABILITY   *In every interactive experience, three mental pictures come into play: the designer's model, or what the designer has in mind when creating the system; the user's model, or what the user expects from the system; and the system's image, or the actual appearance of the system itself. A project design should be tested to determine where the three pictures overlap the most; those areas of overlap result in natural mappings between required actions and their effects, and between visible information and the user's interpretation of the system. By following those natural mappings, a designer can create an intuitive system.*

In Star Trek IV: The Voyage Home, *the Star Trek crew travels back to the year 1986. Scotty expects to be able to talk to the computer. He instead encounters a Macintosh...*

Scotty:
Computer!
Computer!
Computer?
Hello, computer!

Man in Tie:
Just use the keyboard.

Scotty:
Keyboard? Oh, great.

CONSISTENCY   *It's more important for a system to interpret user behavior consistently than to appear consistent; in other words, it's more important for interactive products to respond to a user's actions in predictable ways than it is for the elements on a screen to have a uniform appearance.*

PROGRESSION *Everything in an interactive system should progress from simplicity to complexity. A user should never be confronted with more complexity than necessary; unasked-for complexity diminishes a user's interest and involvement. The default should always be the simplest level of information, with details accessible only at the direction of the user. A user should be able to set the beginning level of information, too, avoiding the repeat of the same actions every time he or she logs onto the system.*

Data:
The input levels are currently at 53 percent of tolerance.

Geordie:
That's too low Data. I won't be able to do anything down there.

Doctor:
I want to start with as wide a margin of safety as possible; we can adjust upward later. Ready?

Geordie:
Go ahead.

When Geordie uses a virtual reality suit to conduct a remote operation, Dr. Crusher adjusts the input levels of the environmental data so Geordie is able to process at maximum efficiency without being exposed to harmful information levels.

NATURAL CONSTRAINTS *A user should be prevented from making many mistakes – that is, a system should be designed to anticipate error and correct the interface, just as the nozzles of gas hoses are designed so that cars that run only on unleaded gas can't accidentally be filled with leaded gas.*

VISIBILITY *The correct elements must be visible, and their function must be apparent. Making an element visible doesn't mean showing every possible control all the time, but the functions applying to what's on the screen at any given time should be accessible without a user having to search for them. Making a function apparent means that elements in the interface should look like what they are. Controls, such as buttons, should have visual attributes that strongly identify them. Other controls should be available if a user requests them, but users should never have to wonder where they are.*

TRANSPARENCY *A user's focus should be on the content of an interactive product, not on format or navigation. An interface should allow users to concentrate on the task at hand, not remind them that they're working on a computer. Designers shouldn't just package information, they should give users a way to get at it.*

In the children's storybook CD-ROM Just Grandma and Me, *there's no imposed GUI with windows and menus. A child simply clicks on parts of the pictures to interact with the story.*

FEEDBACK *Each action a user takes should have an immediate and obvious effect. People need to know the results of their actions immediately.*

This is the status window for file transfer in the Windows 95 operating system: the user knows the result of the action initiated.

MODES OF OPERATION *People use three main modes when they interact with a computer. One is command mode – telling the system to do something, looking up a word, going to a section or chapter, or marking a place. Another is manipulation mode – accomplishing tasks by manipulating objects, "dissecting" an image on the screen, running a simulation, or changing variables. A third is recording mode – entering data, making annotations, highlighting text, or recording thoughts in a notebook.*

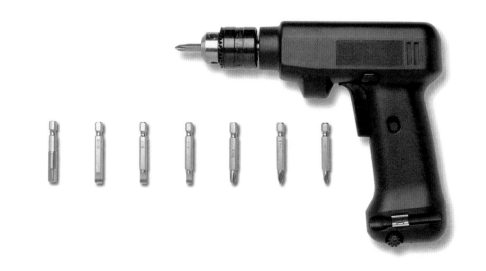

PACE   *A user should be able to control the speed at which he or she moves through material, whether that means scrolling through text or navigating to a different section. For that matter, users shouldn't feel as if they're navigating, or going, anywhere; rather, an interface should give users the impression that they're summoning the information.*

APPROPRIATENESS   *Most of all, an interface should be designed to accommodate its users. A designer should make no assumptions about what a user can or cannot do, or what a user will want to do; those decisions should be left to the user. A design should be as customized as possible, in as many ways as are reasonable.*

Who Is the User?

Who are the users? What are they accustomed to and what do they want? What is the user model? These are the most important questions for designers to ask when they're putting interactivity and interface design into a context.

People don't all fit the same mold, which means that their interactivity requirements vary. Where do they work? What do they do? Are they professionals? Students? Designers can provide different interactive experiences; people accustomed to getting information from print sources may like to browse through information on screen, whereas people who use online news wire services may prefer to use search functions, but any interactive piece should provide both kinds of interactivity. Whether an interactive piece presents information as text or as a full-on multimedia extravaganza, designers should begin their work by thinking about how to make the piece adapt to the needs of all its users.

Remembering Who the User Is

Just because it's possible to implement every configurable option doesn't mean that it's wise to do so. The standards for interactivity design are still making interactivity appropriate and keeping users' wants and needs in mind. A designer creating a customized interactive piece – that is, a piece with a specific user in mind – should consider the following principles.

PATH The path through information should be self-evident, if not intuitive. "Intuitive" does not mean "GUI for dummies." An intuitive path implies structured reasoning with logical steps or actions.

ABSTRUSENESS The level of information presented should respect users' knowledge level, not just their intelligence. Just because a user may be a physicist doesn't mean an interface should present highly technical terms about medical information. Choices should be provided so the user can determine the appropriate level of information.

GUIDANCE The controls and tools used to get through information should be scalable in relation to the complexity of the information presented. Relevant controls and support should be presented as they're needed. No one wants a personal coach all the time.

ACTIVITY LEVEL How much passive reading or watching is appropriate? How much active participation?

PREFERRED MEDIA TYPES Some users may prefer to browse through text and bring up accompanying graphics, video, and animation at will. Others may want to see graphics with text explanations available on demand.

SPECIAL CIRCUMSTANCES A user may be right- or left-handed, color blind, or vision- or hearing-

> In a very real sense, the places in our lives get "under our skin" and influence our behavior in ways that we often don't suspect.
> Winifred Gallagher, *The Power of Place*

impaired. A GUI can be designed to accommodate people's needs through large text, controls arranged on one side of the screen or the other, high audio levels, and so on.

MODE OF EXPRESSION A user should find it easy to view whatever is important to him or her. In a medical reference CD-ROM, for instance, female users should have access to a female anatomical rendering – not just the default white-male depiction.

LOCALITY Material in an interface should be localizable for countries and regions, and easily translated into other languages. For a global audience, an interface should be as modular as possible, allowing developers to update specific features without having to apply their work to every file.

INTELLIGENCE In addition to allowing a user to customize it, a system ideally has the intelligence to customize itself. That is, it should be able to "learn" about its users, "remembering" between sessions where a user has been and where he or she might want to begin next time.

Customizing an interface design adds complexity to the work of designing it, but the reward of that work is a valuable product or service. The ultimate system adapts to the outside limits of a user's wishes without allowing flexibility to invite chaos.

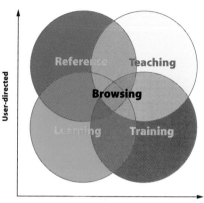

One way to understand design parameters and user definitions is to assess a project's content to determine the functions the user will perform, and then use the *x* and *y* axes to plot the specific behaviors of the interface. The diagram above shows functions specific to an online medical information service. Each represents a somewhat different experience, yet they overlap substantially. A person can be in learning mode and in reference mode at the same time. The main differences are how user-structured and how sequential the activities tend to be. Reference is the most user-structured and least sequential mode. All four modes involve browsing.

Profiling Users

Once it's clear what users' wants and needs are, the design process can address user profiles. If it's not possible to determine a preference that will satisfy all users, the designer should find a way to give users a prompt; on a personal computer, PDA, or interactive television, users might both hear and see a prompt. If the complexity of a program requires more than one piece of information from users, the interface should guide them through their choices.

AGE   What age groups do potential users fall into?

PERSONAL HISTORY   What kind of information should a system allow users to enter about themselves? How should questions be phrased? How will each user's privacy be protected?

ACCESS SELECTOR   How will a user understand the differences among the ways to access information and make informed choices?

FLEXIBILITY   What happens if a user changes his or her mind at any point?

TERRAIN   How can a user navigate from choice to choice? How can a user return to the point of origin? Should a user be able to move around within a program?

HELP   What kind of assistance is available? Is it appropriate for every user?

SUBJECT SELECTOR   How are choices made clear to a user? What if a user doesn't know which choice to make?

MODE OR KNOWLEDGE LEVEL   Interactive products and services can fill reference, training, teaching, or learning needs. How can a system elicit the appropriate information from a user? How can a user be made to accurately describe his or her own knowledge level? What if a user is highly educated but looking for relatively simple information?

DELIVERY CHANNEL   A system shouldn't have to prompt a user to tell it whether it's being used on a personal computer or a television. It won't be long before interactive products are used on multiple platforms, so that a user can, say, retrieve information from a computer-based product and transfer it to a PDA, or switch from a personal computer to a television screen.

PREFERENCE   How can a system let a user choose media types or a level of interaction? How can a user define how "passive" or "active" an experience he or she wants?

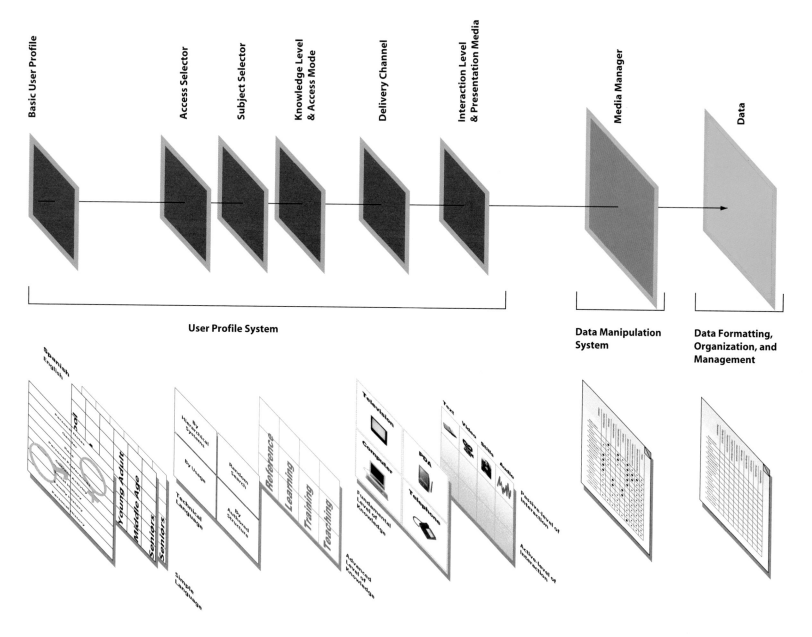

Basic User Profile

Access Selector

Subject Selector

Knowledge Level & Access Mode

Delivery Channel

Interaction Level & Presentation Media

Media Manager

Data

User Profile System

Data Manipulation System

Data Formatting, Organization, and Management

Effective interactivity is created only when adaptability to user needs and preferences are taken into account. The top half of this schema represents all the information used to build an interactive system; the left section are people-centric considerations. The lower half shows detailed matrix views of the categories above. This schema is a means of evaluating project priorities as well as scope.

Content Directs,

Design Mediates

It's always content that should drive the implementation of technology and design. Content and purpose form an anchor that the computing medium's "what-ifs" and "what's-possibles" tend to obscure, but they're the bottom line of every project. Interactivity design is the process of choosing the interactivity arts that best mediate between content and users.

The new and necessary factor in the process of interactivity design is usability testing. Traditionally, designers evaluate usability in graphic terms: How big is the type? Is it readable? But an integral aspect of interactivity design – a necessity not currently well understood in most marketing and design communities – consists of performance testing, usability testing, and debugging. Product testing is important in evaluating interaction in digital information design.

When the government deregulated banks in the early 1980s, banking was no longer tightly restricted within state boundaries and banks were allowed to offer a variety of investment services. That increase in market reach generated demand for more choices, including the option of customer banking at home via modem. One of the first banks to take advantage of deregulation was a California bank that extended its existing online banking service to the Prodigy online service.

The bank wanted to make the transition from the existing system to the Prodigy service as seamless as possible from the perspective of its customers. However, the differences between a system driven by a floppy disk and accessed in a closed environment and the open environment of an online service raised questions about whether it was appropriate simply to drop the interface of the existing system into the new system. Would it be necessary to develop a custom version of the interface, or would that confuse longtime customers?

The structure of the Prodigy service groups information into categories, which a user threads through until the banking option appears. Where Prodigy organizes information by category, the bank's existing system (as well as its ATM system) was driven by function – by a customer's desire to make transactions like transferring money or paying bills. Driving the product by category instead of function would mean reversing the order of choices in the existing product: instead of choosing a transaction type first and then specifying which accounts to apply that choice to, a customer would first choose an account, then specify which function to apply to it, and then specify a second account.

The bank and the design studio grouped the navigational system into two logical directions. One was portfolio based and included liquid portfolios, investment portfolios, credit portfolios, and services such as bill paying. The bank suggested the portfolio-based system as a way to better market those accounts; if customers had to first choose an account before performing a transaction, they would be more likely to think in terms of portfolios and build additional accounts. The portfolio-based system had marketing goals, whereas the transaction-based system was oriented toward the specific tasks that a customer might want to perform. The marketing agenda required a mix of both, which raised the issue of consistency; how could a system let customers switch modes at any time so they could approach the system either by function or by category?

The solution was to implement a scenario that carried both functions all the way through. The design studio conducted usability studies on two prototypes – one portfolio based and one transaction based – to see how people interacted with each system. Testing showed what users looked at first and how they moved through a system to get money or transfer money. Users were asked to find an account balance and transfer money from one account to another, as well as more general questions, such as "if you were doing this, what features would you like?"

A third prototype, the one the bank chose, was a hybrid that gave customers the option to review a portfolio – review their overall financial situation, pay bills, check their account status, and look at interest rates – or simply make a transaction. Customers only had to make one choice; the point of interactivity for that particular function was at the top level of the interactivity structure.

Social Science,

Not Rocket Science

This book devotes substantial space to various principles and models, as well as to considerations for the use and the users of interactivity design. Interactivity design may seem complex and difficult to master, but the truth of the matter is that interactivity is social science, not rocket science. This book's dissection of the computing medium is really a means to an end, and that end is engaging people with the forms of expression that computing makes possible.

Cooking Up an Interactive Experience

A good interactive experience is like a successful dinner party: good cooks and good interactivity designers both plan ahead. Who will the guests be? Will the party have a theme? A host invites people to contribute their personalities to a dinner party

setting, and perhaps asks them to bring a bottle of wine or a pot luck dish. On Web sites or online services, varied interactions, like scavenger hunts or chat sessions and conferences, make different kinds of experiences possible. Planning a supper on the theme of, say, Italian cooking is very much like defining a premise for interactivity. Will the party be formal? How many courses will be served? When should preparation start for each dish so that it's ready to be served at the right moment? Overcooked filet mignon, or too long a pause between courses, or foods that don't go together can ruin an evening for everyone. Whether an interactive experience is instructive or intriguing or just plain fun, it's orchestrated within well-defined parameters, and its structure and navigation are well thought out. Will any of the preparation require special utensils? Will there be enough chairs and place settings for everyone? What kinds of music and lighting and flower arrangements will help create the right ambience? In an interactive experience, an illustration that worked well in a printed book might be infinitely more effective expressed as a moving picture, and tabular material might serve users better in database format. Just as a good host makes guests feel comfortable no matter what their eccentricities, good interactivity design accommodates users' preferences and human error.

When an experience is just right, whether it's a meal or a CD-ROM, people don't question why; they just come away feeling satisfied. It's the way that events are orchestrated that makes for a memorable experience.

The Designer's Trust

At the heart of all the talk about the virtual world, connectivity, and the tremendous amounts of information available, is people's desire for the ultimate interaction – social interaction. A designer has an important responsibility: to keep in mind that people need to communicate and express themselves. A designer's work must always be focused on the people who will experience the interactivity and on what is appropriate for a particular community; the technology employed is always a secondary consideration. The ultimate task of every designer is to create ways for people to communicate with each other and share common interests.

Although online communities have only been possible within the last few years, they're already extremely popular: 50,000-plus participants log onto AOL every weekday evening specifically to chat– the equivalent attendance of a typical rock concert. The Utne Reader established its online site with the uppermost thought of publishing exclusive online content; they were very surprised when the most visited part of their site turned out to be Cafe Utne, where users chat and exchange ideas and opinions.

Integrated Views: Case Studies

Publishing
HarperCollins
24 Hours in Cyberspace

Broadcasting
National Broadcasting Company – Intercast

Online Communities
MSN, The Microsoft Network
iQVC

Entertainment
Sony New Technology

Commerce
Herman Miller, Inc.

HarperCollins

HarperCollins (www.harpercollins.com) is one of the largest book publishers in the world, with one of the industry's most extensive backlists. Its major strengths are in popular, education, reference, software, and religious titles. The many divisions of HarperCollins are each responsible for a multitude of products and services, which in turn have different branding and identity needs. Interactive software products have different marketing and delivery specifications from paper-based products.

BUSINESS GOAL
HarperCollins had a long-term goal of establishing an overall Web presence under a corporate umbrella. It wanted to initiate that presence with a Web site for its newly created HarperCollins Interactive division.

TECHNOLOGY MANDATE
The technology mandate was to make the service work in a browser-based environment that would reach as many people as possible.

DESIGN CHALLENGE The design challenge was to create an identity and a Web site for the HarperCollins Interactive division that would serve as a flexible model for other HarperCollins divisions and that would accommodate any future expansion and reorganization.

Start Small, End Up Big

This case study illustrates how a well-conceived system can accommodate the needs of even the largest and most diverse corporation. HarperCollins asked us to develop an overall Web presence, beginning with a site for one division under a corporate umbrella and eventually expanding into an integrated presence for all HarperCollins divisions, present and future. The HarperCollins list is one of the most diverse in the publishing world, and this project required us to work with people from all parts of the organization and fill needs in both print and computing media. Constructing a plan for a company that represents such a diversity of product and effort was a challenge. Yet – as this case study shows – it is

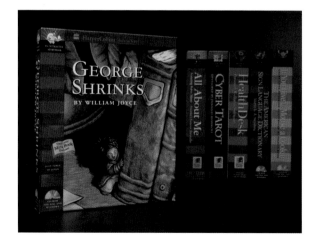

REFERENCE
TOOL

INTERACTIVE
STORYBOOK

INTERACTIVE
STORYBOOK

The design work for the software titles in 1992 was the starting point of our work for HarperCollins. This look was eventually carried through to the Web site.

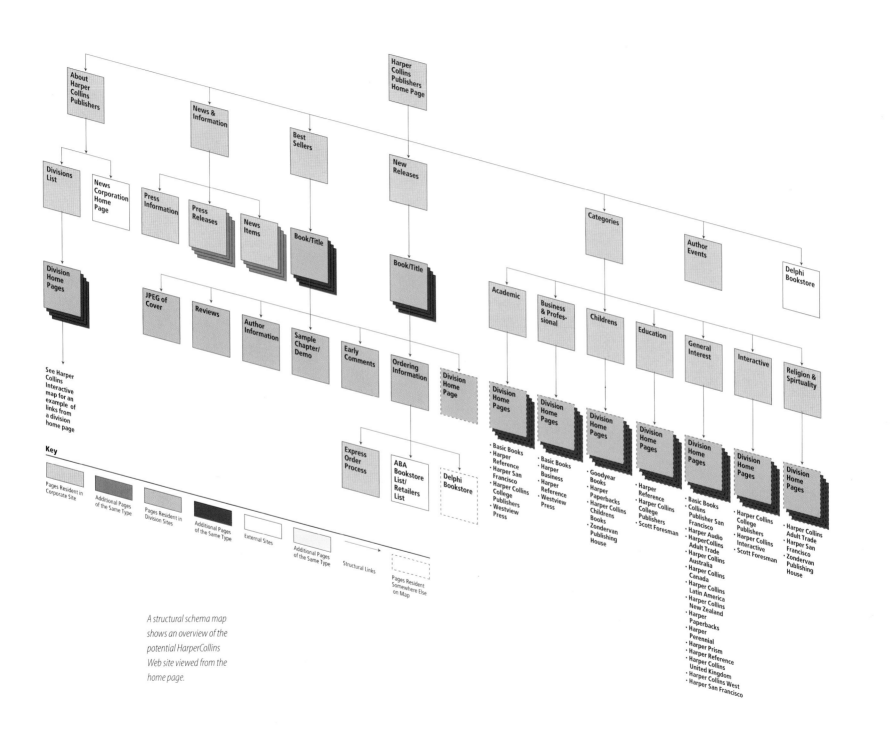

Harper Collins Publishers Home Page

About Harper Collins Publishers
- Divisions List
  - Division Home Pages
    - See Harper Collins Interactive map for an example of links from a division home page
- News Corporation Home Page

News & Information
- Press Information
- Press Releases
- News Items

Best Sellers
- Book/Title
  - JPEG of Cover
  - Reviews
  - Author Information
  - Sample Chapter/ Demo
  - Early Comments
  - Ordering Information
    - Express Order Process
    - ABA Bookstore List/ Retailers List
  - Division Home Page
    - Delphi Bookstore

New Releases
- Book/Title

Categories
- Academic
  - Division Home Pages
    - • Basic Books
    - • Harper Reference
    - • Harper San Francisco
    - • Harper Collins College Publishers
    - • Westview Press
- Business & Professional
  - Division Home Pages
    - • Basic Books
    - • Harper Business
    - • Harper Reference
    - • Westview Press
- Childrens
  - Division Home Pages
    - • Goodyear Books
    - • Harper Paperbacks
    - • Harper Collins Childrens Books
    - • Zondervan Publishing House
- Education
  - Division Home Pages
    - • Harper Reference
    - • Harper Collins College Publishers
    - • Scott Foresman
- General Interest
  - Division Home Pages
    - • Basic Books
    - • Collins Publisher San Francisco
    - • Harper Audio
    - • HarperCollins Adult Trade
    - • Harper Collins Australia
    - • Harper Collins Canada
    - • Harper Collins Latin America
    - • Harper Collins New Zealand
    - • Harper Paperbacks
    - • Harper Perennial
    - • Harper Prism
    - • Harper Reference
    - • Harper Collins United Kingdom
    - • Harper Collins West
    - • Harper San Francisco
- Interactive
  - Division Home Pages
    - • Harper Collins College Publishers
    - • Harper Collins Interactive
    - • Scott Foresman
- Religion & Spirituality
  - Division Home Pages
    - • Harper Collins Adult Trade
    - • Harper San Francisco
    - • Zondervan Publishing House

Author Events

Delphi Bookstore

Key

- Pages Resident in Corporate Site
- Additional Pages of the Same Type
- Pages Resident in Division Sites
- Additional Pages of the Same Type
- External Sites
- Additional Pages of the Same Type
- Structural Links
- Pages Resident Somewhere Else on Map

A structural schema map shows an overview of the potential HarperCollins Web site viewed from the home page.

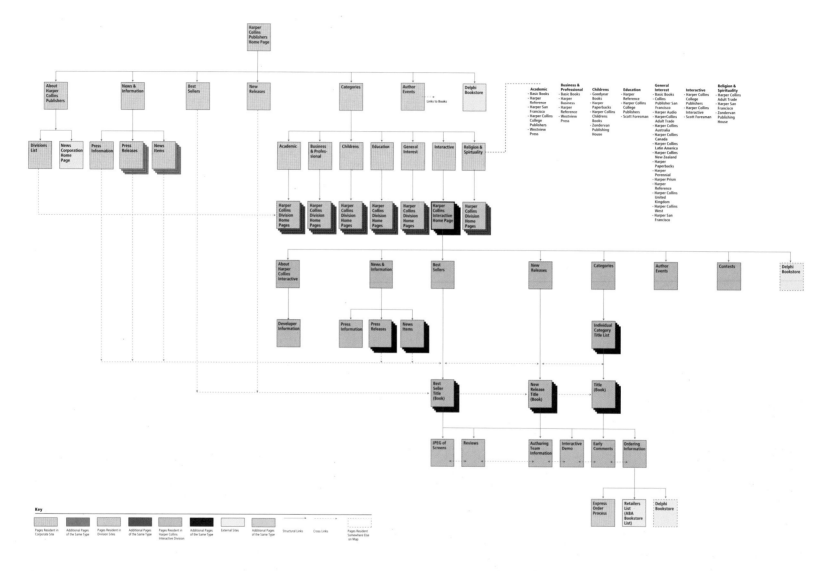

This next level of mapping is expanded to show the HarperCollins Interactive division's pages. A detail from it (right) shows the HarperCollins Interactive section which outlines the information and components on each page. This helped identify the size of the site and the information the client had to provide. This diagram was presented to the client for clarification, and then to the HTML programmers so they could build the pages. This was a common document so the programmers didn't have to think about steps like how many and what kind of buttons there would be; it was also the blueprint from which the design planning and development began, and from which the GUI was developed. We have had the experience of not performing this step, directed by clients who don't "need" the architecture and planning – the result was a disjointed site, and we eventually had to go back and do it anyway.

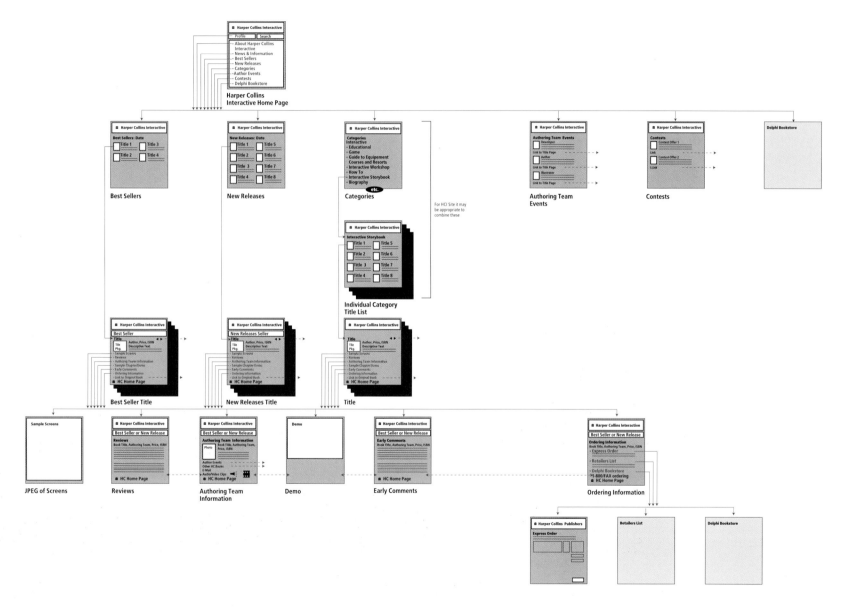

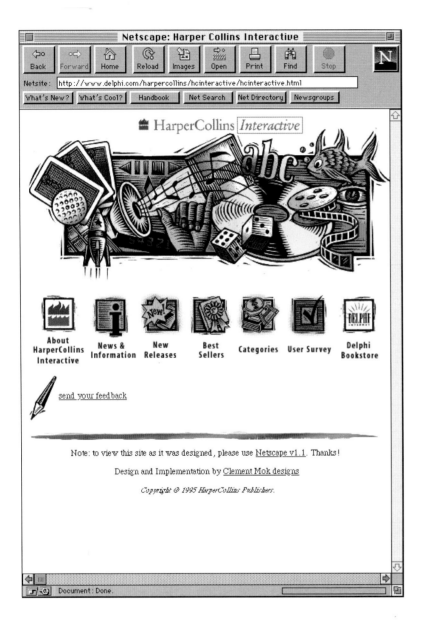

possible, and in fact necessary, to execute such a project without first gaining a complete overview of the corporate context; the speed with which business evolves makes it virtually impossible for any business or designer to know the complete extent of many projects at their outset. The key to such a project is working within a defined scope.

We began our work with HarperCollins by designing product packaging for the newly formed HarperCollins Interactive division. To create the new division, HarperCollins pulled in staff from existing divisions in both the New York and San Francisco offices. The dispersion of authors and editors in time and space, along with sparsity of the new division's list, made it unusually tricky to design an identity that would encompass all the division's titles. The division's first offering was a slightly disjointed list of six titles from various subject areas, including children's, health, new age, and reference, but the list promised to expand to hundreds of titles in the not-too-distant future.

HarperCollins' goal for their identity system was to make people aware of HarperCollins Interactive not only as a new division of HarperCollins – leveraging the parent company's reputation for quality among customers already familiar with HarperCollins book titles – but as a distinct subset

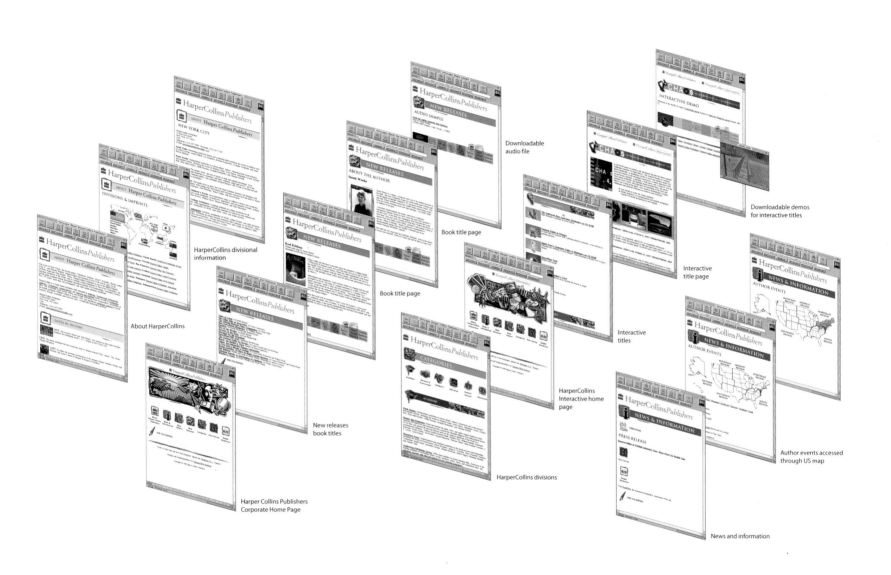

HarperCollins divisional information

Downloadable audio file

Downloadable demos for interactive titles

Book title page

About HarperCollins

Interactive title page

Book title page

New releases book titles

Interactive titles

HarperCollins Interactive home page

Author events accessed through US map

Harper Collins Publishers Corporate Home Page

HarperCollins divisions

News and information

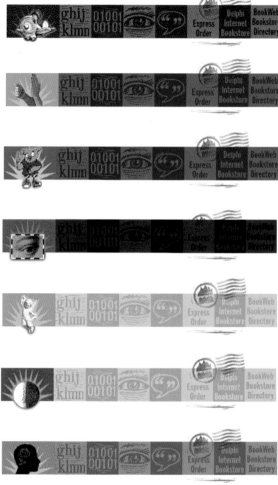

of the HarperCollins family. The market for CD-ROM titles is so new that few CD-ROM publishers have had time to establish brand loyalty; people who purchase CD-ROM titles make buying decisions mostly on the basis of their interest in the titles' content. The packaging, which combined the look of a book cover with the look of consumer electronics software packaging, both conveyed the hybrid identity of the titles and helped address the need to display compatibility and performance information on the packaging.

Tying It All Together

HarperCollins wanted to take advantage of the Web's unique strengths in supporting marketing and promotion efforts, servicing field representatives, and promoting better relationships with customers from retailers to consumers. Two years after the product identity project, HarperCollins asked us to create a Web site for HarperCollins Interactive and develop a long-range Web plan for the entire company. The aim of the project was to establish a framework for HarperCollins' corporate presence and to set up navigational structures and guidelines that would preserve the unity of HarperCollins' image as each division went online. The worldwide HarperCollins empire encompasses about sixty groups, so we developed an overall structure map (see page 151)

showing how all the divisions' sites could be related to each other in the context of HarperCollins' overall corporate Web presence; the map made the eventual value of the company's Web presence comprehensible to all the divisions as well as to executives. It was natural to begin development with the HarperCollins Interactive site, not only because it was logical to promote digital media titles on the Web, but also because its promotional material was all in digital format.

We based the infrastructure and GUI of the site around potential content and functions, which included ordering information, a link to the bookstore at Delphi Online, e-mail links to authors, and news about recently released titles. In the course of three lengthy planning sessions, we gained an understanding of HarperCollins' structure – what each division was responsible for, and how the divisions were organized.

The structure map served as a preliminary outline for the HarperCollins Interactive site. A later map (see page 153) showed how the interactive division site could work in the context of the entire site. This second map clarified the scope and size of the undertaking for everyone involved; we had initially estimated it at a small fraction of its actual size.

HarperCollins wanted the interactive division's Web site to act first as a billboard and second as a reference for customers looking for particular titles, perhaps even helping customers to find dealers and distributors specializing in hard-to-find books from HarperCollins. It also wanted to include reviews and write-ups about each title. What the site needed was a search engine so that visitors and book distributors could search for books by title, subject, author, and year.

Unfortunately, HarperCollins stored all of that information in separate databases for each division, and those databases were not linked. We spent half a day with the HarperCollins team mapping out a workaround structure to compensate for the lack of a central database. We categorized books so that visitors could initially choose a book topic and then follow links to all the divisions carrying books under that topic. The workaround was awkward because a visitor to the site might have to search through several divisions to find the book he or she was looking for. The HarperCollins team hoped that the site's launch would spur funding for linking the databases. It wasn't the scope of the plan or the reality of implementing it that was the challenge here, but simply the location of the data.

GUI Design

To design the GUI, we developed tagging schemes, or ways of identifying each level in the overall structure of the site, from divisions to groups. Defining those levels was far more time consuming than anyone on the project had imagined.

Working with the HarperCollins team, we set out to identify the levels of all of the components of the corporate site, and the interactive division site, the subset of the division, and so on down to the smallest subcategories. The overall site contained a huge amount of information and had a very deep structure. Furthermore, HarperCollins wanted to link press releases and hot lists of recent titles to pages for individual titles at the very lowest levels. Visitors to the site were more than likely to give up if they had to click through ten pages to get to the information they were looking for. How could we structure the site so that a visitor could dive all the way down to information at the lowest level of a division site with just one or two clicks? After studying the structure carefully, we tried collapsing the smaller parts of a section into a single Web page. That worked, and it quickly became obvious which of the other groupings should be collapsed.

Each division site had different kinds of information to disperse and unique functions to perform. We designed graphics that were modular and therefore easily adapted to different division sites. The graphics not only gave the site its visual style and served as navigation elements, they imposed a consistent look and feel throughout the site. The modularity of the graphics minimized the time it took for users to move through the site, and it also allowed HarperCollins to add onto the site later – adding a new search function, for instance – in ways that we hadn't envisioned in our original plan.

The mapping, planning, and structure and navigation phase lasted about six weeks; design, illustration, and approval took another six weeks.

The HarperCollins project showed how it's possible to start with a portion of a project and build it into a unified whole – there's no need to be paralyzed by the impossibility of implementing a definitive solution. Finding a way to carry out such a project can be daunting, but the only way to get somewhere is to step forward.

24 Hours in Cyberspace

Part event, part publication, part broadcasting, 24 Hours in Cyberspace was an online experiment that took place during the twenty-four hours of February 8, 1996. It resulted in the real-time publication of feature stories, photographs, and interviews from all over the world in a Web "magazine" updated every thirty minutes. Funded with $3 million and over $2 million in loaned equipment, the 24 Hours project was staffed by professional editors and photographers from *Time, Life, Newsweek,* National Public Radio, and the Associated Press, among others. Engineers, technicians, and equipment were provided by Sun Microsystems, Adobe Systems, Kodak, NEC, Illustra, NetObjects, and many others. Eighty people worked each eight-hour shift in 6,000 square feet of equipment-jammed space.

BUSINESS GOALS

A Web site with the capability to publish human interest stories in real time.

TECHNOLOGY MANDATE

Create a system that could accept huge volumes of information, process it into page form, and then distribute a new version of it (in Web site form) worldwide every thirty minutes.

DESIGN CHALLENGES

To develop an automated Internet publishing system for "non-techies" that provided the site with a clean, professional magazine layout and high-quality graphics.

Publishing:

The Next Generation

The 24 Hours in Cyberspace project was the brainchild of Rick Smolan, founder of Against All Odds Productions. Smolan is the creator of "Day in the Life" books, a series developed from the orchestration of one-day photo shoots in Japan, Australia, the United States, and other countries. This time Smolan dispatched more than a hundred photographers to every corner of the world to document the ways in which "the Internet is transforming people's lives." To display the photographs and tell the stories behind them, it took a large team of editors backed by the best technical expertise and equipment. The resulting full-color journalistic "magazine" on the Web was something like a newspaper, and something like broadcasting – only faster. This was a truly collaborative effort forged into a hybrid of event and location-based computing and publishing.

When Smolan hatched the idea for the project, the Web was a relatively new phenomenon and he envisioned Web pages with well-designed text, beautiful graphics, and true-to-life photographs. Some of the technology required to implement this vision didn't even exist at the time.

24 HOURS IN CYBERSPACE: HOW IT WORKS

CREATE
On February 8th, 100 professional photographers and thousands of others worldwide shoot photos and transmit them to San Francisco.

COLLECT & EDIT
At Mission Control in San Francisco, teams of judges, editors, designers, and technicians sift through incoming pictures and audio clips, and build a World Wide Web site the same day.

PUBLISH
The work is published at the 24 Hours in Cyberspace Web site (http://www. Cyber24.com), and "mirrored" around the world.

"Mirror" sites at the Internet 1996 World Expo, MCI, BBN Planet, and Sun Microsystems.

Photographers
Assistants
Students
Amateurs
The Military

Kodak Digital Science Camera, Kodak Film and Processing

NEC Versa Notebook Computer, Adobe Photoshop, SWCC PIK, Polaroid Scanner

Kodak Digital Science Camera, Adobe Page Mill, Adobe Photoshop, Adobe Acrobat, Netscape Server

MFS Communications

MAE West*

MAE East*

* MFS Internet connections, with Internet

MISSION CONTROL, SAN FRANCISCO

Collect Data
Judges

Traffic Team

Sonic Solutions Team

System Administration Team

Audio Interviewer

Technical Support

Senior Editors

Proof Readers

floating support for all groups

Make Story Pages (Six teams)
Photo Editor

Text Editor

Adobe Photoshop Technician

Adobe Photoshop, Illustra, Netscape Navigator, NetObjects Technology

Network

60 Sun Ultra Sparc Workstations and Servers

Illustra Database

25 NEC Powermate Systems

Revise

Publish

Web Site

MFS Communications

Update the Homepage
Editor-in-Chief

Executive Photo Editor

Web site Designer

Adobe Photoshop, Illustra, Netscape Navigator, NetObjects Technology

Make Table of Contents Pages
Table of Contents Team

Adobe Photoshop, Illustra, Netscape Navigator, NetObjects Technology

Additional technology:
Power Computing's systems
Cyberports for Business' connectivity
The Software Construction Company's (SWCC) Photoshop Plug-in
Best Power's UPS
US Robotics's modems
Cisco Systems' routers
Bay Networks' hubs
Telos Systems' interfaces
Telex headsets
Spider Island Software's Telefinder BBS

Nigel Holmes' diagram describing the technology and information paths of the 24 Hours site.

One month before the 24 Hours in Cyberspace project, a Web site was launched to solicit story ideas; the site also provided submission guidelines for potential contributors.

The Nuts and Bolts

Two requirements influenced the technology mandate: the Netscape 1.2 delivery platform and the accommodation of 14.4 modems. The bulk of the technology research was in the domain of Against All Odds Productions, who determined, during September and October, the technologies that would make the project a reality.

The building blocks of the 24 Hours in Cyberspace site were the pictures and text the photographers and others would transmit from around the world. The stories were created from rough copy prepared ahead of time; audio recordings of interviews conducted in the China Basin Building in San Francisco – where the 24 Hours operation took place – were also story material. We knew these building blocks had to be put into a database, and also that the editors needed a way to pull them out of the database and turn them into finished stories and pages very quickly. What we had to figure out was what digital tools the editorial team required to bring those pieces to life over the Internet.

The central part of the system was the Illustra database, which collected and held all the data from on- and off-site (Illustra has a relational and object search engine, and a web tool that allows viewing of specific photos and written material). We needed to find a way to automate the process of identifying and moving each editorial item from Illustra to some kind of document the editors could work from.

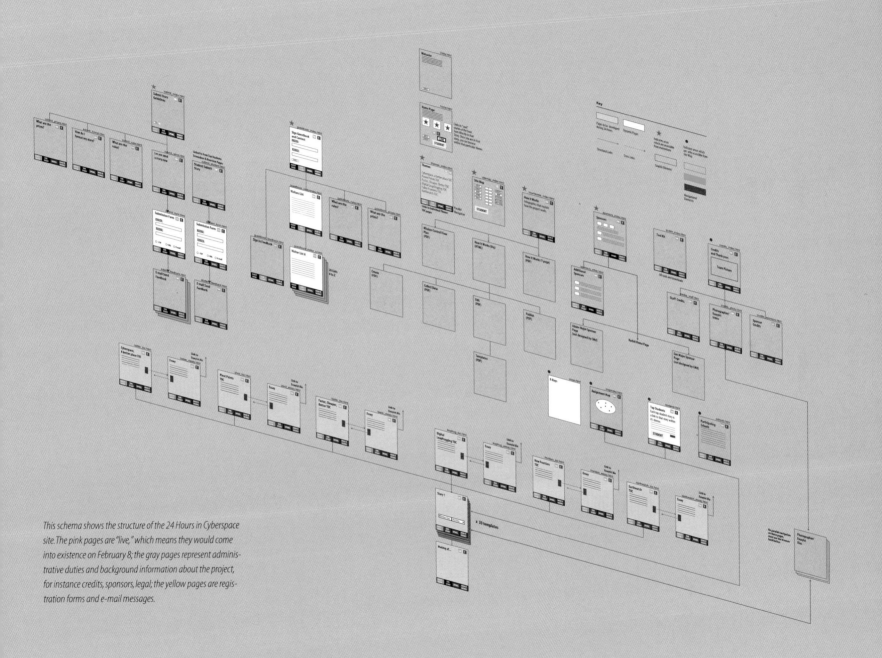

This schema shows the structure of the 24 Hours in Cyberspace site. The pink pages are "live," which means they would come into existence on February 8; the gray pages represent administrative duties and background information about the project, for instance credits, sponsors, legal; the yellow pages are registration forms and e-mail messages.

The technical team came up with the idea of templates, which would accommodate stories with different numbers of photos, amounts of text, and headline emphasis in a variety of format combinations; the templates also specified character and word counts for the headline, text, and caption boxes along with their pixel dimensions. In addition, they relieved the editors of having to cope with HTML (computer code required for all Internet material). We designed thirty story templates for the project (see page 167).

We then needed an application that would efficiently relay the editorial material to and from the templates and Illustra. We turned to NetObjects, which developed an application especially for this project called SitePublisher. SitePublisher allowed editors to choose one of the rough stories from the database, select one of the thirty templates from a pull-down menu, view the story in the template, and then edit the text and headlines. As editors made changes to text, SitePublisher updated the database automatically. SitePublisher also allowed the editors

Case Studies

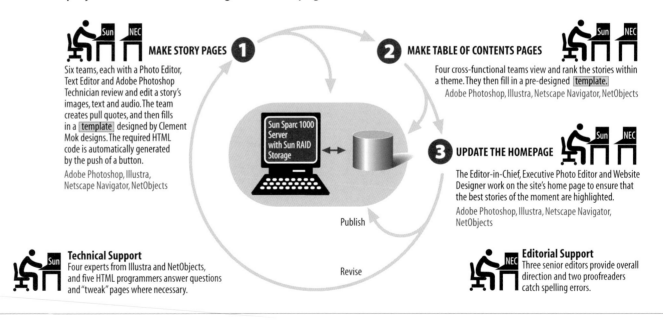

At Mission Control, teams of editors, designers and technicians build the web pages that are the heart of the project. There are three stages for each page:

MAKE STORY PAGES ❶
Six teams, each with a Photo Editor, Text Editor and Adobe Photoshop Technician review and edit a story's images, text and audio. The team creates pull quotes, and then fills in a template designed by Clement Mok designs. The required HTML code is automatically generated by the push of a button.
Adobe Photoshop, Illustra, Netscape Navigator, NetObjects

❷ **MAKE TABLE OF CONTENTS PAGES**
Four cross-functional teams view and rank the stories within a theme. They then fill in a pre-designed template.
Adobe Photoshop, Illustra, Netscape Navigator, NetObjects

Sun Sparc 1000 Server with Sun RAID Storage

❸ **UPDATE THE HOMEPAGE**
The Editor-in-Chief, Executive Photo Editor and Website Designer work on the site's home page to ensure that the best stories of the moment are highlighted.
Adobe Photoshop, Illustra, Netscape Navigator, NetObjects

Publish

Revise

Technical Support
Four experts from Illustra and NetObjects, and five HTML programmers answer questions and "tweak" pages where necessary.

Editorial Support
Three senior editors provide overall direction and two proofreaders catch spelling errors.

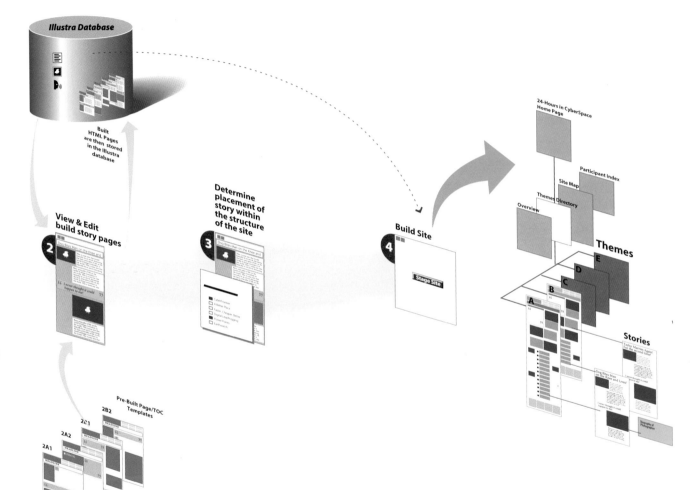

Illustra Database

Built HTML Pages are then stored in the Illustra database

Select Story & Template

1 NETObjects *SitePublisher*

View & Edit build story pages

2

Determine placement of story within the structure of the site

3

Build Site

4 Stage Site

2A1

2A2

2B1 2B2

Pre-Built Page/TOC Templates

24-Hours in CyberSpace Home Page

Participant Index

Site Map

Themes Directory

Overview

Themes

E

D

C

B

A

Stories

This diagram shows how SitePublisher, the Illustra database, and the templates worked together in the 24 Hours in Cyberspace site.

to instantly generate HTML code by simply clicking on a button – they could then preview their work on Netscape Navigator to see how it would look on the finished Web site. SitePublisher kept the code out of the editors' way so that they could concentrate on what they were best at – shaping the copy and choosing appropriate photographs.

Express Publishing

The publishing process involved the following steps: collect data, edit data, select template, edit data, finish story, gather stories, create table of contents, and publish. When the site opened on February 8th, photographs and their captions began streaming

in from all over the world. When the photographs were chosen and the related story was brought up, the editors selected a template and then the appropriate text or caption, and clicked on the space in the template allotted for each particular type of material.

SitePublisher allowed editors to change the layouts of their stories simply by clicking on another template – all the editorial and photographic material was automatically transferred to the right place in the new layout. When the time came to assemble the first "magazine," the table of contents editor chose the desired material from a list provided by SitePublisher. The stories were posted, prioritized,

From left to right: the first screen offered the editors a choice of story and template; the second shows the template the editors worked from; the third displays a preview of the finished page on the Web site.

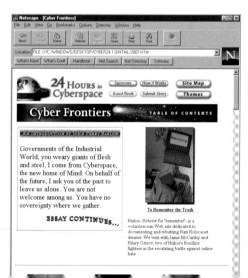

5-Photograph Story Templates

Light Text Scenario　　　　　　*ModerateText Scenario*　　　　　　*HeavyText Scenario*

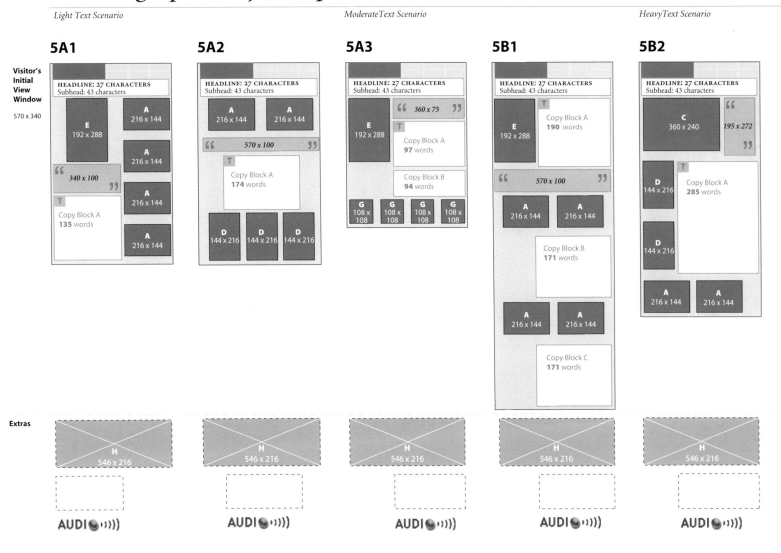

5A1　　　**5A2**　　　**5A3**　　　**5B1**　　　**5B2**

Visitor's Initial View Window

570 x 340

5A1
HEADLINE: 27 CHARACTERS
Subhead: 43 characters
E 192 x 288
A 216 x 144
A 216 x 144
340 x 100
A 216 x 144
T
Copy Block A
135 words
A 216 x 144

5A2
HEADLINE: 27 CHARACTERS
Subhead: 43 characters
A 216 x 144
A 216 x 144
570 x 100
T
Copy Block A
174 words
D 144 x 216
D 144 x 216
D 144 x 216

5A3
HEADLINE: 27 CHARACTERS
Subhead: 43 characters
E 192 x 288
360 x 75
T
Copy Block A
97 words
Copy Block B
94 words
G 108 x 108
G 108 x 108
G 108 x 108
G 108 x 108

5B1
HEADLINE: 27 CHARACTERS
Subhead: 43 characters
T
E 192 x 288
Copy Block A
190 words
570 x 100
A 216 x 144
A 216 x 144
Copy Block B
171 words
A 216 x 144
A 216 x 144
Copy Block C
171 words

5B2
HEADLINE: 27 CHARACTERS
Subhead: 43 characters
C 360 x 240
195 x 272
D 144 x 216
T
Copy Block A
285 words
D 144 x 216
A 216 x 144
A 216 x 144

Extras

H 546 x 216　　AUDIO))) 　　H 546 x 216　　AUDIO))) 　　H 546 x 216　　AUDIO))) 　　H 546 x 216　　AUDIO))) 　　H 546 x 216　　AUDIO)))

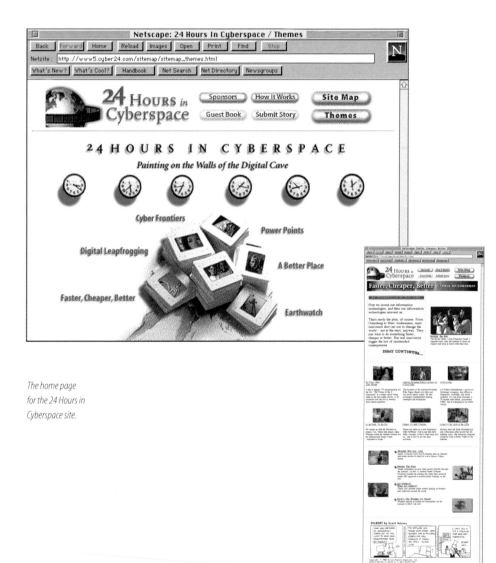

*The home page
for the 24 Hours in
Cyberspace site.*

and sequenced (which determined the pagination of the "magazine") by the senior editors. When it was time to publish the site, the table of contents editor clicked on a button called "stage," which told SitePublisher to retrieve all of the HTML pages, and photo and sound files from Illustra for that issue; SitePublisher then compiled the pages, added navigational controls and links, and positioned the new pages in the context of the Web site.

The new magazine/site was tested within mission control by logging onto a separate web server to make sure everything worked. It was "pushed" out to Mae West (the largest Internet hub in the world); as the new issue was fanned out to fourteen mirror sites across the globe, the editorial staff was already working to meet the next deadline, only thirty minutes away.

A Web Site Disguised as a Magazine

Giving the site the look of a magazine required the adaptation of magazine publishing conventions to Web browser capabilities. For one, it wasn't possible

*There were six theme areas
in the 24 Hours site; these table
of contents pages list stories,
features, cartoons, etc.*

Left: a table of contents
page with a listing and
description of stories;
to the right are samples
of finished stories.

to specify type the way it's done in print; browser software generally defines type in relative sizes – small, medium, and large. We could, however, specify typefaces, and we chose Myriad and Joanna because of their clean lines and overall legibility; we also designed initial drop capitals for the beginning of each story. The graphics were kept simple to accommodate the variety of user screens. We had a staff on site to help photo editors with the placement of the work.

The templates were not constructed as conventional pages, but were instead created so stories could be long or short with many or few photographs. At the beginning of the project, some editors suggested there be double columns – a recommendation perfectly plausible just about anywhere else – but in this medium just not relevant because of the scrolling nature of the screen. Another publishing rule that changes once the format becomes digital is the size of the text space, which we had to design and format down to the single pixel in order for the database to parcel it out and for SitePublisher to manipulate it.

We kept the navigational graphics simple to prevent them from competing with the various story layouts. SitePublisher automatically assigned the correct theme banner and footer to each page. All the editors had to worry about was the story.

On the day of the event, the Communications Bill was signed at 11:00 A.M. Eastern Standard Time. Three hours later, the blue ribbon freedom-of-speech campaign was in full swing and the 24 Hours site was already being criticized for not responding quickly enough to the story.

24 Hours in the Future of Business

The 24 Hours in Cyberspace project played out a number of the scenarios that businesses find themselves enacting when they publish and maintain Web sites. Managing and maintaining huge amounts of data is one. Another is that the Internet's real-time features give businesses unprecedented opportunities to instantly publish a message – this requires all aspects of a communication to be carefully thought out. A corollary to instant publication is the immediate response it generates; businesses who aren't used to having their customers talk back to them

The choice of the blue ribbon was inspired by the red HIV/AIDS and yellow POW/MIA ribbons used to show support for these causes: displaying the blue ribbon indicates support for freedom of speech in the electronic world. Some organizations asked that the 24 Hours site be blacked-out as a more radical display of support. Freedom of speech is obviously fundamental to the realization of experiments such as the 24 Hours project; the blue ribbon was quickly inserted in the first letter of the first word on the first page of the Web site.

Visitors List

ON FEBRUARY 8, 1996...

We asked visitors to sign the site's Guestbook. By doing so, they added their names to the walls of our digital cave.

We're still tallying the totals, but at this point, 21,221 people have signed the guestbook! If you were one of these people, thanks for signing!

We asked each person for their age and gender, since we thought it would be interesting to get a snapshot sample of Net surfers that day. Our findings:

- 73% were men
- 27% were women

- 13% were under the age of 20
- 37% were between 21 and 35 years old
- 45% were between 36 and 59 years old
- 3% were older than 60 years old

To see who has visited the site, click on a letter to see those last names:

A B C D E F G H I J K L M N O P Q R S T U V W X Y Z

If you have Netscape Navigator 2.0 and can support Java check out our Project X-RAYS

now have to be prepared to quickly handle the sometimes overwhelming feedback (see sidebar on page 171). Finally, the look and feel of the 24 Hours in Cyberspace project – graphics, type, color, and especially interactive qualities – played an important role in its impact and in the way people interpreted its message.

This project marked the inception of a new media hybrid – essentially a cross between newspaper publishing and broadcasting – one site to many millions instantly. The computing medium allowed editorial choices, pacing ability, and audience participation and response. The publishing model provided a variety of ways for the delivery of the editorial material. Too frequently on computing projects, the content is shaped by technological constraints. On this project, however, it was the other way around – content was the force behind most of the decisions made about equipment, personnel, and the general dynamic of the project. That force represents a hopeful sign that content and technology development are at last coming closer together.

Back to TOC

HTTP ACCESS

GUEST BOOK

www.realaudio.com
www.bluestone.com
www.cyber24.com
www.adobe.com
www.kodak.com
www.netobjects.com
www.nmc.org
www.sun.com
www.illustra.com
www.macromedia.com
www.acme.com
www.pcworld.com
www.realaudio.com
www.bluestone.com
www.cyber24.com
www.adobe.com
www.kodak.com
www.netobjects.com
www.nmc.org
www.sun.com
www.illustra.com
www.macromedia.com
www.acme.com
www.pcworld.com
www.realaudio.com
www.bluestone.com
www.cyber24.com
www.adobe.com
www.kodak.com
www.netobjects.com
www.nmc.org
www.sun.com

John Doe, Denver CO
Jane Doe, San Mateo CA
Chris Doe, Oakland CA
Rick Jones, Manchester England
Paul R, Dorchester, GB
Bill Platz, Dusseldorf
Larry Moe, Wacko TX
Marylou H, Austin FL
Maddy Y, Lexington KY
KP Wong, Sydney, Australia
John Doe, Denver CO
Jane Doe, San Mateo CA
Chris Doe, Oakland CA
Rick Jones, Manchester England
Paul R, Dorchester, GB
Bill Platz, Dusseldorf
Larry Moe, Wacko TX
Marylou H, Austin FL
Maddy Y, Lexington KY
KP Wong, Sydney, Australia
John Doe, Denver CO
Jane Doe, San Mateo CA
Chris Doe, Oakland CA
Rick Jones, Manchester England
Paul R, Dorchester, GB
Bill Platz, Dusseldorf
Larry Moe, Wacko TX
Marylou H, Austin FL
Maddy Y, Lexington KY
KP Wong, Sydney, Australia

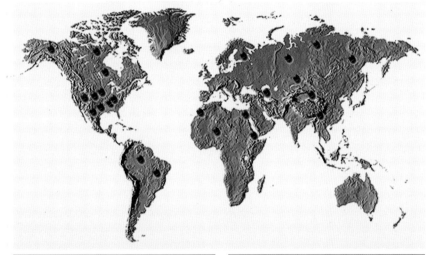

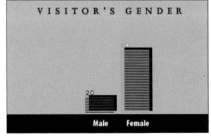

VISITOR'S GENDER

Male   Female

VISITOR'S AGE

-20   21-35   36-45   45-59   60+

*This screen was live on the 24 Hours site and showed a
scrolling list of visitors and their point of origin.*

Television on Your Computer

National Broadcasting Company – Intercast _____

Intercast technology merges the Internet with broadcast television. Broadcasters can use it to transmit digital information – like Web pages and e-mail – along with an analog television signal. It lets viewers get more out of television by making it possible to view television programming and use the Internet at the same time, in different windows on the same computer screen. To receive Intercast signals, which are transmitted in the same way as televised signals, a viewer needs an Intercast-enabled computer. After Intel initiated the Intercast project, it was joined by Viacom/Paramount, NBC, and Turner Broadcasting. Each partner had a vested interest in making Intercast an accepted technology; the consortium's goal was to create a broadly accepted, open system that would make possible rapid, industry-wide implementation.

Intercast technology makes possible an array of fantastic features, showing the power of the convergence of the Internet and broadcasting. Customer communication and business models are different in each medium, though, and Intercast technology introduced a bewildering mix of both. The Intercast consortium needed an effective way to get the attention of potential investors and content providers.

Intercast technology is based on content programming and computer code programming; each has distinct modes of operation. What, we asked, could happen when television content and Web-like content appeared together on one screen? How could we design Intercast applications that would be the basis for a valid business proposition and a solid communication structure?

BUSINESS GOAL
The Intercast consortium wanted a way to show potential content providers, partners, and the press what Intercasting was and how it could work, and why Intercast was a viable business proposition.

DESIGN CHALLENGE
The design challenge was to visualize the deployment of the technology and create examples of its applications that would make it real for people.

TECHNOLOGY MANDATE
The technology mandate was to show that Intercast could work.

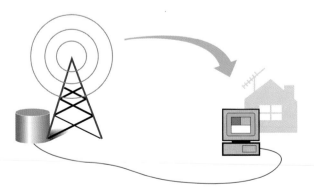

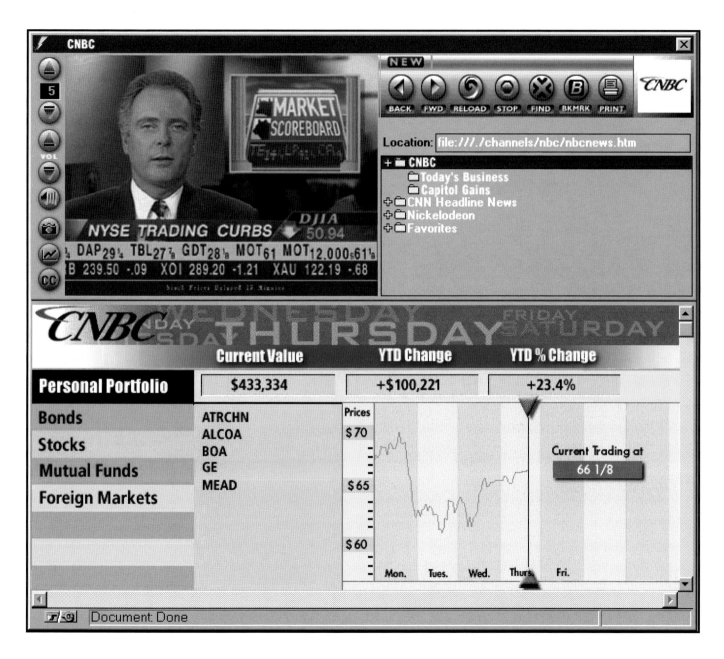

CNBC displays the concept of mass customization with the Intercast technology. The user can set up his or her own financial portfolio and determine what kind of data he or she wants, and in which order it is received.

Technology or media-focused businesses are usually developed in three sequential stages: technology, then product, then market development. Generally, a certain amount of technological activity must take place before the other stages can begin. In the case of the business of interactive television, for instance, a considerable amount of underlying enabling technology was already available, such as cable networks and fiber optic systems.

In the same vein, it wasn't long after personal computers became prevalent that the idea for putting television content on the computer moved into the product phase. The business goal of the Intercast consortium was to take the technology into the marketplace by making its development a viable business proposition. Because Intercast's backers have means and influence, they could kick-start the market and front its development.

To design the look and feel of the screens, the different scenarios, and the applications, we had to understand the broadcasting medium – how a signal gets to its destination and how much control can be exerted over it. Intercast technology is based on an Intel chip that lets broadcasters send digital data through the VBI channel, the same band used to transmit closed captions such as sign language translation. When a viewer turns on the computer and sets it to television mode, the computer acts like a television. When the viewer changes to Intercast mode, HTML-formatted information streams in through the VBI channel and shows up in another window on the screen as Web pages.

Our task was to discover how the two modes – linear television narrative and the highly interactive environment of the Internet – could cohabit the same space without confusing users. We used "what if?" scenarios to insinuate possibilities, a technique used at Apple during the development of the HyperCard technology to imagine and plan real-life circumstances. (It wasn't long after HyperCard's launch that some of these dream scenarios became real services.) Marrying a little futurist thought with real situations is a good way to explore the possibilities of technology. What if a viewer could watch an Intercast cooking show? What if the viewer could

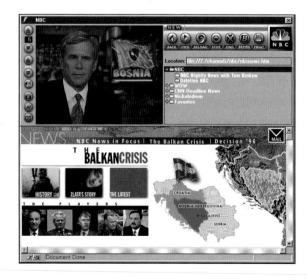

The "Tonight Show" is a promotion showcase for movies, books, videos, and music CDs. We showed how the Intercast medium could supply a merchandising supplement to television programming, offering direct product ordering from a television show or commercial.

While watching this television drama, a viewer could try to solve the mystery before the show is over. This application showed how the Intercast medium could extend the narrative in television programming and build another level of storytelling.

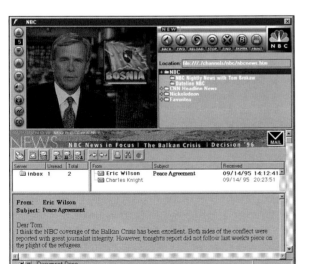

The three screens on the left show how Web content and the Internet's interactivity could supplement television programming such as a news program.

print out the recipes that Julia Child was preparing on screen by clicking on a button? What if the viewer could download a digital video version for future reference?

Our prototype applications included business applications, entertainment, and drama. The "NBC Nightly News" application depicted news show host Tom Brokaw reporting on a political crisis in Bosnia. On the same screen, our Intercast interface allowed a viewer who wanted an update on Bosnia's current boundaries or background information on the crisis to call up a customized Web site. It also allowed a viewer to send Tom Brokaw an e-mail message about his coverage of the issue.

What if, we asked, a viewer of a business program could not only browse through a financial magazine supplement on the Web, but could update a stock portfolio or find its current value?

The Intercast medium would have no set format, so interactivity could vary from program to program, adapting to each program's format. What if, while watching Bryant Gumbel interviewing the surgeon general on "Today" about nascent viral infections, viewers could go to the Centers for Disease Control Web site to check whether Gumbel had done his homework? What if viewers could take advantage of bargains advertised during commercials by printing out coupons on the spot? That kind of inventive approach to business propositions may be relatively new, but it isn't far-fetched to say that some of these scenarios will produce models for viable businesses.

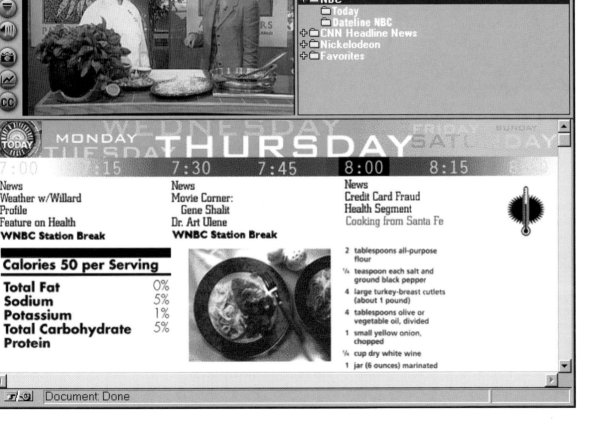

In this application, viewers can browse through and print recipes for dishes being prepared on a cooking show. This scenario shows the importance of real time as an aspect of combining television and the Internet. It also shows why television on the computer makes more sense than a computer on television: television cannot produce a printout.

Interface or Identity?

This online project brought together the disciplines of information, identity, and interactivity design by addressing identity design within an information system with set interaction parameters. We began the project by evaluating it on the basis of guidelines in a two-page brief from Microsoft. This initial evaluation normally would have taken considerable time and been part of the definition stage of the design process, but on this project it was necessary to complete the evaluation before we won the account. Although the project was presented as a question of interface design only, as we continued to analyze Microsoft's request for proposal, we determined that the primary challenge was to solve a *branding* problem through *interface* design. In addition, the project had to stay within the interactivity parameters of the Windows 95 operating system.

Preliminaries

Microsoft's online service was to establish the company in the online marketplace as a global service provider offering a wide range of PC industry and general consumer content and services. What was the competition? America Online, certainly, and the Internet also was a competitor for online content and services. When we started on the project (which Microsoft had code-named Marvel), Microsoft was a

MSN™ *The Microsoft Network* ——————————————

Microsoft® is the world's largest software company. Until recently, its focus was on creating software for computer operating systems and electronic productivity software applications such as Microsoft® Word and Microsoft® Excel. CD-ROM titles such as Microsoft Encarta® and The Microsoft Art Gallery™ marked an expansion into the publishing arena, and a recent corporate reorganization produced an Internet division as well as MSN, The Microsoft Network – the online service described here.

BUSINESS GOALS
With The Microsoft Network, Microsoft wanted to create a distribution vehicle for reaching new audiences, as well as a way to support future service and business endeavors.

TECHNOLOGY MANDATE
The technology mandate was to make Microsoft's online service a transparent extension of the Windows 95™ operating system, from the perspective of both technical and functional performance.

DESIGN CHALLENGES
Orchestrate the evolution of the company's product sector image into an online service.

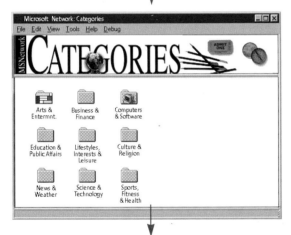

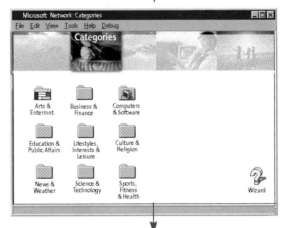

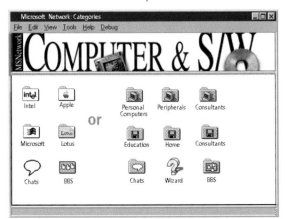

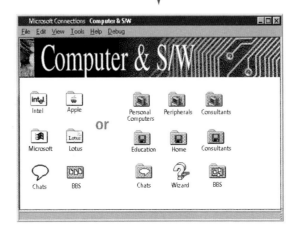

The screens in the two columns here are two initial concept presentations of The Microsoft Network (at first code-named Marvel) interface; the top screens are main menus, and the second and third screens are from different main sections of the service.

The GUI shown in the column on the left takes its cue from corporate identity and the identity of Microsoft's product line – it incorporates the comfortable look of Microsoft's packaging and advertising, with its familiar typography and all-white background. Its look incorporates a literal interpretation of the service's functions: it depicts e-mail functions with a letterbox, varied categories of service with an apple and an orange.

The GUI shown in the column on the right, on the other hand, depicts not the service's functionality but a collection of moods. The GUI conveys a look driven less by corporate identity than by the characteristics of typical future Microsoft Network subscribers and by the service's benefits. When service sector companies create brands and image, they don't come right out and say "We also sell flowers" or "We also sell chairs;" instead, they emphasize the value of their products and the ways in which that value can enhance customers' lives. The L.L. Bean brand, and the imagery in its catalogs, for instance, projects a distinctive value system and lifestyle.

The designs of the screens for the main sections were restricted to a banner area at the top of the screen. (These comparatively elaborate GUIs were proposed before the 10K restriction on banner graphics was imposed.)

This identity organization schema indicates each category's depth and its location within the structure of the service. We worked out this macro view to understand ways in which the Microsoft identity could coexist with the identities of third-party vendors residing in the service. The schema identified the third-party issues that Microsoft had to contend with and helped Microsoft make sure that third-party branding was a value-added proposition.

Engineers define identity in terms of information architecture and the way code is built – in other words, as the relationships between screens, and how one screen leads to the screens that follow. The schema shows the project's structural underpinnings – how its identity structure was nested within the information structure, which in turn was nested in the project's technology structure.

Sub-category

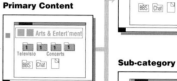

Primary Content

The identity bands for Primary Content Categories include a Service Category identity element (e.g. Categories) and feature an identity element for the Primary Content Category (e.g. Arts & Entertainment). The folder, BBS, chat, and document icons are in the Primary Content Category style. Sub-categories are identified by the name under the file.

Sub-category

Third-Party Information Provider

A third-party information provider screen is identified by a third-party branding band. The branding band must include an identity element for the Sub-category, (e.g. Television) be a specific size, and fit in a specific area. Beyond these guidelines, the third party can determine how the band identifies their brand.

The branding band is downloaded from the server as a metafile.

The third-party has two options for folder, BBS, chat, and document icons:
1. They can use the Primary Content Category set of icons.
2. They can create their own.

Icons must be applied consistently within the the third-party area. For example, MTV can have a unique chat icon, but all MTV chats must use it. Each MTV chat can't have its own chat icon.

Icons are downloaded from the server as bitmaps.

Sub-categories identity bands include a Primary Content Category element (e.g. Arts & Entertainment) and feature an identity element for the sub-category (e.g. Television).

Third-party brands are identified by unique icons on a standard folder.

Primary Content

Each Primary Content Category has its own identity band and icon style. The icons are used throughout the category.

Service Category

All Service Categories have an identity band that includes the MSN brand identity and features an identity element for the Service Category. Under the category, *Categories*, the user can access the nine Primary Content Categories. At that level, consistent with the Windows convention, each category is represented by a unique icon on a Windows folder. This icon establishes the style for a set of icons for each Primary Content Category.

The category identity bands and all icons are downloaded from the server as bitmaps.

Service Category

At the Service Category level, and below, the user can access sub-categories, bulletin board services (BBSs), chats, and documents. Each is represented by a folder or icon. Sub-categories will have unique icons on their folders. BBSs and chats will use a standard MSN icon either on a folder, when the icon represents a group of BBSs or chats, or separately when the icon represents a single BBS or chat.

Splash

The Splash screen introduces the user to the Microsoft Network (MSN) brand identity and reinforces the Microsoft and Windows 95 identities. MSN's optimum window size of 512 x 384 pixels allows the user to have easy access to the standard desktop icons and tool bar. The MSN identity is displayed on the desktop as an icon. The Windows 95 identity is displayed on the desktop Tool Bar.

The Splash screen graphic is stored on the client as a bitmap.

Log-On/Off

The Log-On/Off screen reinforces the Microsoft and MSN brand identities. The Title Bar at the top of the screen displays the MSN icon and the Microsoft Network name. This Windows 95 convention will serve as a consistent identity element throughout the product.

The Log-On/Off screen graphic is stored on the client as a bitmap.

Home Base

The Home Base screen continues to reinforce the Microsoft and MSN identities and introduces identity elements for each of the five Sevice Categories. The categories are:
• Categories
• What's New
• Electronic Mail
• Member Services
• Favorite Places

The Log-On/Off screen graphic is stored on the client as a bitmap.

Key to Branding and Identity Elements

▪ Microsoft Branding Element

▪ MSN Branding Element

▪ Windows 95 Branding

▪ A Service Category Identity

▪ A Primary Content Category Identity

▪ A Sub-category Identity

▪ A Third-Party Information Provider Branding

Splash Screen   **Sign-On**   **Home Base**   **Service Category**   **Primary Content**

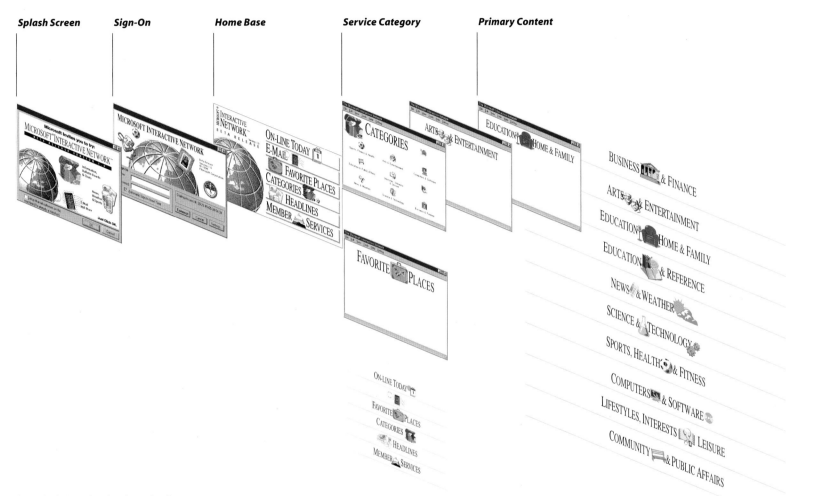

This graphical schema shows how the interface design
(left) was carried through part of the service for the pre-
beta release. At release, sub-category and third-party
information provider sections had not been put in place.

Eight-bit color palette
(256 colors)

Four-bit color palette
(16 colors)

software company that produced applications and titles. With Marvel, it would spread into the service sector, a extension that would fundamentally change the perception of Microsoft as a company and make it necessary for Microsoft to reconsider its established identity.

The way we developed the GUI for Marvel would have a direct impact on Microsoft's corporate identity. That gave us much to consider: once the Windows 95 operating system was released, the elements of Microsoft's identity would include the Microsoft logo and tag line, the Windows 95 operating system logo, and the distinctive look of the operating system's GUI. Just as the smiling face in the Mac OS logo evoked the personality of Apple as a company, the no-nonsense character of the Windows 95 GUI would help identify Microsoft as a company for Everyman (or Everywoman). Microsoft wanted the service to exemplify the idea that Microsoft was "the place to go for information." But just what did that mean? Was Microsoft really the place to go, or was it the Windows-platform that enables one to go places?

Functionality and performance, as well as GUI design, also play an important role in identity. How did these identity components apply to a service business? Microsoft products have virtual emissaries called wizards; users familiar with the Windows environment are familiar with the concept of valets, or

The way we addressed color (see Pre-Release Issues on pages 189 and 193) is an example of why design solutions can require a firm grasp of a computer's workings. We experimented first with bit depth. The images here (left and facing page) show the results of tests we performed by converting images from an eight-bit color palette to a four-bit palette. The black-and-white image translated well, as did the images with high contrast.

The images in the pastel spectrum, however, did not fare as well in the test, and flesh tones are notoriously difficult to express in four-bit color. The images in the more "literal" depiction of categories (see the left column on page 181) could be easily rendered as illustrations, which would fall within a four-bit color palette and a 10K file size. The other interface, however, conveyed moods that demanded a photographic approach. The results of the test led us

to examine the possibility of creating illustrations with a photographic feeling. We eventually found an illustrator whose style was photo-realistic and who also could execute work in sixteen colors. Our solution greatly affected the look of the interface; the final results are shown on page 192.

Bitmapped images index-colored to a eight-bit color palette (256 colors).

Bitmapped images index-colored to a four-bit color palette (16 colors).

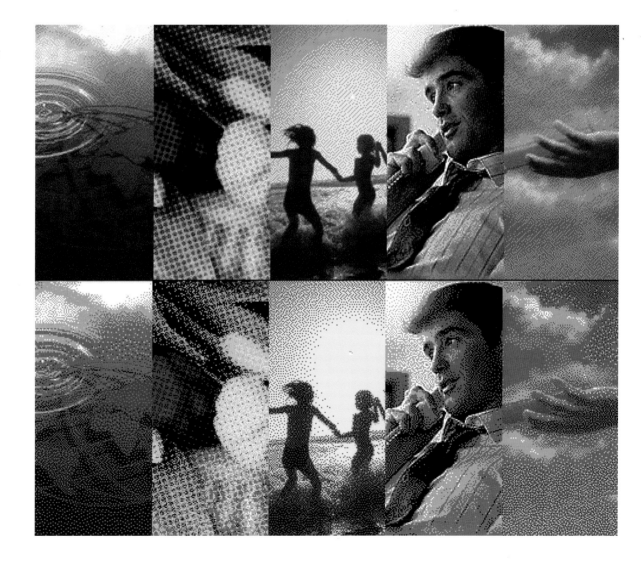

agents, that find and filter information and lead the user through complex processes. Wizards themselves have a distinct look and feel, which we had to consider as we designed the overall look and feel of the service.

Should Marvel's brand identity focus not on functionality and performance but on benefits? In the product world, ads for jeans and perfume don't focus on functionality; they're directed at those products' benefits, on the results of using them, on how those products affect and reflect people's lifestyles. Was that the way to approach a service brand, too?

We also considered the question of the appropriate distance between the service brand and the corporate brand. Because of the close relationship between Microsoft's company identity and the product identity of the Windows 95 operating system, one way to gauge that distance was to analyze the relationship between Marvel and Windows 95. What were the differences in their interface requirements? We began to explore two alternative GUIs in terms of branding: one was focused on Microsoft the company, with a look similar to the Windows 95 operating system; and another was focused on the service, with a look that distanced it from the

This exercise in counting syllables helped us make naming recommendations for the service. People have a strong tendency to nickname expressions with more than a few syllables; even though "Microsoft Word" is only two words, people still shorten it to "Word." People would certainly coin some short form of a long name like "The Microsoft Interactive Network." We suggested that Microsoft take the reins and do the coining itself – which it did, settling on "MSN."

the‑mi‑cro‑soft‑in‑ter‑ac‑tive‑net‑work
❶ ❷ ❸ ❹ ❺ ❻ ❼ ❽ ❾ ❿

mi‑cro‑soft‑in‑ter‑ac‑tive
❶ ❷ ❸ ❹ ❺ ❻ ❼

mi‑cro‑soft‑net‑work
❶ ❷ ❸ ❹ ❺

e‑world
❶ ❷

What constitutes the identity system of online services? The first three thumbnails show how we looked at the ways other online services (America Online, e-World, CompuServe; right, top to bottom) depicted themselves on screen. We also examined the consistency in the way other software companies (such as Adobe; far right, top) and Microsoft (far right, middle) expressed their brands not only on the computer but through other media, in magazine ads, on television commercials, and on packaging. Finally, we examined the individual components of Microsoft's system and how they related to other Microsoft products (far right, bottom). The thumbnail compares the iconography and depictions of drives and directories in the Windows 95 environment with The Microsoft Network GUI.

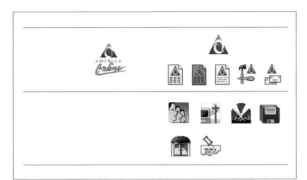

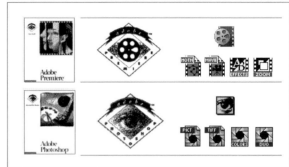

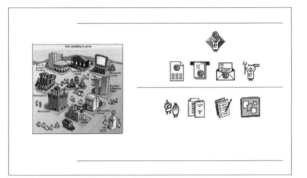

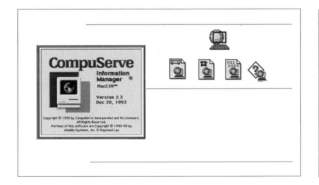

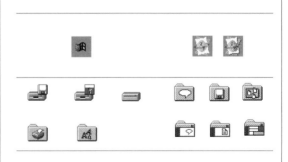

Pre-beta release. November 1994 —four-bit color. The GUI for the beta release of The Microsoft Network was based on many of the elements of Microsoft's established identity. Microsoft's advertising agency was still working on an identity for the service when this GUI was developed. We took a practical approach of leveraging the identity equity that Microsoft had built instead of bringing a different identity and voice into the ring.

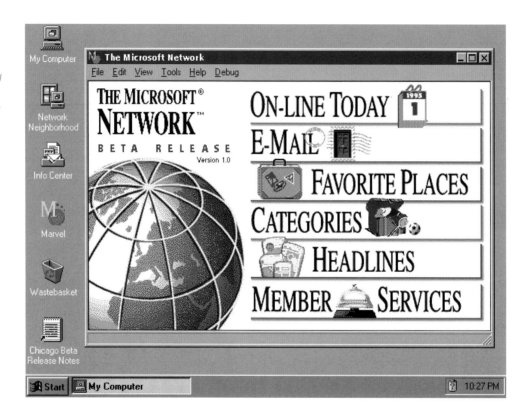

company identity. In developing either alternative, we had to take into account that the service didn't yet have a name; Microsoft's advertising agency was still developing an identity for it.

Third-Party Brands

Another identity consideration was the depiction of the brands of all of Marvel's content providers. Third-party branding was unfamiliar in the Windows environment, and it was an identity issue that required some examination. At what point should Microsoft's identity recede into the background? Should it disappear altogether? The answers to these questions determined icon placement and Marvel's visual conventions. Part of the design problem was building an identity system and structure for The Microsoft Network that could accommodate any other brand without letting users forget that they were using Microsoft's service. That aspect of branding, as it turned out, was so closely related to navigation that we essentially had to treat identity and navigation as a single design issue.

Pre-Release Issues

Microsoft wanted its service to be "user friendly, global, credible, immediate, old, new"; it wanted the service to offer "grounded, inviting destinations, communities, and meeting places." It wanted users to feel drawn in by a familiar kind of atmosphere, as if they were spending time in their grandfather's house in the country; it wanted users to feel nostalgia for someplace they had never been. How should those ideas manifest themselves on the splash screen, log-on screen, main menu, and throughout the interface for The Microsoft Network? Once we had succeeded in portraying the sum of those concepts in the look of the interface's introductory screens, we carried aspects of the look into other parts of the interface, creating a visual vocabulary for the service (see page 183).

Sometime before the beta release, approximately six weeks after the start of the project, Microsoft made several major decisions affecting The Microsoft Network's identity and interface. The service acquired a real name, MSN, The Microsoft Network, and Microsoft launched the "Where do you want to go today?"™ campaign. Microsoft's visual style changed – new typeface, a new photographic style. This meant that the graphic style of the interface also needed to change while carrying through the same concept.

Another major change concerned the technical issue of bit depth. On the grounds of faster performance, Microsoft had initially specified that images in the pre-beta interface be restricted to four-bit color. The advantage of four-bit graphics is

Splash Screen

Sign-On

**Select
Dial-Up Number**

Registration

Security

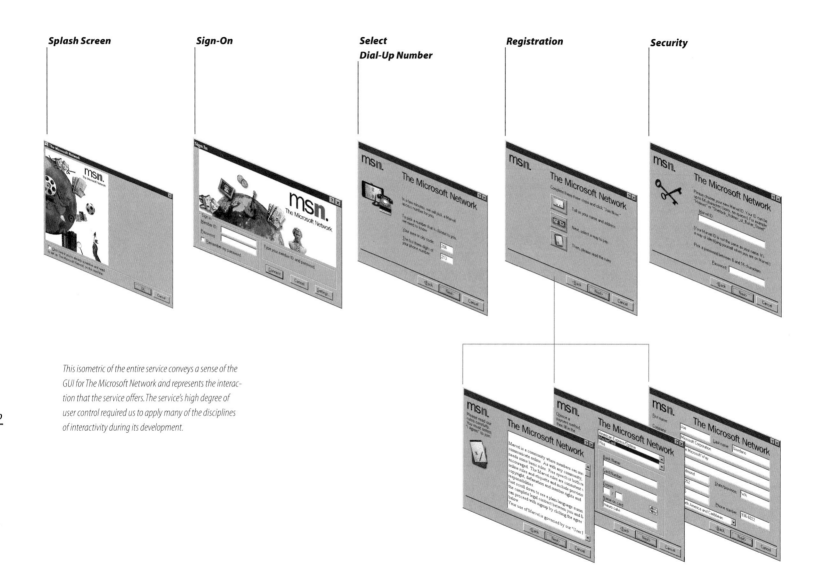

*This isometric of the entire service conveys a sense of the
GUI for The Microsoft Network and represents the interaction that the service offers. The service's high degree of
user control required us to apply many of the disciplines
of interactivity during its development.*

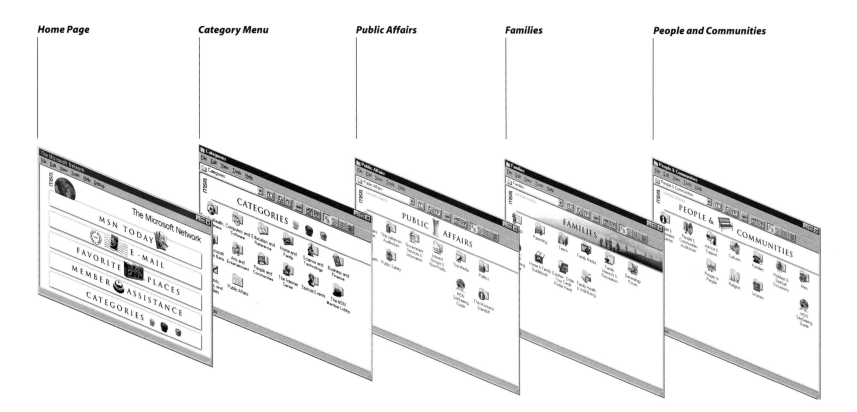

Home Page *Category Menu* *Public Affairs* *Families* *People and Communities*

The Microsoft Network

MSN TODAY

E - MAIL

FAVORITE PLACES

MEMBER  ASSISTANCE

CATEGORIES

*Beta release and
final release using
eight-bit color.*

that their file sizes are smaller than those of eight-bit graphics and travel much more quickly over most telephone networks. The advantage of using eight-bit graphics is that they can carry a much broader range of color information; photographic images cannot be displayed effectively as four-bit graphics. By the time of the beta release, however, the other major online services were moving toward eight-bit color, and it was no longer appropriate to launch a new service using a technology that Microsoft's competitors were abandoning. However, the file size restriction of 10K for banner graphics meant finding creative ways to maintain the image quality that Microsoft was looking for. We also needed to keep the four-bit color format in mind as we developed icons and symbols.

Microsoft asked us to go ahead with our concept of a "literal" look (see page 181). To preserve the photographic look of the graphics while meeting technical requirements, we brought on an illustrator with a realistic style and executed with sixteen colors. Keeping enough of the warmth of the images derived from the concept was a tremendous effort but a successful one.

Marvel, Beta, and the Final Interface

Changing technical and identity parameters midway through product development is not an ideal scenario to work within. We moved forward with the four-bit graphics and the existing Microsoft identity as the working premise for the pre-beta release. Microsoft released the pre-beta version of The Microsoft Network six weeks after the first initial project briefing. Six weeks later, we were asked to adapt the interface for an eight-bit color application incorporating the new corporate and service identities. Again, the adaptation was not easy because of the technical constraints of the 10K graphics files. The graphical user interface for the beta release (left) was completed in January 1995 and distributed in March 1995 and the adapted design utilizing photographic images ultimately became the final graphical user interface for the network.

iQVC ———————————————————————————

QVC's pioneering cable television retailing service has made its name synonymous with televised shopping. QVC's success results from consistent quality, value, and convenience. Open 24 hours a day, 364 days a year, QVC posts sales that define the industry benchmark: one offering of Packard Bell Pentium machines brought in close to $5 million in one hour. Few companies provide a more efficient shipping and tracking service, or have such a convenient return procedure.

BUSINESS GOALS

QVC wanted to extend its brand and expand its customer base by offering its service through The Microsoft Network and eventually over the Internet and Intercast.

TECHNOLOGY MANDATE

To do business online without having to retrench every time a new delivery option became available.

DESIGN CHALLENGE

To design an interface that could remain consistent and sustain QVC's visual appeal both on The Microsoft Network and in other online environments.

Go Figure

QVC made its initial step toward extending its cable television retailing service to the online market by putting its service on The Microsoft Network. As that online service's first large retail merchant, QVC expected its online shopping service, iQVC, to immediately establish itself as *the* place to shop on The Microsoft Network. QVC came to us with an extensive, detailed plan containing its wish list for iQVC and ideas for deploying it on The Microsoft Network. We knew that applying the same features to the Internet version of the interface would be a monumental task because of the dramatic differences between The Microsoft Network and the Internet, in terms of both their GUIs and their technological underpinnings. Mechanisms that are easy to put in place on one system are virtually impossible to implement on the other. Nevertheless, to sustain

Designer's note. The iD System™ is the way we protect our intellectual property, which are proprietary processes and methodologies we invented to work through the DADI system (see pages 54–59). The trademark helps distinguish the techniques we employ on projects from its deliverables.

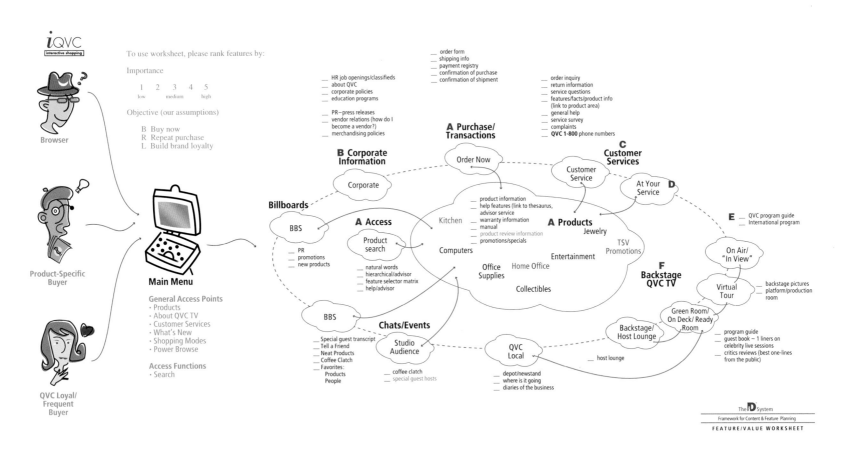

iQVC
interactive shopping

Browser

Product-Specific Buyer

QVC Loyal/ Frequent Buyer

To use worksheet, please rank features by:

Importance

1 2 3 4 5
low   medium   high

Objective (our assumptions)

B Buy now
R Repeat purchase
L Build brand loyalty

Main Menu

General Access Points
· Products
· About QVC TV
· Customer Services
· What's New
· Shopping Modes
· Power Browse

Access Functions
· Search

__ HR job openings/classifieds
__ about QVC
__ corporate policies
__ education programs

__ PR–press releases
__ vendor relations (how do I become a vendor?)
__ merchandising policies

__ order form
__ shipping info
__ payment registry
__ confirmation of purchase
__ confirmation of shipment

__ order inquiry
__ return information
__ service questions
__ features/facts/product info (link to product area)
__ general help
__ service survey
__ complaints
QVC 1-800 phone numbers

A Purchase/ Transactions

B Corporate Information

C Customer Services

Order Now

Corporate

Customer Service

At Your Service **D**

Billboards

BBS

A Access

Kitchen

__ product information
__ help features (link to thesaurus, advisor service
__ warranty information
__ manual
__ product review information
__ promotions/specials

A Products

Jewelry

E __ QVC program guide
__ International program

Product search

__ PR
__ promotions
__ new products

Computers

__ natural words
__ hierarchical/advisor
__ feature selector matrix
__ help/advisor

TSV Promotions

Entertainment

Office Supplies

Home Office

Collectibles

F Backstage QVC TV

On Air/ "In View"

Virtual Tour

__ backstage pictures
__ platform/production room

BBS

Chats/Events

Studio Audience

__ Special guest transcript
__ Tell a Friend
__ Neat Products
__ Coffee Clatch
__ Favorites: Products People

__ coffee clatch
__ special guest hosts

QVC Local

Backstage/ Host Lounge

Green Room/ On Deck/ Ready Room

__ host lounge

__ program guide
__ guest book – 1 liners on celebrity live sessions
__ critics reviews (best one-lines from the public)

__ depot/newstand
__ where is it going
__ diaries of the business

The **D** System
Framework for Content & Feature Planning
FEATURE/VALUE WORKSHEET

This bubble diagram is our assessment of the features and content of QVC's service. We used it to determine iQVC's possible functions, which we then asked QVC to prioritize. We also used the diagram as a worksheet in two ways: to facilitate group discussion with QVC and the programmer, and to set internal priorities before the service's release.

QVC's identity and visual appeal, it was imperative for us to design an adaptable, scalable, and flexible interface.

Although QVC's wish list was long, the service's development cycle was short, so we had to find a quick way to define what features were possible and which of those were critical to the service's success. First, we worked with QVC to group activities into categories. Then, by clustering the activities on a bubble diagram, we essentially translated QVC's wish list into spatial form (page 195). We asked QVC to rate the importance of each cluster, and the activities within each cluster, on a scale from one to five. After tabulating the rating, we determined which functions were technologically simple or complex. Finally, we did another layer of prioritizing to compare the ease or difficulty of implementing each function on The Microsoft Network and the Internet. The bubble diagram served as a communication link throughout the project.

Now the big picture emerged – we could see what the interface should emphasize and how it should work. Just as an architect uses a master plan to lay out spaces and orchestrate traffic patterns in a building, we used the bubble diagram (and later, information mapping; see page 198) to plan and develop the functions that defined iQVC. (A common way to establish priorities is to look at what clients list as important in their request for proposal, but in the past, that approach quickly led us off track.)

People who are used to the Windows environment are comfortable with its folders-and-lists setup. The way users get at information in the Web's page-based system, on the other hand, follows a completely different path, and the Web's interface accommodates a huge variety of look-and-feel effects. In the physical world, shopping – whether it's in a store, on television, or from a catalog – is an immersive experience. An environment full of folders and lists just isn't conducive to the kind of stimulating shopping atmosphere that is so important to QVC's image. It was clear that we had to add an interface on top of The Microsoft Network (MSN) that would allow for rich graphics. Using the bubble diagram to communicate the issues that confronted us, we turned to a software developer who specializes in multimedia applications on The Microsoft Network. The developer created a custom application using MediaView, a proprietary format on MSN, for iQVC.

The MediaView authoring environment has parameters that are different from MSN's and the Web's, and the interface we designed had to accommodate the characteristics of all three. On the Web, for example, screen sizes can vary; on The Microsoft Network, they don't.

The Intercast version of the project didn't require a different Web *interface*. However, in the

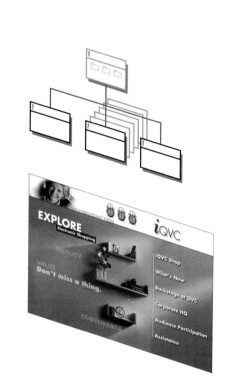

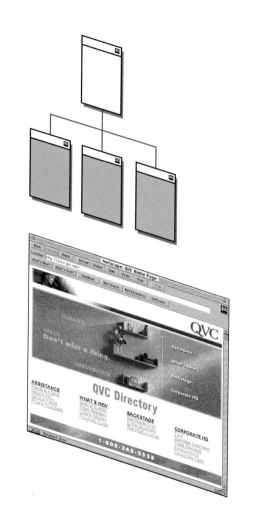

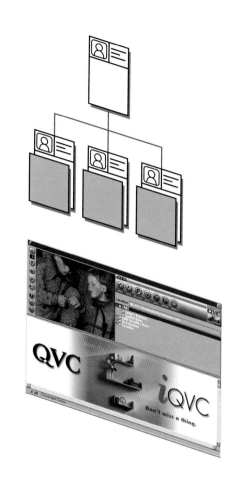

Left to right: The iQVC interfaces for The Microsoft Network, the Web, and Intercast, along with the structures that support them to show what goes on behind the scenes in each interface. A graphical schema goes hand in hand with a structural one. The Microsoft Network schema shows the relationship of the custom MediaView application, which made it possible to give The Microsoft Network version of the service its graphic appeal, to The Microsoft Network structure.

Shown here are the paths that Microsoft Network subscribers can take to browse through iQVC, get detailed information about products, and put the items they select in a "shopping cart." The steps involved in ordering products were kept as minimal as possible.

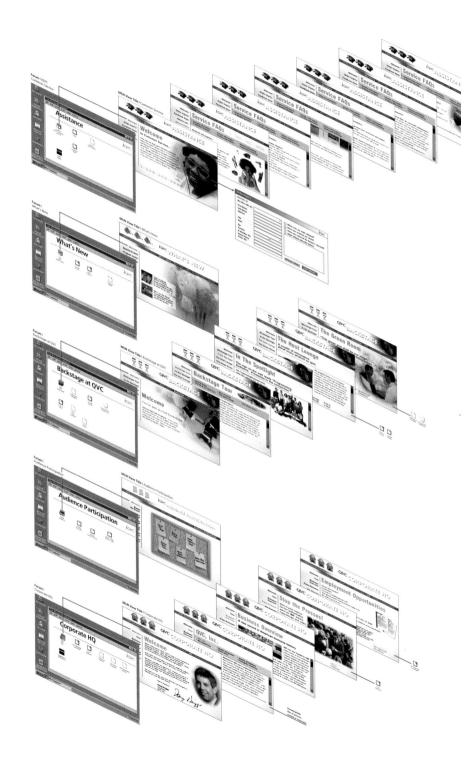

This map of a small part of The Microsoft Network version of iQVC shows the breadth and depth of the service and the overall look of the interface. On this project, because our focus was on taking the feel of QVC's cable service and translating it into online environments, feel – the service's structure and the relationships among its parts – came before look.

context of Intercast, Web *content* would need to provide interactivity that complemented the cable channel. The cable broadcast, being linear, could only be used to promote one "hot item" at a time. The Web window, on the other hand, could show links to all the current promotions at once, giving customers access to more iQVC promotions in less time.

Another important interface design consideration was the transaction process. QVC is known for the speed, quality, and efficiency of its ordering system, so we paralleled QVC's established procedure in iQVC's ordering process. There are no time constraints in the computer environment, and for iQVC shoppers the service's main benefit is its customized, instantaneous responses. That meant that iQVC's service had to be as good as, if not better than, QVC's toll-free phone service. QVC customers are used to instant purchase gratification: – "I want that product, I'm going to order it now" – getting that same kind of confirmation shouldn't take longer than a few mouse clicks. The design challenge was not so much in the interface's look as in its performance.

Once we understood how iQVC would be organized, we could begin working out a graphic design that would show off the products the service advertised. At the same time, because QVC's promotions continue only as long as supplies last, it was important to standardize the graphics so that iQVC personnel could load and change the graphics quickly and easily on all of the interfaces.

The drawers and cubbyholes in the Main Categories
screen of The Microsoft Network version of iQVC
are part of a flexible design that makes the interface
adaptable to new and seasonal promotions, just
like a storefront. It's important for the interfaces
of retail online services to allow merchants to use
established merchandising techniques.

Sony New Technology _____

Sony Corporation of America is a leading manufacturer of audio and video hardware as well as one of the world's most comprehensive entertainment companies. Headquartered in New York City, Sony Corporation of America has holdings in electronics, software companies, music, motion pictures, television, and retail entertainment, and develops location-based entertainment centers.

BUSINESS GOALS
Sony wanted to create the equivalent of the World's Fair or Disneyland (also known as location-based entertainment) on the Internet. The goal was to use that initiative to bring the world of Sony under one umbrella, building brand and extending market reach.

DESIGN CHALLENGE
To create an interactive concept sketch of a three-dimensional environment in a two-dimensional screen-based medium – an environment that would absorb users' attention, a kind of gateway into the fantastic world of Sony products and entertainment.

TECHNOLOGY MANDATE
To temporarily suspend awareness of technological limitations while brainstorming about the destination's look and feel.

A Place Imagined

"In the past, Sony's business was very easy because there was a product, there was a tactile feel, there was image created by the product itself. Now we must create experiences, touch people and form an image of Sony as a company in a different manner." That's how Sony executives described the change in direction that Sony envisioned for its businesses.

Creating new experiences and relationships between customers and products is a constant challenge for any company. For decades, companies have been leveraging their brand identities or properties into new products and services, merchandising everything from Shirley Temple dolls to Coca-Cola clothing. More recently, companies have opened retail theme stores that extend their identities into environmental spaces and convert their stories, titles, movies, and other soft media into new businesses. Nike Town and the Time Warner stores are two great examples of this phenomenon, each proving to be wildly successful in helping these companies extend their brands and reach new customers. In the future, more and more companies will extend these concepts by integrating entertainment, information, and consumer transactions into a single environment.

Sony's businesses are media intensive and it's fitting that they actively pursue the integration of entertainment, information, and consumer products and services. They have already begun by developing location-based entertainment centers. These centers are vehicles for bringing its huge diversity of business franchises – encompassing hardware, software, movies, television, and music – under one roof. The objective of these retail entertainment centers is to bring together retail entertainment like theaters and video arcades with merchandising, resulting in a social focal point that showcases Sony products. The first of these centers, in Lincoln Center in New York City, embodies a small part of the location-based entertainment concept. It has thirteen theaters equipped with state-of-the-art technology, including a nine-story-high Imax theater in which viewers wear 3-D goggles while watching Sony-produced movies.

Sony's eventual goal for location-based entertainment is to turn retail transactions into theatrical experiences, engaging people in the act of purchasing electronics or sports equipment as if they were part of a story. That concept is the non-virtual version of what we were asked to envision. Our task was to imagine incarnations of a cyber-theme park – location-based entertainment on the Web.

We started by considering why such places exist. Exactly why do people spend their time and money in entertainment centers and how could we provide people with the same kind of experience in the digital world? How are themes created, and what kinds of themes would tie into Sony's brand and image?

The parameters Sony gave us were gathered in an informal meeting. Sony wanted visitors to see every attraction at a glance as if they were at the World's Fair, but it did not want the destination to have an old-fashioned atmosphere or look like e-world. Sony also wanted the destination's theme to appeal to a wide audience, from ten-year-olds entranced by the hip and cool and the cutting edge of technology to mom and pop.

On that basis, we developed three possible navigation models for the project, each allowing visitors to approach the destination from a different perspective. (See the diagrams to the right.) From our diagrams and sketches, Sony chose a combination of two of the models, landscape and panoramic, to develop into storyboards and eventually a prototype.

We developed a theme in tandem with the navigation models and storyboards. Deducing that any theme for the project needed to fall somewhere between a realistic environment – which could easily appear trendy or dated – and a completely "made-up" or synthetic one, we developed a theme that included a little of both.

In the prototype (a Director movie), a visitor approaches the park from a bird's-eye view, as if from a plane. After navigating closer, a visitor finds himself or herself inside the park, surrounded by the objects in it (following the panoramic navigation model). The prototype shows a Central Park filled with oversized flying objects (a giant container of popcorn, a soccer ball the size of a tree, a "media shower" of other objects) that are gateways to the attractions beyond – Sony's music, electronics, and other products. The surreality of the objects lent a fantastical feeling to the environment, while the Central Park theme made the surroundings familiar enough that visitors didn't feel disoriented. A video agent accompanied visitors and guided them through the park.

The prototype gave Sony executives a way to grasp the possibilities of our incarnation of the project, some of the most inventive work our studio has produced.

Below: A completely synthetic GUI, obviously pixeled and rendered so it has no references to the real world whatsoever. Instead of the user being in the center of the universe and looking around, he or she steps from the center into one of these places.

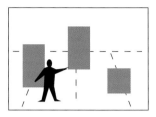

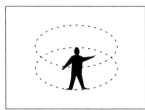

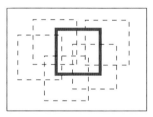

These diagrams show the three navigation models we presented to Sony. Storyboards of each model demonstrated how each structure would appear to visitors. The center diagram shows the structure of the environment in which the panoramic model envelops the user.

Herman Miller, Inc.

Herman Miller has specialized in contract furnishings, furniture, and furniture systems for offices and other workplaces for over seventy years. The company's success is based on a combination of adherence to sound business practices and enthusiastic acceptance of new ideas. Herman Miller's designers have included Charles and Ray Eames; the company's continuing reputation for high-quality products is extraordinary.

BUSINESS GOALS

Herman Miller needed an innovative informational and graphical presentation for use in launching a new product, the Aeron® chair.

DESIGN CHALLENGES

The design challenge was to convey the uniqueness of the chair and the extensive research behind its design and development.

TECHNOLOGY MANDATE

Herman Miller gave us no technological mandate; it was up to us to invent a way to solve a difficult communication problem.

Virtual Information

When Herman Miller introduced its Aeron chair, it had to overcome formidable communication challenges. The market for chairs in workplaces is heavily influenced by cultural biases about the nature of a well-designed and comfortable chair. People who buy chairs for workplaces usually put form, performance, and price at the top of their list of criteria; it probably helps if a chair *looks* comfortable too. The Aeron chair, however, doesn't appear at first glance to exhibit the form, performance, or comfort characteristics people generally expect. Its value lies in the many innovations in form, structural engineering, applied materials, manufacturing techniques and processes, and ergonomic performance that it incorporates. The Aeron chair has enough technological innovations to keep the U.S. Patent Office busy for years. The Aeron chair is the result of two decades of research into the phenomenon of sitting by industrial designers Bill Stumpf and Don Chadwick. Stumpf and Chadwick worked on a variety of seating projects, studying sitting in the minutest detail: body type and size, aeration, hip-pivot motion, weight distribution, circulation, and spinal decompression. In the early 1980s, they collaborated with Herman Miller in the development of the Equa chair. It was a winning combination: the Equa chair dominated the

The Aeron Chair Teaser Video was used to generate curiosity and to create a buzz about the chair. It was designed to set the tone and the focus of the product demonstration to follow. There is no chair, no ergonomic story, just beautiful metaphorical and suggestive images of forms and expressions. View the CD-Rom.

market for nearly a decade. In 1992, Stumpf and Chadwick again brought their wealth of knowledge to Herman Miller, joining a core team from key departments in the company. What followed were two years of exhaustive model building, drawings, presentations, and retooling. Six months before the Aeron chair was launched, we were asked to develop ways to present the chair to corporate facilities managers and contract furniture dealers. To grasp the significance and nuances of the chair's value, it was necessary for us to become part of the Aeron team.

We conducted a series of interviews and working sessions with the entire team and with Stumpf and Chadwick individually. One of the chair's most arresting features is the transparent, membranous,

stretchable mesh, called Pellicle,™ that is fitted precisely into the chair's back support and seat. Thoroughly tested for every imaginable stress factor, the Pellicle distributes body weight so evenly that it produces a floating sensation. Pellicle, however, was only one of the many breakthroughs in seating engineering we had to convey. The multidirectional adjustability of the armrests, the back support, the tilt mechanism, and the seat itself offers many compelling benefits to sedentary workers. The Aeron chair is extremely utilitarian, with as many functions as a Swiss army knife. However, although the extent of the research backing up the Aeron technology was impressive, Stumpf and Chadwick had equally provocative things to say about physical and

Case Studies

Bill Stumpf's and Don Chadwick's concept book was the source from which we developed our communication materials. It covered everything from the psychology of ergonomics to exact measurements of multiple-task posture and "Qwerty" constraints of a keyboard.

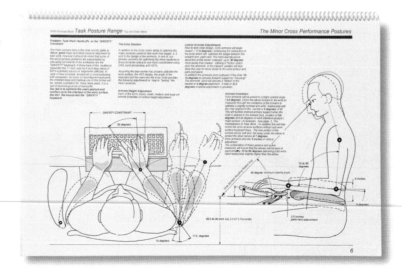

emotional comfort. Stumpf, a great storyteller, related how his observations of people's behavior became departure points for the design. Watching a parent holding an infant and noticing the way the baby's bottom was supported by the parent's forearms, for instance, gave Stumpf the idea that a chair should provide the same kind of comfort. Chadwick spoke at length about the importance of aeration as it relates to comfort. As we studied our notes on the interviews, it became clear that the Aeron chair had no single outstanding feature that could serve as an organizing premise in the presentation.

A Flexible Presentation

If the chair was unconventional, so too was the process of developing and marketing it. As design and development proceeded, the core team made visits to the facility managers of Fortune 500 companies, bringing with them a full-size prototype. The process in many ways resembled software development – trying an idea, testing it, getting feedback, making refinements, and testing it again. We knew that we, too, had to take an unconventional approach as we developed the presentation, which clearly needed to adapt to diverse audiences and accommodate multiple uses.

Stumpf and Chadwick had created a "concept book," which documented the thinking behind the Aeron chair's design, to use as a tool in presenting their solutions to the ergonomic problems they were

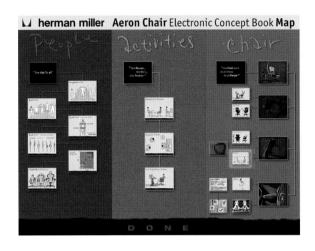

addressing. We grouped the information in the concept book into three categories: (1) concepts that had to do with people and their differences in size and shape; (2) concepts related to work activities supported by the chair; and (3) specific features of the chair. Then we looked at ways to make certain ideas more explicit. Some concepts were simple facts, but others were elaborate ideas about people, time, and space. For instance, Stumpf and Chadwick had measured the temperature increases and changes in weight distribution that take place over time as people remain sitting. That kind of information could be much more clearly expressed in moving pictures than in tables.

The concept book was full of fascinating ideas which made it highly entertaining; realizing that all we had to do was bring it to life, we adapted it into a "digital concept book." Much more flexible and appropriate than an ordered string of presentation points, this collection of dynamic multimedia diagrams and animation would not only capture the Aeron chair's comfort, adaptability to people's bodies and habits, and technological aesthetic; presenters could draw from it in any number of ways depending on whom they were addressing. The sales and marketing groups could try out different portable presentations for different organizations but still make key points consistently. Moreover, the program's modular format allowed Herman Miller to add new concepts and components as it pleased, such as a competitive analysis module and a specification module for ordering.

The digital concept book.
View the CD-ROM.

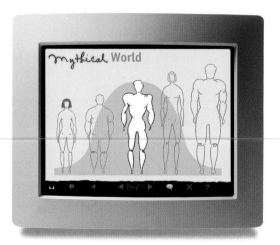

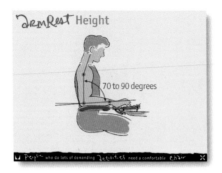

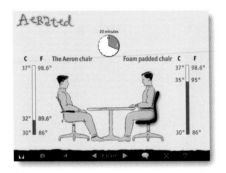

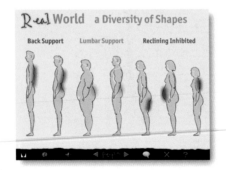

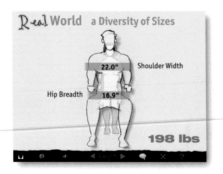

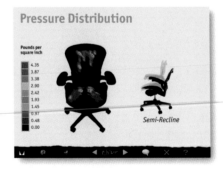

An Aeron Chair for Everyone

One of the additional components for the digital concept book was already under way. When we joined the Aeron chair team, only two sets (small, medium, and large sizes) of the prototype existed. Those chairs were shared by the marketing, engineering, and sales groups, and what with photo shoots, demonstrations, and testing, crating and transport costs were beginning to add up. We suggested exploring the possibility of developing a virtual chair, which for the time being could serve as a demonstration and which later could be included in the digital concept book. The company liked the idea, and we proceeded.

The Advanced Technology Group at Apple had used QuickTime VR technology to make navigable movies that let a user view scenes from either a rotating or a revolving perspective; one movie gave users a 360-degree view from one of the towers of the Golden Gate Bridge, and the other let people examine a teacup from all angles. We wanted to portray the Aeron chair in the same way, except that we wanted potential customers to be able to view the chair from any angle, not just from within one plane. We decided to use a digital camera to take stills of the chair and insert the stills into the movie frames; using a video camera would produce potentially blurred shots. The best way to capture every single required angle was to build a small rotational base into the bottom of the chair and set the chair on a pole. In that way, we took 1,512 photographs of the chair; hundreds of hours of monotonous, painstaking technical work followed. Each picture was scaled, cropped, rotated, and filtered; the part of the chair the pole obstructed in each photograph was meticulously reconstructed using Adobe Photoshop. Once the photos were prepared, our crew went to work making the stills into a three-dimensional navigable movie, a much more difficult task than making a panoramic navigable movie restricted to one plane.

The virtual Aeron chair was not just an extraordinary multiple media feat, though. It allowed Herman Miller sales representatives to "show" the chair to prospective customers without having to crate and transport a chair to the location of each sales pitch. The Aeron chair project was an innovative solution for selling an innovative product. We made the program simple to launch, and we gave it an interface that would let sales representatives go directly to the information they wanted to present

without having to click through many screens. Potential customers could use it to investigate ergonomic features and details of the chair's performance at their own pace.

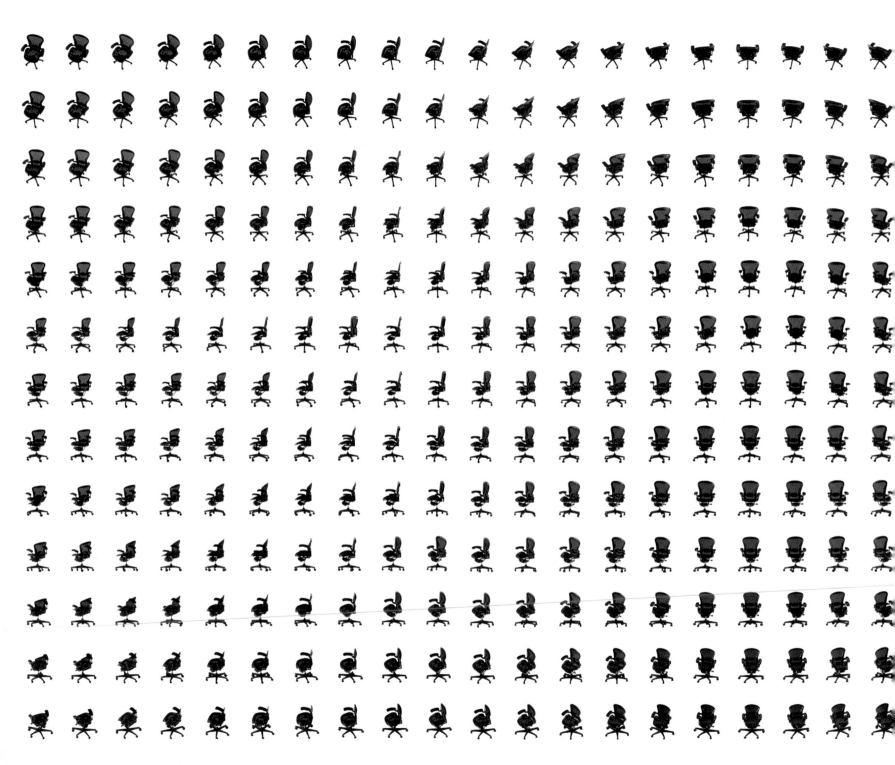

How do you create a world around a chair? The horizontal angle was covered with a Macintosh controlled, precision-calibrated rotating rig; the vertical was conquered with a Kafkaesque rope and pulley contraption that resembled a medieval torture device. As the rig was set up, the photo studio started to look like a Rube Goldberg illustration. Our objective was simple: 1,512 precision photographs taken with a Kodak DCS200

digital camera that was tethered to an eight-foot SCSI cable to a PowerBook 180C strapped on top of a 25-foot ladder, then imaged as high-resolution PICT files directly onto CD-ROM. The work was slow and painstaking. 1,510, 1,511, 1,512... the final shots were finished. Now the serious pixel crunching could begin. Download, rotate, scale, and outline. Drop out the backgrounds and erase all traces of the rig. 14 days, 3 designers, 1 starving student – probably the most monotonous PhotoShop session of all time. All the Aeron's blocked-out five-star bases and casters seamlessly rebuilt and stripped back into position. Compression testing and zooms handled flawlessly. Meanwhile the computer code was being rewritten and

continued

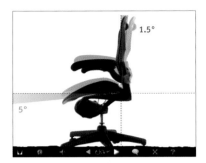

1.5°

5°

A   B&C   B&C

19.5" 495.3 mm   20.8" 528.3 mm   21.5" 546 mm

14.3" 363.2 mm   15.0" 381.0 mm   15.2" 386 mm

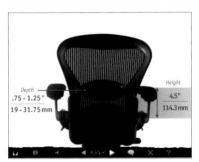

Depth
.75 - 1.25"
19 - 31.75 mm

Height
4.5"
114.3 mm

tweaked to make the chair really fly. Integrated without a hitch and up and running on the 840AV, 32MG Mac playback station. This was some cool stuff. What's next? Let's make this baby really fly right off the screen, full-on 3-D with 5-7 degree vision parallex and those funny little red and blue 3D glasses and everything. Not just a chair – but a digital, user-controlled, navigable chair. View the CD-ROM.

Bibliography

Business

Collins, James C. and Jerry I. Porras. 1994. *Built to Last: Successful Habits of Visionary Companies.* New York: HarperCollins.

Davidow, William H., and MIchael S. Malone. 1992. *The Virtual Corporation: Structuring and Revitalizing the Corporation for the 21st Century.* New York: HarperCollins.

De Bono, Edward. 1985. *Six Thinking Hats.* Boston: Little, Brown and Company.

Fukuyama, Francis. 1995. *Trust: The Social Virtues and the Creation of Prosperity.* New York: The Free Press.

Kao, John J. 1991. *The Entrepreneurial Organization.* Englewood Cliffs, N.J.: Prentice-Hall.

Kaplan, Jerry. 1994. *Startup: The Silicon Valley Adventure.* Boston: Houghton Mifflin.

Schwartz, Peter. 1991. *The Art of the Long View: Planning for the Future in an Uncertain World.* New York: Doubleday.

Design

Berger, John. 1977. *Ways of Seeing.* New York: Penguin Books.

Blackwell, Lewis and David Carson. *The End of Print: The Graphic Design of David Carson.* 1995. San Francisco: Chronicle Books.

Caplan, Ralph. 1982. *By Design: Why There are No Locks on the Bathroom Doors in the Hotel Louis XIV and Other Object Lessons.* New York: McGraw-Hill.

Frutiger, Adrian. 1989. *Signs and Symbols: Their Design and Meaning.* Translated by Andrew Bluhm. New York: Van Nostrand Reinhold.

Garland, Ken. 1994. *Mr. Beck's Underground Map.* Middlesex: Capital Transport Publishing.

Holmes, Nigel. 1991. *Pictorial Maps.* New York: Watson Guptill.

Holmes, Nigel with Rose DeNeve. 1985. *Designing Pictorial Symbols.* New York: Watson-Guptill.

Kerlow, Isaac Victor. 1996. *The Art of 3-D Computer Animation and Imaging.* New York: Van Nostrand Reinhold.

King, Robert. 1995. *Designing Products and Services That Customers Want.* Portland, Ore.: Productivity Press.

Laurel, Brenda. 1993. *Computers as Theatre.* Reading, Mass.: Addison-Wesley Publishing Company.

Mitchell, William. 1992. *The Reconfigured Eye: Visual Truth in the Post-Photographic Era*. Cambridge, Mass.: The MIT Press.

Mitchell, William J. and Malcolm McCullough. 1995. *Digital Design Media*, 2nd Ed. New York: Van Nostrand Reinhold.

Mullet, Kevin and Darrell Sano. 1995. *Designing Visual Interfaces: Communication Oriented Techniques*. Englewood Cliffs, N.J.: Prentice-Hall.

Neuhart, John, with Marilyn Neuhart and Ray Eames. 1989. *Eames Design: The Work of the Office of Charles and Ray Eames*. New York: Henry N. Abrams.

Norman, Donald A. 1988. *The Design of Everyday Things*. New York: Doubleday.

Olins, Wally. 1984. *The Wolff Olins Guide to Corporate Identity*. London: The Design Council, The Incorporated Society of British Advertisers, The Design Management Institute.

Papanek, Victor. 1992. *Design for the Real World: Human Ecology and Social Change.* Chicago: Academy Chicago Publishers.

Rand, Paul. 1985. *A Designer's Art*. New Haven and London: Yale University Press.

Information

Branscomb, Anne Wells. 1994. *Who Owns Information? From Privacy to Public Access.* New York: Basic Books.

Brook, James, and Iain A. Boal, eds. 1995. *Resisting the Virtual Life: The Culture and Politics of Information.* San Francisco: City Lights.

Lutz, William. 1989. *Doublespeak: From "Revenue Enhancement" to "Terminal Living"; How Government, Business, Advertisers, and Others Use Language to Deceive You*. New York: HarperCollins.

Tapscott, Don. 1996. *The DigitaL Economy: Promise and Peril in the Age of Networked Intelligence*. New York: McGraw-Hill.

Tufte, Edward R. 1990. *Envisioning Information*. Cheshire Conn.: Graphics Press.

—— 1988. *The Visual Display of Quantitative Information*. Cheshire Conn.: Graphics Press.

Wurman, Richard Saul. 1996. *Information Architects*. Zurich: Graphis.

—— 1989. *Information Anxiety*. New York: Doubleday.

Media

Brand, Stewart. 1987. *The MediaLab: Inventing the Future at MIT*. New York: Viking.

McKibben, Bill. 1992. *The Age of Missing Information*. New York: Penguin Books.

McLuhan, Marshall. 1994. *Understanding Media: The Extensions of Man*. Cambridge, Mass.: The MIT Press.

Ogilvy, David. 1986. *Confessions of an Advertising Man*. New York: Atheneum.

—— 1983. *Ogilvy on Advertising*. New York: Crown Publishers.

Technology

Katz, Barry M. 1990. *Technology and Culture: A Historical Romance*. Stanford, Calif.: Stanford Alumni Association.

Kelly, Kevin. 1994. *Out of Control: The Rise of Neo-Biological Civilization*. Reading, Mass.: Addison-Wesley Publishing Company.

McNeill, Daniel and Paul Freiberger. 1994. *Fuzzy Logic: The Revolutionary Computer Technology That is Changing Our World*. New York: Touchstone Books.

Mitchell, William. 1995. *City of Bits: Space, Place, and the Infobahn*. Cambridge, Mass.: The MIT Press.

Paepke, C. Owen. 1993. *The Evolution of Progress: The End of Economic Growth and the Beginning of Human Transformation*. New York: Random House.

Postman, Neil. 1992. *Technopoly: The Surrender of Culture to Technology*. New York: Vintage Books.

Negroponte, Nicholas. 1995. *Being Digital*. New York: Alfred A. Knopf.

Norman, Donald A. 1993. *Things That Make Us Smart: Defending Human Attributes in the Age of the Machine*. Reading, Mass.: Addison-Wesley. Floppy Disc New York: Voyager Company. CD-ROM New York: Voyager Company.

Taylor, David A. *Object-Oriented Technology: A Manager's Guide*. Alameda, Calif.: Servio Corporation.

Thinking, Ideas, Invention

Brand, Stewart. 1994. *How Buildings Learn: What Happens After They're Built*. New York: Penguin Books.

Burke, James. 1978. *Connections*. New York: St. Martins.

Canto, Christophe, and Odile Faliu. 1993. *The History of the Future: Images of the 21st Century*. Translated by Francis Cowper. Paris: Flammarion.

Edwards, Betty. 1989. *Drawing on the Right Side of the Brain*. Los Angeles: Tarcher/Perigee.

1994. *Dorling Kindersley Ultimate Visual Dictionary*. London: Dorling Kindersley.

Gallagher, Winifred. 1993. *The Power of Place: How Our Surroundings Shape Our Thoughts, Emotions, and Actions*. New York: HarperCollins.

Lubar, Steven. 1993. *InfoCulture: The Smithsonian Book of Information Age Inventions*. Boston: Houghton Mifflin.

Macaulay, David. 1988. *The Way Things Work*. London: Dorling Kindersley.

Mackay, Judith. 1993. *The State of Health Atlas*. New York: Simon and Schuster.

Minsky, Marvin. 1986. *The Society of Mind*. New York: Simon and Schuster. CD-ROM: 1994. New York: Voyager Company.

Petroski, Henry. 1992. *The Evolution of Useful Things*. New York: Vintage Books.

Robin, Harry. 1992. *The Scientific Image: From Cave to Computer*. New York: Harry N. Abrams.

Rucker, Rudy. 1984. *The Fourth Dimension: A Guided Tour of the Higher Universes*. Boston: Houghton Mifflin.

Seager, Joni, ed. 1990. *The State of the Earth Atlas*. New York: Simon and Schuster.

Van Doren, Charles. 1991. *A History of Knowledge: Past, Present, and Future*. New York: Ballantine Books.

Venturi, Robert. 1992. *Complexity and Contradiction in Architecture*. New York: The Museum of Modern Art.

Periodicals

Design Issues. Tri-Annual. The MIT Press. Cambridge, Mass.

interactions: New Visions of Human-Computer Interaction. Bi-Monthly. Association for Computer Machinery, Inc. New York, New York.

Interact. 1994. Annual. American Center for Design Journal. Chicago, Illinois.

Design Credits

Cover Typography, David Bullen; design, David Bullen and Josh Michels; photography, PhotoDisc Inc.

i

ii, iii

iv, v

vi, vii

viii, ix

x, xi

xii, xiii

xv The Icon Bar, San Francisco: Photograph, Mario Parnell.

page 1 Adapted and reprinted by permission from *The American Heritage Dictionary of the English Language,* Third Edition.

page 2 Photograph, Tom Landecker.

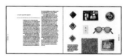

page 5 Photographs of highway signs, sushi, 24-hour clock, RJ11 phone socket, monitor, and circuit board are from CMCD Visual Symbol Library; Revo sunglasses, photograph, Steve Underwood; Botticelli's *Birth of Venus* is from Planet Art CD-ROM Library.

page 7 Photograph, Doug Menuez © 1990. Used with permission.

page 8 Photographic illustration, Studio Archetype © 1992.

page 9 Design, Bob Aufuldish; writer, Mark Bartlett; programming, David Karam; icons, Eric Donelan and Bob Aufuldish. © 1995 by Aufuldish and Warinner.

pages 10 & 11 Design, Hugh Dubberly. Dubberly wishes to acknowledge Charles Altschul for his work on information structures; special thanks to Charles Altschul, Erin Murphy, John Skidget, and Eliot Bergson for their many suggestions. The diagram first appeared on a poster for American Center for Design's 1995 Living Surface Conference, "Design for the Internet." ©1995 Hugh Dubberly. Redrawn for *Designing Business* by Josh Michels. Used with permission.

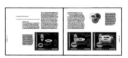

pages 12 & 13 Diagrams based on work of Tony Oettinger at Harvard Business School, 1991. Adapted by Clement Mok.

page 13 The Convergence Diagram developed by Nicholas Negroponte for the MIT Media Lab, interpretation, Clement Mok.

pages 14 &15 Shoelace and exfoliant diagrams, Nigel Holmes. Used with permission. *US Atlas* and *Rome Access Guide,* Richard Saul Wurman. Used with permission.

page 16 *Envisioning Information,* Edward Rolf Tufte. Used with permission.
page 17 Photographic illustration, Clement Mok.

page 19 Photograph of Charles and Ray Eames; diagram, Charles Eames. Used with permission.

page 20 Viable System diagram (partial view), Stafford Beer; interpretation of the Viable System diagram, Clement Mok.
page 21 Illustration, Seymour Chwast.

page 23 Adapted and reprinted by permission from *The American Heritage Dictionary of the English Language,* Third Edition.

page 24 1) The Microsoft Network interface, design, Clement Mok and Lillian Svec, Studio Archetype. 2) Rocket Science Web site, design, Claire Barry, Studio Archetype; program, Sheryl Hampton and Matisse Anzer, illustrations, Studio Archetype & Rocket Science. 3) NBC Intercast prototype, design, Clement Mok and Eric Wilson, Studio Archetype; photographs are the property of National Broadcasting Company. 4) News on Demand prototype, design, Claire Barry and Josh Michels, Studio Archetype. 5) CD-I format of the Mayo Clinic Family Healthbook, design, Doris Mitsch and Clancy Nolan, Studio Archetype. 6) Glencoe/Macmillan Health Textbook prototype, design, Claire Barry, Clement Mok, and Lillian Svec, Studio Archetype. 7) Wolverine Exterior Systems kiosk, development, Doris Mitsch, Studio Archetype. 8) Photograph, Doug Meneuz.

page 26 *Philosophiae Naturalis Principia Mathematica* from the library of John Warnock. Used with permission.
page 27 Photograph, Photodisc, Inc.

page 29 Photographs, CMCD.

page 30 Photograph, PhotoDisc, Inc.
page 31 Left: IVI Publishing Vision Video, creative direction, Clement Mok and Carl Halverson; director, Randy Field; screenplay, Jim Vacarro; executive producer, Katherine Hunter; location production, Edgewater Production; screen designs, Nancy Pinney and Blaire Beebe, Studio Archetype; contribution, Brad Husick and Lillian Svec. Middle: News on Demand prototype, design, Claire Barry and Josh Michels, Studio Archetype; courtesy of IVI Publishing. Right: Movies-on-demand prototype, design, Claire Barry and Josh Michels, Studio Archetype.

page 32 Apple Macintosh Interface poster, design, Lori Barra, Studio Archetype; masks, John Brotzman; photography, John Clayton. Used with permission.
page 33 Top left: Herman Miller Interactive presentation, design, Claire Barry and Clement Mok; programming, Paula Meiselman, Studio Archetype; illustration, Ward Schumacher. Top middle: Apple QuickTime Starter Kit: production, Doris Mitsch and Clancy Nolan; animation, Doris Mitsch, Studio Archetype; videography, Robin Moratti. Top right: Wells Fargo ATM, design, Claire Barry and David Weissberg, Studio Archetype; courtesy of Wells Fargo Bank. Bottom left: Prototype for Internet Shopping Network, design, Claire Barry and Blaire Beebe, Studio Archetype. Bottom right: Sony Wonderland, design, Claire Barry and Andrew Cawrse, Studio Archetype; courtesy of Sony.

page 35 Top left: Courtesy of Random House College Dictionary. Top middle: *The Way Things Work.* Courtesy of David Macaulay. Top right: From the library of E.M. Ginger. Center row: Photographs: Photodisc, Inc. Bottom left: Courtesy of Adobe Systems. Bottom middle: Quicken images courtesy of Intuit © 1996. All rights reserved. Quicken is a registered trademark of Intuit Inc. Bottom right: Courtesy of Rick Smolan, Against all Odds Productions.

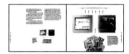

page 36 Left: Screen courtesy of Adobe Systems. Right: Screen, design, Claire Barry and Josh Michels, Studio Archetype. Yellow Pages photograph, Charles Cormany.
page 37 Left: Screen courtesy of Adobe Systems. Right: Screen, design, Claire Barry and Josh Michels, Studio Archetype; book composite photograph, Hunter Freeman; photographic illustration, Michael Conti.

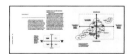

pages 38 & 39 Diagram, Clement Mok; contributors, Brad Husick and Lillian Svec, Studio Archetype.

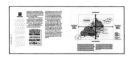

page 40 Netscape logo © Netscape Corporation. Used with permission. Magazine image courtesy of *Fast Company*.

page 41 Diagram, Clement Mok; contributors, Brad Husick and Lillian Svec, Studio Archetype.

page 42 Diagram, Clement Mok; contributors, Brad Husick and Lillian Svec, Studio Archetype.

page 43 Photograph, Steve Underwood. CMCD identity and packaging system, design, Clement Mok and Josh Distler. Visual Symbol Library photographers, Steve Underwood and Mario Parnell.

page 45 Left: Brochure, design, Samantha Fuetsch, Studio Archetype. Right: Interactive leasing worksheet, art direction, Samantha Fuetsch; design and animations, Paula Meiselman and Nancy Pinney, Studio Archetype; programming, Terry Schusler of Grey Matter; illustrations, Mick Wilton. Courtesy of Hewlett Packard.

page 46 Diagram, Clement Mok; contributors, Brad Husick and Lillian Svec, Studio Archetype.

page 47 Looking Inside a Storm from *USA Today*; design, Richard Curtis. Used with permission. Musical notation, photograph, Mario Parnell; circuit board mechanical drawing of Apple II computer, Steve Wosniak; photograph, Mario Parnell. Used with permission of Apple Computer Inc.

page 48 Diagram, Clement Mok; contributors: Brad Husick and Lillian Svec, Studio Archetype.

page 49 Graphical user interface of Net.radio's Net Companion, design, John Grotting, Studio Archetype.

page 50 Illustration, Seymour Chwast

page 53 Illustration, Seymour Chwast.

page 55 Photograph, Photodisc, Inc. Diagram, design, Mark Crumpacker and Lillian Svec, Studio Archetype. DADI™ process diagram is a trademark of Studio Archetype.

page 56 Typographic illustration, Clement Mok, Studio Archetype.

page 57 Hierarchy tree diagram, Josh Michels, Studio Archetype.

page 58 Illustration, Scott Matthew. Courtesy of Lotus Development Corp.

page 59 Corporate Design Foundation Web site, design, Clement Mok; production, George Chen and Lorraine Beebe, Studio Archetype.

pages 60 & 61 Web sites and online services, definition, architecture, design, and implementation, Studio Archetype: Chuck Adsit, Emma Ainsworth, Jennifer Anderson, Mark Anquoe, Claire Barry, Blair Beebe, Lorraine Beebel, Stephen Bugaj, Matt Carlson, Andrew Cawrse, George Chen, Michael Clasen, Michael Conti, Mark Crumpacker, Raul Diaz, Josh Distler, Brian Forst, Samantha Fuetsch, Carl Goldschmidt, Anastacio Gomes, John Grotting, Sheryl Hampton, Paula Meiselman, Josh Michels, Clement Mok, Michael Morgan, Beth O'Rourke, Judith Romero, Karen Sivak, Greg Shoemaker, Wendy Smith, Lillian Svec, Hallie Warshaw, David Weissberg and Eric Wilson.

page 63 Adapted and reprinted by permission from *The American Heritage Dictionary of the English Language*, Third Edition.

page 64 Photograph, Roy Shigley. Used with permission of Apple Computer, Inc.

page 65 Tracking screen from FedEx Web site. Used with permission of Federal Express Corporation.

page 66 Icons for iQVC on MSN, design, Mark Crumpacker, Studio Archetype.

page 67 Top left: UB Network identity, logo, Joshua Distler, Studio Archetype. Top right: Remote control device, courtesy of Logitech. Center left: MFactory identity, design, Samantha Fuetsch, Studio Archetype. Center right: Mirage Hotel and Casino identity, design, Clement Mok, Sandra Koenig, and Dale Horstman; illustration, Clement Mok, Studio Archetype. Bottom left: Signage at Apple Computer corporate headquarters, Cupertino, California; photograph courtesy of Sussman Prejza; design, Sussman Prejza. Used with permission. Bottom right: Graphical user interface for MacPaint, 1982-83, Bill Atkinson and Susan Kare, Apple Computer; pixel rendering of Japanese Lady originally adapted by Susan Kare of Apple Computer; derivative rendering on adapted work by Clement Mok, Apple Computer. Used with permission.

page 68 Elevator button to Clement Mok designs, Inc. (renamed Studio Archetype); company logo design and illustration, Clement Mok; photograph, Mario Parnell.

page 69 Top: Caere Corporation's Omnipage product identity, design, Chuck Routhier and Clement Mok, Studio Archetype; photograph, Hunter Freeman. Omnipage booth, design, Mitchel Mauk of Mauk Design; advertising, Clement Mok; photograph, Tom Zimberoff. Bottom: Photodisc Web site, design, Clement Mok, Bill Heston, Thaddeaus Brophy, and Mark Anquoe. Photodisc service on MSN, design, Clement Mok.

page 71 Courtesy of Flightlink and America West.

page 72 3Com logo, design, Dale Horstman; 3Com Park logo, design, Andrew Cawrse, Studio Archetype.

page 73 Republic of Tea logo, design, Nancy Bauch and Clement Mok, Studio Archetype; calligraphy, Georgia Deaver.

page 74 Power TV logo, design, Josh Distler, Studio Archetype.

page 75 Farallon Computing's packaging, illustration, Mark Penberthy; design, Chuck Routhier, Studio Archetype.

page 76 Context Media logo, design, Clement Mok, Jennifer Anderson, and Josh Michels, Studio Archetype.

page 77 Illustration, Studio Archetype; characters, Doris Mitsch, Studio Archetype; derivative rendering, Clement Mok, Studio Archetype.

page 79 Kodak Motion and Television Imaging division's organization chart, design, Mark Crumpacker, Studio Archetype.

page 81 Mayo Clinic and IVI Publishing's Family Pharmacist CD-ROM, design, Clement Mok, Studio Archetype; Carl Halverson, IVI Publishing; and Bill Felke, Georgia Tech; prototype development, Caroline Sloan; documentation, Sascha Geissendoerfer, Studio Archetype.

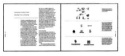

page 83 Top row: Network General, illustration, Beth O'Rourke, Studio Archetype. Center row: pure wool logo, courtesy of The Wool Bureau; Adobe logo and the Adobe Postscript logo, courtesy of Adobe Systems; the Sony logo, used with permission. Bottom row: One Server logo is the trademark of Connect, Inc.; design, Jennifer Anderson, Mark Crumpacker, and Samantha Fuetsch, Studio Archetype; Sanctuary Woods logo, design, Andrew Cawrse and Joshua Distler, Studio Archetype.

page 84 Logo for Connect, Inc., design, Clement Mok, Studio Archetype.

page 85 Photograph, courtesy of Studio Archetype and Motorola.

page 87 Mayo Clinic and IVI Publishing's Family Pharmacist CD-ROM, design, Clement Mok, Studio Archetype; Carl Halverson, IVI Publishing; and Bill Felke, Georgia Tech; prototype development, Caroline Sloan; documentation, Sascha Geissendoerfer, Studio Archetype.

page 88 Icons courtesy of Studio Archetype.

page 89 Mayo Clinic and IVI Publishing's Family Pharmacist CD-ROM, design, Clement Mok, Studio Archetype; Carl Halverson, IVI Publishing; and Bill Felke, Georgia Tech; prototype development, Caroline Sloan; documentation, Sascha Geissendoerfer, Studio Archetype.

page 91 Graphical user interface for automatic teller machine, design, Clement Mok and Claire Barry, Studio Archetype; production, Emma Ainsworth, Paula Meiselman, David Weissberg. Courtesy of Wells Fargo Bank.

page 92 Apple's Knowledge Navigator, producers, Hugh Dubberly, Doris Mitsch, and Michael Markman, Apple Computer; director, Randy Field; production, The Kenwood Group. The1984 commercial, courtesy of Chiat/Day Advertising Agency and Apple Computer.

page 93 IVI Publishing vision video, creative direction, Clement Mok and Carl Halverson; direction, Randy Field; screenplay, Jim Vacarro; executive producer, Katherine Hunter; location production, Edgewater Production; screen designs, Nancy Pinney, Studio Archetype; contributions, Brad Husick and Lillian Svec, Studio Archetype. Courtesy of IVI Publishing.

page 95 Adapted and reprinted by permission from *The American Heritage Dictionary of the English Language,* Third Edition.

page 96 Illustration, David Weisman; co-producer, Eric Brown.

page 99 Information architecture diagram, design, Clement Mok; ideas and contributions, E.M. Ginger, Lillian Svec, and Vic Zauderer.

page 100 Nature of information diagram, design, Clement Mok; derived from information structure work, Studio Archetype; original work, Charles Altschul.

page 101 Top row: Water cycle art, Art Parts; photographic illustration composite, Clement Mok and Josh Michels, Studio Archetype. Center row: Annual report graph, Josh Michels, Studio Archetype; Interactive map, American Center for Design journal interact CD, design, Peter Spreenburg of IDEO; music composer, Gordon Kurtenbach. Bottom row: Wire frame diagram, Matt Carlson; *Vizibility* CD, executive producers, Kristina Hooper Woolsey and Bill Hill; authors, Kristina Hooper Woolsey, Scott Kim, and Gayle Curtis; developer, MetaDesign West; producer, Bill Purdy; associate producer, Cindy Rink; creative direction, Terry Irwin and Jeff Zwerner; video direction/producer, Wendy Slick; programming, Marabeth Harding; digital video design, Don Ahrens; design production, Jym Warhol; sound design, Earwax Productions.

page 102 Top: Beebe Interactive logo, design, Andrew Cawrse. Bottom: Sentence syntax diagram based on original work from Bill Mitchell's book *Digital Media,* interpretation, Josh Michels, Studio Archetype,.

page 103 Left column, 1st. row: Photograph, CMCD Visual Symbol Library. Left column, 2nd row: Babushska dolls from the private collection of Clement Mok; photograph, Mario Parnell. Left column, 3rd row: Random House College Thesaurus.© 1984 by Random House, Inc. Used with permission. Left column, 4th row: TV guide illustration, Josh Michels and Andy Stachler, Studio Archetype. Middle column, all rows: Organization model diagrams, Hugh Dubberly and Clement Mok. Right column, 1st row: Selected screen from *A Passion for Art,* design, Corbis Publishing; creative director and production, Curtis G Wong; interface design and art direction, Pei-Lin Nee; writers, Karyn Esielonis, Mary Tavener Holmes, Chiyo Ishikawa, Carol Ivory, Suzanne Kotz, Susan L'Engle, Heather McPherson, Hal Opperman, Christopher Riopelle, Peter Selz, Martha Smith, Janis Tomilson, and Carol Troyen; developer, James C. Gallant; graphic designers, Pei-Lin Nee and Cecil Juanarena; photographers, Dennis Brack, Nicholas King, Edward Owen, Tess Steinkolk, and Gradon Wood; sound editors, Ella Brackett, Eileen H. Monti, and Curtis Wong; additional programmers, Patrick O'Donnell and Bill Radcliffe; editor, Lorna Price; segment editor, Lisa Anderson; segment production, Ted Evans and Vince Peddle; assistant producer, Eileen H. Monti; Macintosh version producer, Eileen H. Monti; Macintosh version developer, Jennifer Tobin. Right column, 2nd row: Selected screen from *Maus,* design by the Voyager Company; creative director/editor, Elizabeth Scarborough; programming, Jim Cornacchia, Brock LaPorte (Windows), John Cromie, and Derek McDermott; design, Peter Girardi and Robbie Meyn; manager, Sandra Benedetto; quality assurance, Todd Farbraner, Tom Green, Elissa Keeler, Drea Marks, and Wendy Martin; audio production, Current Sounds Studio, Bob Ward. Based on the book by Art Spiegelman. Right column, 3rd row: *Riddle of the Maze,* design, Fathom Pictures Inc.; art direction, Hennie Farrow; illustration, Christopher Manson; producer, Colin Andrews. Right column,4th row: Closed caption image, Photodisc, Inc.

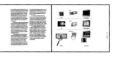

page 105 Left column, all rows: Images, CMCD Visual Symbol Library; photographic illustration, Josh Michels and Michael Conti, Studio Archetype.
Right column, 1st row: Selected screens from *Interactive Thumbnail Index,* design, the Voyager Company; creative director, Jane Gorrell; interface design, Jane Gorrell, Paul Schrynemakers, and Colin Holgate; programming, Colin Holgate; graphic design, Paul Schrynemakers; sound editing, Paul Supkof; series director/producer, Jackie Kain; director of original film, Jon Else. Right column, 2nd row: Selected screens from *The Human Body;* design, Dorling Kindersley, Multimedia London; managing editor, Andrean Pinnington; design manager, Caroline Murray; technical lead, Sharon Bambaji; design, Emma Ainsworth, Des Plunkett, David Wall, Patrick Schirvanian, and Salatore Tomaselli; digital animation and imaging, Richard Greenland, Lai Marsh, Patrizio Semproni, and Paul Stefka; cell animation and illustration, Ruth Linggford; medical illustrators, Joanna Cameron, Lydia Umney, Simonne End, Tony Graham, and John Temperton; audio, Sid Wells, Ian Hawkridge, Patch McQuaid, and Tim McQuaid; software manager, Roy Margolis; software development, Katy Disley, Graham Westlake, Jilan James, and Philip Miller; product testing supervisor, Isabel Whitfield; picture research, Kate Fox, Catherine O'Rourke, and Christine Rista; writers, Richard Walker PhD, Susan Sturrock, and Diane Jakobson PhD. Additional help provided by medical illustrators and medical consultants. Right column, 1st row: Selected screen from *A Passion for Art,* design, Corbis Publishing; creative director and production, Curtis G Wong; interface design and art direction, Pei-Lin Nee; writers, Karyn Esielonis, Mary Tavener Holmes, Chiyo Ishikawa, Carol Ivory, Suzanne Kotz, Susan L'Engle, Heather McPherson, Hal Opperman, Christopher Riopelle, Peter Selz, Martha Smith, Janis Tomilson, and Carol Troyen; developer, James C. Gallant; graphic designers, Pei-Lin Nee and Cecil Juanarena; photographers, Dennis Brack, Nicholas King, Edward Owen, Tess Steinkolk, and Gradon Wood; sound editors, Ella Brackett, Eileen H. Monti, and Curtis Wong; additional programmers, Patrick O'Donnell and Bill Radcliffe; editor, Lorna Price; segment editor, Lisa Anderson; segment production, Ted Evans and Vince Peddle; assistant producer, Eileen H. Monti; Macintosh version producer, Eileen H. Monti; Macintosh version developer, Jennifer Tobin.

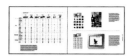

page 106 Organization model matrix, design, Lillian Svec, Brad Husick, and Clement Mok, Studio Archetype.

page 107 Top: 1987 HyperCard brochure, Apple Creative Service; design, Clement Mok and Hugh Dubberly; writing, Linda Bradford, Eric Stouffer, and Rich Binell; illustrations, Alan Cober, Michael Schwab, and Ward Schumaker. Front cover photographs Cadillac Fin © Cindy Lewis/The Stock Market; Beduin Woman ©Albano Guatti/The Stock Market; Earth© Allan Lee Page/The Stock Market; Cypress Tree © David Muench 1987; Dry Lakes © W. Warren. Additional photographs courtesy of The Bettmann Archive and Ernie Frielander. Used with permission from Apple Computer. Bottom: Herman Miller navigable movie, design, Claire Barry, Paula Meiselman, Dan O'Sullivan, and Blair Beebe, Studio Archetype. Courtesy of Herman Miller, Inc.

page 109 *The Way Things Work* by David Macaulay. Used with permission from the publisher. CD-Rom version, design by Dorling Kindersley; Multimedia; David Game, editorial lead; Tony Foo, design lead; Helen Dowling, Sarah Larter, and Tony Pearson, editorial; Sarah Cavan, Alison Donovan, and Andy Walker, design; Matt O'Brian, Russell Harding, Eugene Jordan, Sarah Nunan, and Iain Pusey, digital animation and imaging; Alan Green, Sarah Koegh and Tony Walters, cell animation; Mick Barrett, David Fathers, and Derek Worrell, illustration; Sid Wells and Ian Hawkridge, audio; Roy Margolis and Graham Westlake, software development; Tom Forge, senior technical lead; Clifford Rosney, managing editor; Susie Breen, managing editor; Jack Challoner BSC (HONS) ARCS, PGGW; Katie Evans BA (CANTAB) and David Glover PhD, Richard Platt BA, writers; Bob Clayton, Tim Crone PhD, Jeff Harding, and Robin Loerch, voice talent. Based on the book by David Macaulay.

page 110 Clement Mok designs Web site, design, Claire Barry and Andrew Cawrse; production and scripting, Sheryl Hampton, Studio Archetype.

page 111 1989 Farallon packaging system, design, Clement Mok and Chuck Routhier, Studio Archetype; illustrations, Mark Penberthy; PhoneNet packaging courtesy of Farallon Computing.

page 112 Time and place diagram, design, Clement Mok and Lillian Svec, Studio Archetype.

page 113 Screen Illustration, Andrew Cawrse; art direction, Mark Crumpacker, Studio Archetype. Background illustration, Mark Crumpacker.

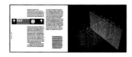

page 114 Sign Illustration, design, Clement Mok, Studio Archetype.

page 115 Information system, design, Lisa Strausfeld. Used with permission, Visible Language Workshop, The Media Laboratory.

page 117 London Underground diagrams. Courtesy of London Transport Authority.

page 119 Bubble diagram, Josh Michels; information design, Clement Mok, Brad Husick, and Lillian Svec, Studio Archetype.

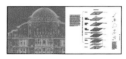

page 121 Information structure diagram, design, Clement Mok, Studio Archetype.

page 122 Architectural image, Planet Art Architecture CD-ROM.

page 123 Information architecture diagram, design, Clement Mok, Studio Archetype; contributions, Samir Arora and E.M. Ginger; Eric Shank and Brad Husick, Studio Archetype. Network configuration diagrams adapted from Bill Mitchell's and Malcolm McCullough's book *Digital Design Media*.

page 125 Adapted and reprinted by permission from *The American Heritage Dictionary of the English Language*, Third Edition.

page 126 Interactivity experience diagram, adapted and interpreted from the work of Tony Oettinger, Harvard Business School.

page 128 Illustration, Clement Mok, Studio Archetype.

page 129 Diagram is an adapted work based on *Peter Gabriel's Secret World*; design, RealWorld Multimedia and Brilliant Media Inc.; concept and artistic direction, Peter Gabriel, Steve Nelson, Michael Colson, Nicholas Bruce and Mike Large; executive producers, Peter Gabriel, Mike Large, and David Eno.

page 130 Left to right: DOS screen capture, Studio Archetype. Alto System screen, Xerox PARC, photograph courtesy of Xerox PARC. MacPaint® GUI, design, Susan Kare and Bill Atkinson, Apple Computer; courtesy of Apple Computer, Inc.

page 131 Left to right: Windows GUI courtesy of Microsoft, Inc.; MagicCap user interface, graphics, Susan Kare; programming, Andy Hertzfeld and Bill Atkinson. Bob is a registered trademark of Microsoft, Inc. e•World, design and art direction, Cleo Huggins and Mark Drury; illustration, Mark Drury; screen courtesy of Apple Computer, Inc.

page 133 CollegeView® interactive catalog, design, Clement Mok, Steve Simula, Blair Beebe, and Paula Meiselman, Studio Archetype. Used with permission.

page 140 Photography, Mario Parnell.
page 141 Diagram, Clement Mok, Lillian Svec, and Brad Husick, Studio Archetype.

page 150 Package design system, Mark Crumpacker, Samantha Fuetsch, and Gregg Heard.
page 152 Information architecture, Lillian Svec, Studio Archetype.

page 158 Web site, design, George Chen and Claire Barry; implementation, Sheryl Hampton, Emma Ainsworth, and Kathleen Egge; illustration, Dave Danz.
page 159 Web site, design, George Chen and Claire Barry; implementation, Sheryl Hampton, Emma Ainsworth, and Kathleen Egge; illustration, Dave Danz.

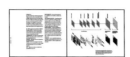

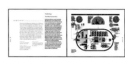

page 134 Photograph courtesy of Studio Archetype.
page 135 Star Trek IV, ©1996 Paramount Pictures. All rights reserved. Televisions, CMCD Visual Symbol Library.

page 143 Diagram, Clement Mok, Lillian Svec, and Brad Husick, Studio Archetype.

pages 152 & 153 Information architecture, Lillian Svec, Studio Archetype.

page 161 Information graphics, Nigel Holmes,© 1996. Information design contribution, Tom Melcher, Against All Odds Productions, and Lillian Svec, Studio Archetype.

page 136 Star Trek: The Next Generation, ©1996 Paramount Pictures. All rights reserved. Stop lights, CMCD Visual Symbol Library.
page 137 Images courtesy of Photodisc. *Grandma and Me,* courtesy of Broderbund.

pages 145 & 146

pages 154 & 155 Web site, design, George Chen and Claire Barry; implementation, Sheryl Hampton, Emma Ainsworth, and Kathleen Egge; illustration, Dave Danz.

page 162 Pre-launch site of 24 Hours in Cyberspace, information architecture, Clement Mok; producer, Eric Wilson; design and production, Matt Carlson, Studio Archetype. Photography, Mario Parnell.
page 163 Site architecture, Eric Wilson and Clement Mok; information mapping, Hallie Warshaw, Studio Archetype.

page 147 Web site, design, Clement Mok and Lillian Svec; implementation, Sheryl Hampton and Kathleen Egge. Cover courtesy of *Utne Reader.*

page 138 Windows dialog box used with permission. Drill and bits photographs, Charles Cormany.
page 139 Tetris from Shareware.com. Hands and scissors, photograph, Charles Cormany.

page 156 Web site, design, George Chen and Claire Barry; implementation, Sheryl Hampton, Emma Ainsworth, and Kathleen Egge; illustration, Dave Danz.
page 157 Web site, design, George Chen and Claire Barry; implementation, Sheryl Hampton, Emma Ainsworth, and Kathleen Egge; illustration, Dave Danz.

page 149

page 164 Diagram, Nigel Holmes © 1996.
page 165 Information diagram, Vic Zauderer and Clement Mok, NetObjects.

page 166 NetObjects site publisher screens graphical user interface design, Vic Zauderer and Greg Brown; programming, Sal Arora. Table of contents from 24 hours in Cyberspace Web site, art direction, Samantha Fuetsch and Matt Carlson, Studio Archetype; and Rick Smolan, Against All Odds Productions.
page 167 Template design, Hallie Warshaw, and Matt Carlson; producer, Eric Wilson, Studio Archetype.

pages 168 & 169 Created by Rick Smolan. Produced by Against All Odds Productions; PR and marketing team publicity director, Patti Richards; student underground and promotions coordinator, Gina Privitere; publicity coordinator, Molly Schaeffer; publicity assistants, Jennifer Friedman, Sophie Deprez; sponsor coordinator, Amy Bonetti; contest coordinator, Laura Zung; production director, Jennifer Erwitt; Mission Control coordinator, Anne Murray; office manager, Katya Able; project controller, Rita Dulebohn; production coordinator, Corey Hajim; production assistants, Erik Fox, Deno Prokos, and Eric Rosenberg; office systems, Dave De Graff; television consultants, Mike Cerre, and David Avery; accounting support, Bob Powers; administrative assistants, Gina Carfora, and Sunny Woodall; general counsel, Barry Reder; counsel, Rick Pappas; counsel, Jonathan Hart, Dow, Lohnes & Associates; editorial development team, director of photography & assignments, Karen Mullarkey; associate photo editor, Judith Siviglia; assistant photo editor, Julie Coburn; managing editor, Spencer Reiss; assignment editors, Paul Andrews, Kathy Dalle-Molle. J. Carl Ganter, Jane Gottesman, Dogen Hannah, Acey Harper, Millane Kang, Sumiko Kurita, Alex Lash, Janice Maloney, Tripp Mikich, Lisa Napoli, Evan Nisselson, Mindy Ran, Beth Rickman, Mark Rykoff, Barry Sundermeier, Kaz Tsuchikawa, and Karen Wickre; assignment writers, Carol Blaney, Cecilia Deck, Ken Siegmann, Steve Silberman, Miriam Silver, and Mark Frost; essayists, John Perry Barlow, Stewart Brand, Esther Dyson, Al Gore, Howard

Rheingold, and Paul Saffo; information architect, Clement Mok; design coordinator, Eric Wilson; book designer, Lori Barra; Studio Archetype designers, Chuck Adsit, Matt Carlson, Michael Conti, Brian Frost, Samantha Feutsch, Carl Goldschmidt, Kevin Morrison, Bob Skubic, Lillian Svec, Halle Warshaw; infographic designer, Nigel Holmes; overall coordinator, Tom Melcher; systems integrator, John Graham; technical assistant, Marc Escobosa; photographer technologies, Don Winslow; audio technologies, Carl Gante;r Eastman Kodak, Karen Kozak; Sun Microsystems, Carl Meske; Adobe Systems, Levon Peck; America Online, Jennifer Schmidt; Netscape Communications, Elyssa Edwards; MFS Communications, Bob Barbour; Illustra, Bill Ray; NEC Technologies, Dale Fuller; NetObjects, Sal Arora; Internet 1996 World Exposition, Carl Malamud; Sonic Solutions, Paul Lefebvre; Cyberports for Business, Bill McCauley; InternetMCI, Vinton Cerf; Polaroid, Isidro Gonzales; The Software Construction Company, Mike Evans; Associated Press, Neal Ulevich; Progressive Networks, Rob Glaser.

page 170 See above entry.

page 172 Visitors list, design, Matt Carlson; 3D modeling, Brian Forst, Studio Archetype.
page 173 Java application, Vlad Lyubovny. Screen design, Clement Mok and Matt Carlson, Studio Archetype.

page 173 Illustration, Clement Mok, Studio Archetype.
page 174 CNBC Intercast screen, design, Clement Mok and Eric Wilson, Studio Archetype.

pages 176 &177 NBC News, design, Clement Mok; producer, Eric Wilson, Studio Archetype. Photographs courtesy of NBC.

page 179 "Today" show Intercast, design, Clement Mok; producer, Eric Wilson, Studio Archetype.

page 181 Design development sketches for pre-release beta of Microsoft Network, design, Clement Mok, Lillian Svec, and Paula Meiselman, Studio Archetype.

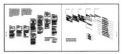

page 182 Branding schema for The Microsoft Network, design, Lillian Svec, Studio Archetype.
page 183 Graphic schema and screens for The Microsoft Network, design, Clement Mok and Lillian Svec; icons, Claire Barry and Josh Distler, Studio Archetype; illustrations, Nancy Stahl.

page 184 8-bit and 4 bit color icons/illustrations, Nancy Stahl and Claire Barry.
page 185 Photographs for 8-bit and 4-bit color tests, Digital Stock CD-ROM Library.

page 186 Syllable diagram, Mark Crumpacker, Studio Archetype.
page 187 Identity studies. America Online, e-world, Compuserve, Adobe, Microsoft logos are registered trademarks of their respective companies.

page 188 Main screen of the pre-beta release of The Microsoft Network, design, Clement Mok, Lillian Svec, Claire Barry, Paula Meiselman, and Nancy Stahl, Studio Archetype.
page 189 Photograph, Steve Underwood. Microsoft logo used with permission.

pages 190 & 191 Beta and final release of The Microsoft Network, design, Clement Mok and Lillian Svec, Studio Archetype; photograph, CMCD.

page 192 Home page of the final release of The Microsoft Network, design, Clement Mok and Lillian Svec, Studio Archetype; photograph, CMCD.

page 195 iQVC bubble diagram, design, Clement Mok and Lillian Svec; illustration, George Chen, Studio Archetype.

page 197 iQVC on The Microsoft Network, information architecture, Clement Mok, Samantha Fuetsch, and Lillian Svec; producer, Eric Wilson; design, Brian Forst and Paula Meiselman; Web site information architecture, Eric Wilson and Lillian Svec; iQVC on Intercast, design, Samantha Fuetsch; diagrams, Josh Michels, Studio Archetype.

pages 198 &199 iQVC on The Microsoft Network, information architecture, Clement Mok, Samantha Fuetsch, and Lillian Svec; producer, Eric Wilson; design, Brian Forst and Paula Meiselman; Web site, information architecture, Eric Wilson and Lillian Svec; iQVC on Intercast, design, Samantha Fuetsch; isometric, Emma Ainsworth, Studio Archetype.

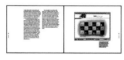

page 201 Main categories screen of iQVC on The Microsoft Network, design, Clement Mok and Brian Forst, Studio Archetype; photography, Scott Peterson.

page 203 Sketch, Andrew Carwse, Studio Archetype.

pages 204 & 205 Sony Wonderland prototype, Claire Barry, Blair Beebe, Andrew Carwse, and Clement Mok, Studio Archetype.

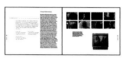

page 206 Herman Miller Aeron chair teaser, creative direction, Clement Mok; producer, Cathy Carolan; director, Terry Heffernan; production, Good Pictures.

page 208 Aeron Concept book, Bill Stumpf and Don Chadwick.

page 209 Aeron chair electronic concept book, design, Claire Barry and Clement Mok; illustration, Ward Schumacher; director of programming and animation, Paula Meiselman; video digitalization, Blair Beebe; audio engineering, interactive audio voice-over, Gary Levenberg; PC version, Terry Schsler, Grey Matter.

page 210 & 211 Aeron chair electronic concept book, design, Claire Barry and Clement Mok; illustration, Ward Schumacher; director of programming and animation, Paula Meiselman; video digitalization, Blair Beebe; audio engineering, interactive audio voice-over, Gary Levenberg; PC version, Terry Schsler, Grey Matter.

page 212 Aeron chair electronic concept book, design, Claire Barry and Clement Mok; illustration, Ward Schumacher; director of programming and animation, Paula Meiselman; video digitalization, Blair Beebe; audio engineering, interactive audio voice-over, Gary Levenberg; PC version, Terry Schsler, Grey Matter.

pages 213 Photographs, Hedrich Blessing. Courtesy of Herman Miller.

page 214 Photographs, Hedrich Blessing. Courtesy of Herman Miller.
page 215 Electonic concept book. Chair section, photograph, Terry Heffernan; calligraphy, Ward Schumacher.

pages 216 & 217 Photography, Claire Barry, Stan Musilek, Dan O'Sullivan and Dave Weissberg; candid shots of photo session, Doug Meneuz. Aeron chair electronic concept book, design, Claire Barry and Clement Mok; illustration, Ward Schumacher; director of programming and animation, Paula Meiselman; video digitalization, Blair Beebe; audio engineering, interactive audio voice-over, Gary Levenberg; PC version, Terry Schsler, Grey Matter; photograph, Doug Meneuz.

pages 218 & 219 Aeron chair electronic concept book, design, Claire Barry and Clement Mok; illustration, Ward Schumacher; director of programming and animation, Paula Meiselman; video digitalization, Blair Beebe; audio engineering, interactive audio voice-over, Gary Levenberg; PC version, Terry Schsler, Grey Matter; photograph, Doug Meneuz.

pages 222 & 223

pages 224 & 225

pages 226 & 227

pages 228 & 229

pages 230 & 231

pages 232 & 233

pages 234 & 235

pages 236 & 237

pages 238 & 239

pages 240 & 241

pages 242 & 243

pages 244 & 245

page 247 Indi, photograph, Steve Underwood.

page 248

Design Credits

Index

Colophon

This book was produced digitally using Adobe software. Prepress consisted of PostScript® computer-to-plate technology (filmless process) by Shepard Poorman Communications Corporation. Soy-based inks were used throughout the printing process to avoid environmentally damaging chemicals. Printed on Potlatch Corporation's Northwest 80lb Text Dull, an acid-free, minimum 10% post-consumer fiber recycled paper. Printed by Shepard Poorman Communications Corporation.

Text design by David Bullen. Text typography uses numerous instances of Adobe Myriad, a two-axis multiple master typeface, designed by Carol Twombly and Robert Slimbach. Quotations use the Tiepolo typeface, designed by Cynthia Hollandsworth. Typeset by Michael Conti.

Art Direction by Clement Mok. Layout by Josh Michels.

CD-ROM Contents _____

Adobe Acrobat® files

Six industry and discipline overlap diagrams showing current professional and technological trends.

Two diagrams showing how information systems are built.

"Earthwatch", one of the six themes from the 24 Hours in Cyberspace project

Interactive presentations

animations

digital sketches of prototypes

videos

Herman Miller Aeron chair presentation

A library of visual images from Photodisc